Praise for *The Love Trauma Syndrome*

"*The Love Trauma Syndrome* reaches out to the many who have suffered the heart-wrenching pain that accompanies the loss (or potential loss) of a significant relationship. Dr. Rosse's conceptualization of the aftermath of a broken heart and the road to recovery will be thought-provoking to both mental health practitioners and the lay reading public."

> —**Jane Vogt Buongiorno, Ph.D.**, Licensed Clinical Psychologist, Virginia and North Carolina

"I cannot imagine the book not being helpful to clients or professionals interested in learning about Love Trauma Syndrome. Dr. Rosse's wit, knowledge, and desire to help those in distress—characteristics well known to those close to him—come through in the text."

> —**John Mastropaolo, Ph.D.**, Psychologist, Silver Spring, Maryland

"By the end of this book, you will not only become an expert in recognizing Love Trauma Syndrome but also you will understand what to do and why you're doing it."

> —**Regina Ottaviani, Ph.D.**, Cognitive Therapist, Chevy Chase, Maryland; Co-Author, *Cognitive Therapy of Personality Disorders*

"A masterpiece of self-help and psychoeducational literature! This book should certainly be added to the list of good self-help books that contribute to the overall effectiveness of any psychological or psychiatric therapy."

> —**Paul Buongiorno, M.D.**, Psychiatrist, Private Practice, Wilmington, North Carolina

The Love Trauma Syndrome

Free Yourself from the Pain of a Broken Heart

The Love Trauma Syndrome

Free Yourself from the Pain of a Broken Heart

Richard B. Rosse, M.D.

INSIGHT BOOKS

PLENUM PRESS • NEW YORK AND LONDON

Library of Congress Cataloging-in-Publication Data

Rosse, Richard B.
    The love trauma syndrome : free yourself from the pain of a broken
heart / Richard B. Rosse.
        p.   cm.
    Includes bibliographical references (p.   ) and index.
    ISBN 0-306-46006-8
    1. Lovesickness.   2. Separation (Psychology)   3. Grief therapy.
I. Title.
RC543.R67   1999
616.85'21--dc21   99-19372
                                                                CIP

This book was written by Richard B. Rosse, M.D. in his private capacity, and the views expressed herein are entirely the author's and do not represent the views of the Department of Veterans Affairs or Georgetown University. Additionally, the treatment recommendations made in this book should never supersede those made by mental health workers or other clinicians directly involved in a patient's care. The ideas and suggestions contained in this book should not be regarded as an appropriate substitute for consulting with your physician or other trained health care workers. Furthermore, statements made by the author regarding specific medications do not constitute a recommendation or endorsement by the product manufacturer. The author and publisher disclaim any liability arising directly or indirectly from the use of this book, or any of the recommendations, procedures, products, medications, or devices described. With future advances in psychiatric and psychological research and practice, the diagnostic and therapeutic recommendations made in this book may change. Finally, in all the case histories in this book, the names of the patients, their circumstances, and any other identifying characteristics, have been altered to protect their confidentiality. Furthermore, certain facts in each case have been rearranged by the author to further protect patient privacy.

ISBN 0-306-46006-8

© 1999 Richard B. Rosse
Insight Books is a Division of Plenum Publishing Corporation
233 Spring Street, New York, N.Y. 10013

10 9 8 7 6 5 4 3 2 1

A C.I.P. record for this book is available from the Library of Congress

Printed in the United States of America

For those who read this book
and know all too well what it is about

Contents

Foreword

I have spent much of my academic and professional life studying the effects of stress and trauma on the mammalian brain. The more severe the stress, the more an animal is overwhelmed and unable to "cope," or adapt. An emotional *trauma* is a type of severe stress that causes serious and long-lasting, unwanted emotional changes. When stress severity reaches the level of being a trauma, brain changes occur that are persistent (if not permanent). For instance, the structure, activity, and distribution of brain neurotransmitter receptors are altered by trauma events. Associated with these brain alterations are corresponding behavioral changes (e.g., increased arousal and vigilance for future threats).

Research has shown that there are differences in the way different animals of the same species respond to the same stress. Whereas some animals respond to a particular stress with evidence of profound neurophysiological and behavioral alteration, other animals of the same species might demonstrate trivial changes. Because of the wide range of genetic variation that exists in nature for a given population, and the probable large number of genes involved in conferring trauma "resistance" versus vulnerability, there is a wide spectrum of responses to a trauma. How a particular animal, or person, will respond to a trauma is not only dependent on the genes they happened to inherit from their parents, but also on the environmental support and protection they received during their early life experience. So an animal's responses to similar stresses is a function of both complex genetic and environmental influences (e.g., a nurturing versus harsh upbringing).

We also know that although there are predictable brain responses to stress and to trauma in general, the specific nature of a traumatic event seems to influence the exact pattern of receptor, neurotransmitter, and behavioral changes evoked by a particular type of stress. The book that Dr. Rosse has written concerns a specific type of stress; one that involves a threat to a person's mating—or love—interests. Dr. Rosse calls this specific stress (when sufficiently severe) a "love trauma." Whether the threat to a relationship is "traumatic" (i.e., a love trauma) is based on a person's reaction to the threat event. One person's love trauma can be another person's liberation from an unhappy relationship. Additionally, one person's love trauma can result in years of misery; another's can dissipate after a night on the town.

The specific brain changes associated with such stress have recently begun to be studied by Thomas Insel's group at the Department of Psychiatry and Behavioral Sciences at the Emory University School of Medicine. Their "animal model" of this stress involves the study of the monogamous prairie vole (*Microtus ochrogaster*).[1] For instance, the Insel group has compared the behavior and brain changes of males of this species who mated with a female in their cage (and were hence more "attached" males) to males who did not (i.e., less attached males). When the males who did mate were exposed to a male intruder, the males exhibited more aggression toward the intruder (i.e., more vigorous "mate guarding"), and demonstrated more evidence of activity in their medial amygdala—a limbic system brain structure involved in mediating aggression. The amygdala is also a brain structure involved in generating brain arousal. Dr. Rosse describes brain hyperarousal as important for the development of Love Trauma Syndrome.

Hence, the work of Thomas Insel's group has begun to elucidate the cascade of brain changes associated with emerging and established mating relationships, as well as the profound brain changes associated with exposure to threats to that relationship. Of course, it is premature to suggest that what goes on in the brains of prairie voles is similar to the brain events in humans, but the work raises important questions as to whether analogous events occur in us. Additionally, there is no doubt there are gender-based differences.

The constellation of behavioral changes associated with a threat to a love interest is labeled by Dr. Rosse as the Love Trauma Syndrome. I am convinced that other more traditional psychiatric diagnoses that have been used to classify such people, such as grief reaction, adjustment disorder, depressive disorder not otherwise specified or obsessional or pathologic jealousy, are inadequate for fully describing the nature of their suffering. None of these separate diagnoses adequately captures the full range of emotional reactions to a love trauma. Love Trauma Syndrome seems to share features of posttraumatic stress disorder, grief reactions, and anxiety, depressive, obsessional and dissociative disorders. The designation of Love Trauma Syndrome helps advance the description, understanding, and treatment of the condition.

The Love Trauma Syndrome so eloquently described in this book by Dr. Rosse is based on his clinical experience with patients over the years. Dr. Rosse, using an intensive case study methodology, has observed a predictable clustering of symptoms in people who have experienced a love trauma. He describes some variability in presentation among sufferers of the condition, as well as a wide range of symptom severity and time courses. Dr. Rosse offers us a vivid and detailed description of the phenomenology of the syndrome that can serve as a more than adequate starting block for further discussion of the idea.

Dr. Rosse is a careful and perceptive student of human behavior. He has published numerous articles in the academic psychiatric literature utilizing an intensive case study approach. One example of his keen abilities as a psychiatric phenomenologist was when he described in the psychiatric literature the syndrome of "geeking" in crack cocaine addicts.[2,3]

Like the Love Trauma Syndrome story, the story of crack addicts who develop geeking is fascinating, and is worthy of briefly reviewing here. After a crack cocaine binge and the exhaustion of the addict's crack cocaine supply, Dr. Rosse discovered that many addicts compulsively search for pieces of crack cocaine they obsessionally believe were dropped accidentally in the area where they were using crack (hence the term "compulsive foraging" used by Dr. Rosse and colleagues). The behavior often has a desperate appearance, as if the geeking person is looking for some life-sustaining substance that if not found will result in their demise. Geeking people might spend hours systematically picking through the pilings of a rug in search of even small pieces of crack. Their minds become completely focused on the search for misplaced cocaine. They might inspect tables, chairs, couches, or the path they took to get to the using environment. Anything that resembles crack cocaine, such as food crumbs, plaster, candle wax, small stones, pieces of soap, or drywall, is carefully inspected, sniffed, and often tasted. If it passes these initial tests, an attempt is made to smoke it on the off-chance that it is crack.

Dr. Rosse and colleagues proposed that compulsive foraging might serve as a drug-induced model of obsessive–compulsive disorder. Geeking seemed to be a stereotypic obsessive–compulsive-like phenomenon seen in people addicted to crack cocaine. Keeping with Dr. Rosse's interests in behavioral evolution, he proposed that geeking might represent the behavioral expression of a primitive brain program where the brain gets the individual to maximize their extraction of "rewarding" resources from the immediate and known environment. This decreases the person's need to venture into novel environments in search of resources. In this way, the geeking behavior decreases the addict's chances of encountering danger in alien environments, such as life-threatening competitors and predators. Only after the person is absolutely certain that resources cannot be found in the immediate environment does his or her brain "turn off" the geeking and let the individual move out into novel but potentially dangerous environments in search of replenishing depleted resources.

When Dr. Rosse and his colleagues found that up to 80% of crack addicts experienced "geeking," and often for more than one hour at a time, they were amazed to discover that the phenomenon had not been well described in the available psychiatric, addiction, or medical literature. Every crack addict seemed to know the phenomenon well—but clinicians were pretty much in the dark about it. Geeking was right under every clinician's and researcher's nose—yet it was Dr. Rosse and colleagues who first brought it to our medical attention. So it does not surprise me that another condition that was right under our noses—the Love Trauma Syndrome— is being more fully brought to our attention by Dr. Rosse.

Interestingly, geeking and Love Trauma Syndrome are similar in that they both involve an inability to "shift" focus, or redirect mental activity away from something "lost." In the case of geeking, the person has lost all of his or her cocaine; in the case of Love Trauma Syndrome, the person has lost someone with whom they were in love. Both cocaine and feelings of love are capable of providing a person with substantial psychological "rewards"—that is, feelings of pleasure and euphoria. As Dr. Rosse points out in the book, love is one of the most rewarding and pleasurable experiences there is. In both geeking and Love Trauma Syndrome, there is the dysphoric anticipation of the loss of future rewards. Geeking addicts anticipate no longer being able to remain "high"; Love Trauma Syndrome victims anticipate the loss of future rewards from the desired relationship.

In both geeking and Love Trauma Syndrome, people are looking for something that is usually no longer there. If they find something, it is typically not in its desired form. The crack cocaine that the geeker finds is not really crack; if it is, it is of insufficient quantity to get him or her high. The love the Love Trauma Syndrome sufferer finds is tainted—it is not the love they desired.

As important as the geeking phenomenon is to improving our understanding of cocaine addiction (and perhaps obsessive–compulsive disorders as well), geeking has never been a target of treatment. In this regard Love Trauma Syndrome is different—it is a treatment target. It is important that Love Trauma Syndrome be adequately described, as effective treatments are available, and they are exhaustively outlined in this book.

When Dr. Rosse first proposed the concept of Love Trauma Syndrome, I was inclined to listen carefully. Similar to his experience with geeking, he was dismayed by the lack of medical literature on Love-Trauma-Syndrome-like reactions, and found that the literature that was available did not fully describe what he was seeing in his clinical practice. He was amazed at how frequently he encountered vivid descriptions of Love Trauma Syndrome in music, in cinema, and in the fiction literature. Indeed, what he found in the arts related to people's reactions to love trauma events helped inform some of his conceptualization of the Love Trauma Syndrome. Additionally, I also have seen patients in my clinical practice who seemed to suffer from the syndrome described by Dr. Rosse, and agreed that medical literature describing their "broken heart disease" was lacking.

Influenced by his interests in behavioral evolution, Dr. Rosse makes a credible proposal that threats to "love interests" represent a threat to our genetic material being "propelled into future generations." This threat, argues Dr. Rosse, is experienced by our brains as "tantamount to death." Hence, "brain alarms" (e.g., limbic system structures such as the amygdala) are activated, and a cascade of other brain events ensue. In vulnerable individuals, Love Trauma Syndrome is born.

The syndrome is especially interesting in light of some recent notorious, violent episodes well publicized in the news media where individuals committed murder and mayhem after a love trauma event. Some of the people who committed these atrocities were teenagers and children. As a trained child psychiatrist who has done considerable research in child psychiatry, and who published one of the first textbooks of pediatric psychopharmacology in the early 1980s, I feel obligated to suggest that preventive education about Love Trauma Syndrome in our schools might be needed to preclude such tragedies from occurring in the future. The syndrome is not being proposed as an excuse for sufferers who commit repulsive and outrageous acts against others, but rather as a way for us to increase our understanding of such people (and to develop strategies to prevent future occurrences). Thankfully, most people with the syndrome do not act violently against others.

As mental health workers know, love trauma events are reported all too commonly by our patients and clients—the young and the old alike. They complicate many of the psychological and psychiatric conditions we treat. I am convinced that by increasing our awareness of the condition, and ways to treat its sufferers, we will improve the quality of our patients' lives.

Again, as the case of "geeking syndrome" taught me, I do not underestimate Dr. Rosse's ability to detect novel clinical conditions that have been right under clinicians' noses for decades. Clinicians and patients alike will have to read this book to determine the usefulness of the Love Trauma Syndrome concept for themselves. However, I am convinced that they will find the reading an enlightening and productive use of their time. I know I did.

I want to emphasize how honored I am to write the Foreword to this important book. I regard Dr. Rosse as a stellar clinician and academician at our medical school and medical center. He has published over 100 original contributions to the scholarly literature, and his publications have concerned themselves with a wide range of clinical and basic science issues. His wide-ranging skills are evidenced by his ability to lecture and supervise medical students, physicians, and mental health trainees on issues from the recognition and resolution of psychodynamic conflicts to novel nondopaminergic mechanisms in the pathophysiology of psychotic disorders.

Finally, on a very personal level, in addition to Dr. Rosse's many outstanding accomplishments, I would like to emphasize his extraordinary sensitivity and considerateness, and his often anonymous efforts on the behalf of others. He is someone whom I admire personally and who serves as my role model for interpersonal behavior and for standards of conduct. This book reflects his fine qualities, and it offers the reader an opportunity to be instructed by one of the best teachers—and healers—I know.

Stephen I. Deutsch, M.D., Ph.D.

Preface

During the height of the O.J. Simpson trial, one patient asked me why someone like O.J. Simpson might be driven to murder. This was a sophisticated patient who was an active member of a number of psychology book clubs. He had been a fan of O.J. Simpson throughout his football and acting careers. "He always seemed like such a nice a guy," he said to me. The patient was retired and followed the Simpson trial closely on a daily basis. "There is no book out there that helps me understand why this man might have done what others say he did," he complained. My patient suspected that O.J. was guilty.

This patient, knowing that I was a psychiatrist who had written extensively in the academic psychiatric literature, asked me half-jokingly, "Why don't you write a book that answers this question for us laypeople? We just want to better understand what makes us tick. We need a book by a psychiatrist that helps people understand why someone like O.J. Simpson could commit such a heinous crime."

My patient went on to describe another instance in his life that reminded him of the O.J. Simpson case. He related the case of an office colleague in Germany who had married a beautiful German woman. They seemed to have a good relationship, and when he saw them together at parties they appeared happy. He was even envious of his acquaintance's successful marriage. Then one day he went to work and was told that this acquaintance had murdered his wife, and later hanged himself. It seemed that the colleague discovered his wife was having an affair. My patient reminded me that O.J. Simpson had written a suicide note and was contemplating killing himself in the week following the murder of his wife. My patient speculated that O.J. wanted to kill himself to punish himself for what he did to his wife. And my patient rightly speculated that what appeared to have occurred in the O.J. Simpson case was not an isolated occurrence. Intimates in problematic relationships sometimes kill each other.

I listened to my patient and wondered how I would answer his question. I had already suspected—based on the information from the media I had about O.J. Simpson and his relationship with his wife—that O.J. suffered from a *Love Trauma Syndrome*. I had loosely formulated the concept years earlier, based on my clinical experience with men and women experiencing intensely dysphoric (i.e., unpleasant) reactions to the breakup of desired romantic relationships. I had been particularly impressed with some lines from the opening statement of O.J.'s suicide note written on June 15, 1994, where he wrote, "I loved her [Nicole Brown Simpson], always have and always will. If we had a problem it's because I loved her so much." I believe it. People have Love Trauma Syndrome only when they are in love. There is no Love Trauma Syndrome if the person is not in love.

I later found myself beginning to think about how someone would write a book about how a person so much in love could murder the object of their affection—a book about Love Trauma Syndrome. The desire to commit murder represented one of the most serious complications of the condition. Although the syndrome is quite common, fortunately only a few individuals go on to commit violent acts because of it.

I did not think that I would have the time to write a book about Love Trauma Syndrome. However, about a year later my life situation changed. My father was rapidly consumed by a very aggressive cancer. As he lay on his deathbed, I sat by his side and felt helpless and sickened. I knew that I was losing the strongest ally I ever had, and probably the strongest ally I would ever have. I knew nobody would support my hopes and dreams more than my father. Nobody was more committed to me, or would sacrifice as much for me. I loved my father. At times it felt difficult for me to move, and I experienced what psychiatrists call "leaden paralysis." My ambitions and desires left me, and I sat weakened and afraid.

In the aftermath of his death my bereavement and depression included a problem that involved waking up around two or three in the morning and being unable to again fall asleep. Rather than tossing and turning in my bed, I decided to keep myself distracted and occupied during these early morning hours by beginning to write the book that my patient requested.

Indeed, over the years I had been impressed by how broken hearts had figured so prominently in my patients' life courses. I found that "love trauma events" associated with failed romances was a major life issue for over 10% of the men and women I saw, be they straight, gay, or lesbian. I have been shocked by the profound negative impact love trauma events have had on my patients' quality of life. Using my skills as a psychiatric phenomenologist, I formulated the description of Love Trauma Syndrome outlined in this book. The presence of the syndrome can make the rich and powerful feel like paupers; the absence of the syndrome can make the poor and powerless feel like kings and queens.

I have not only recognized many cases of Love Trauma Syndrome, but I have also developed treatments for people afflicted with the condition. The treatments include education about the syndrome, the use of self-help techniques, and a variety of standard strategies used by mental health professionals. These treatments are discussed in this book. Many people have suffered from Love Trauma Syndrome without knowing its name, and many have successfully treated themselves by engaging in a full range of healthful activities.

When I began to speak with friends and colleagues about my concept of Love Trauma Syndrome, I was amazed by how many of them immediately knew what I was talking about, and I found that the concept of such a syndrome rang true. Person after person told me of their experiences with the syndrome, of patients they were treating with serious cases of the condition, or of friends or relatives who were afflicted. On more than one occasion I was told of people who had committed suicide in the throes of a severe Love Trauma Syndrome. I too had observed this tragic consequence of the syndrome. With my impressions about the importance of Love Trauma Syndrome confirmed by others, my enthusiasm for writing the book was enhanced.

Love Trauma Syndrome is a distinct clinical entity fully described in this book. It is a common condition, and exists in various forms and along a continuum of severity and duration. The long duration of some cases of Love Trauma Syndrome demonstrates that time does not heal all wounds. It is not a trivial condition, as it can be associated with intense emotional distress and social and occupational impairment.

The syndrome can be complicated by other psychiatric disorders, such as depression, anxiety, and substance or alcohol abuse. When severe, Love Trauma Syndrome can markedly diminish the sufferer's quality of life and ability to perform socially, academically, and occupationally. Some people with Love Trauma Syndrome end up committing suicide, whereas others might stalk or even murder the people they love the most (and many then kill themselves—"homicide–suicide" or "dyadic death").

Another motivation for me to write this book was the lack of literature on the subject. This deficiency of reading material on Love Trauma Syndrome left many of my patients feeling isolated and alone in their suffering. Many feel ashamed that they are not able to adequately get over the loss of love on their own. This book is written for the millions of people with Love Trauma Syndrome—most of whom are aware of their suffering, but not aware of the syndrome from which they suffer. The book is designed to help people understand the condition and to help them understand what they can do to break the cycle of their misery.

Richard Rosse, M.D.

Acknowledgments

I would like to thank my patients over the years. They have been my best teachers. They have taught me to be a better listener and to appreciate that nothing they say about how they feel is wrong—it is only my understanding of the significance of what they say that can be in error. In this book I describe some of these patients, but in all instances their identities have been obscured.

I would also like to thank my family, friends, and colleagues who have supported me during this writing effort. They have excused my absence from other important familial, social, academic, and occupational responsibilities while I focused on completing this book. Without their support and forgiveness, this book would not have been possible. I would also like to thank Frank K. Darmstadt, editor of Insight Press, and Richard Johnson, production editor, for their time and vast assistance in making this book a reality.

Figures and Tables

FIGURES

TABLES

The Love Trauma Syndrome

Free Yourself from the Pain of a Broken Heart

Chapter One

Introduction

L ove hurts—sometimes intensely, and sometimes for a long time. This book is about the *profound* emotional pain that can be associated with damaged or failed love relationships. When the loss of love is very distressing, the experience is a *love trauma*. A love trauma is a form of psychological stress that produces an emotional disturbance that is both severe and prolonged. It interferes with the sufferer's social and occupational functioning and diminishes their quality of life. This more profound reaction to the loss of love—or to the threat of such a loss—I call the *Love Trauma Syndrome*.

A *syndrome* is a group of symptoms that appear together in a predictable fashion. In Love Trauma Syndrome, these symptoms include sleep disturbance, nervousness, intrusive painful love-trauma-related memories and thoughts, anger, and avoidance of reminders of the love trauma. When a Love Trauma Syndrome develops in response to the loss of love, the syndrome that appears will not be identical in all people. In some people, problems with sleep and intrusive memories might predominate. In others, anger or avoidance of love trauma reminders dominate the clinical picture.

The intense emotional reaction seen in Love Trauma Syndrome is in contrast to the milder degrees of emotional distress that can be associated with romantic failure. I classify these lesser emotional reactions to the loss of love as the "relationship blues." Relationship blues are a less severe and less prolonged psychological response to romantic failure. With relationship blues, the intense emotional distress and significant negative impact on social and occupational functioning is absent. The spectrum of emotional pain that can be experienced after the loss of love is illustrated below in Figure 1.1.

To get a better sense of just how pervasive intense pain associated with broken hearts is, turn on any radio station where popular songs are played and carefully listen to the lyrics. Although you sometimes hear songs relating the joys of love, you will probably hear more songs depicting love's pain. The songs portray different nuances of this pain, including expressions of sadness, disappointment, fear, surprise, anger, and hurt.

I began to appreciate the potential severe and long-lasting impact of romantic failures on people after years of listening to the life stories of some of my older patients. As a geriatric psychiatrist, I have treated many older men and women. I have had the opportunity to examine the major life events and issues for these people over the course of their whole lives and I have been impressed with how broken hearts have so prominently affected many patients.

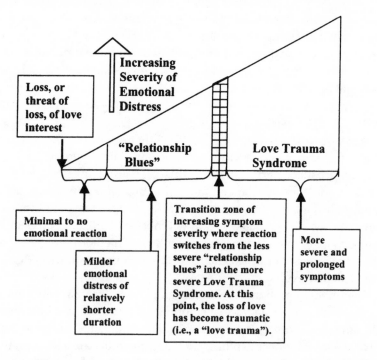

Figure 1.1 *The spectrum of emotional reactions in response to a loss—or threat of loss—of a love relationship.*

Many of my patients were combat veterans with some degree of post-traumatic stress disorder (PTSD) related to military combat. Combat-related PTSD can be a severe, chronic, and disabling condition that affects every aspect of a patient's life. They can become nervous, become unable to sleep, have nightmares related to their combat experiences, and withdraw from the people around them that they love. Combat-related PTSD can ruin a person's life.

With this in mind, I was amazed at how often these patients—decades after combat—would plop themselves into the easychair in my office and tell me stories of their failed romantic relationships *before* describing to me the horrors of war. Some of these patients had actually joined the service after romantic failures and hoped that they would be killed in combat so they could be liberated from their heartache. They performed heroic deeds in the throes of a Love Trauma Syndrome, not caring whether they lived or died. And long after their unhappy combat and romance experiences, it was often their love-trauma-related distress that weighed heavier on their minds than the pain of their traumatic combat-related memories and feelings. The intensity of some of these patients' misery related to their defeats in love was astounding to me, especially in light of the horrific combat traumas they had endured.

For instance, one patient described returning from combat after World War II to discover that his wife was living and sleeping with his older brother. My patient had loved both his wife and his brother, and he had dreamed of being reunited with them after the war. However, his homecoming was anything but welcome. My stunned patient quickly moved to a city in another state. He never saw his wife or anyone in his family again.

This veteran had seen considerable combat in the Pacific, and for years after his return from the war he reported that he slept poorly and had nightmares related to combat. However, he said that for decades after his return, his main preoccupation was his ex-wife and her adultery with his brother. In his old age, this was the major source of distress in his life. When he initially spoke to me about his love trauma, it was as if it had happened yesterday. His mind seemed stuck in the events of 50 years ago. When describing his life story, he described the events of his 50 years *after* the love trauma in broad brush strokes. However, the more distant past love trauma events, and the period immediately surrounding the love trauma, were described in excruciating detail. Additionally, he never re-married. "I had enough," he told me.

In classic PTSD, the traumatic event to which the patient is exposed needs to involve *life-threatening* situations, where the person witnesses the actual or threatened serious injury or death of others or personally experiences serious injury or the threat of death. Such traumas occur in the context of robberies, muggings, sexual assaults, automobile accidents, and natural (e.g., earthquakes, floodings, tornadoes, hurricanes) or manmade disasters (e.g., plane crashes, explosions).

However, I have also seen intense and sometimes prolonged PTSD-like psychological reactions to love traumas in people who *never* had PTSD, either related to combat or to other life-threatening events. These love traumas did not involve any threat of death or of serious injury. Nevertheless, the problematic romantic situations were experienced as traumatic—with severe and durable psychological distress.

With these patients, I started using the label Love Trauma Syndrome. Similar to PTSD, Love Trauma Syndrome appeared to be a disorder of "too much memory." In both conditions, conscious and unconscious memories of the past intrude upon the present and influence thoughts, feelings, and behaviors to a much greater extent than would be expected. And after experiencing seemingly similar love traumas, it is often difficult to predict who will develop a Love Trauma Syndrome and who will be spared. However, a prior history of Love Trauma Syndrome does seem to predict future similar reactions to love trauma events.

I have worked with men and women with Love Trauma Syndrome, including gay males, lesbians, and straights. Some of the most severe and persistent cases of Love Trauma Syndrome I have seen have been in gays. The young and the old, the gay and the straight, the married and the single, and the rich and the poor—anyone with the capacity to fall in love—all seem vulnerable to Love Trauma Syndrome. Only those unable to fall in love seem to be spared. Love is the critical ingredient for the development of the syndrome.

Why a Book on Love Trauma Syndrome?

Over 10% of the people I see in my clinical practice suffer from some degree of Love Trauma Syndrome. Yet there was no book to which I could refer my patients that adequately captured the full character of the way they felt. They needed a book. The lack of available literature on the subject left many of my patients feeling isolated and alone in their suffering. Some of my patients described themselves as feeling weak, inadequate, and ashamed for not being able to get over their distress quickly and on their own. The condition is a major source of unhappiness and shame. I have found that many patients—especially men—will not talk about their love trauma because of the shame and humiliation involved.

This book is written to help those afflicted with Love Trauma Syndrome. It is an affliction that, when severe, has the capacity to markedly diminish the sufferer's quality of life and their ability to perform socially, academically, or occupationally. More important, Love Trauma Syndrome often precipitates or exacerbates other psychiatric conditions such as depression, anxiety, and alcohol or substance abuse.

At the extremes of possible reactions to a love trauma, the syndrome can result in tragic and horrible outcomes. Some patients end up committing suicide. Others might murder the person they love the most, then kill themselves (homicide–suicide or dyadic death). It is reported that "jealous love" is the motive in about two-thirds of homicide–suicides.

People need to become aware of this potentially devastating and serious psychological condition. This book is designed to educate people about the condition and to help sufferers of the syndrome understand what they can do to break their cycle of misery. I also wanted to provide a healing environment whereby people can maximize their recovery from their Love Trauma Syndrome.

Not only is the syndrome mistakenly trivialized by the sufferer and the layperson, its importance is also minimized by practiced mental health clinicians. The book is designed to help clinicians better detect and treat syndrome sufferers. Clinicians need to become more aware of the condition so they can ask the right questions of patients when a Love Trauma Syndrome is suspected. Some psychological treatments become stuck at an impasse because clinicians fail to recognize the importance of a Love Trauma Syndrome in a patient's life. Indeed, Love Trauma Syndrome sufferers, their families and friends, and the clinicians who care for them all need to be educated about the syndrome, its different manifestations and continuum of severity, and the treatments available to relieve suffering.

Because of the potential for violence associated with extremely severe (and thankfully rare) cases, law enforcement officers and judicial officers need to be made aware of the syndrome. For instance, in March 1998, two junior high school boys—ages 13 and 11—opened fire on a crowd of their fellow students and killed three girls and a teacher. The motivation for the shooting spree was supposedly the breakup of the 13-year-old boy and his girlfriend *a year earlier*. She was one of girls killed.

There are many other, less notorious, crimes committed in the throes of a Love Trauma Syndrome. However, violence against others should *never* be considered an appropriate response to a love trauma. Similarly, the impulse to commit such violence in the context of the syndrome should not be considered irresistible. All temptations and all impulses are resistible.

Fortunately, the consequences of the syndrome are almost always less tragic. People with a Love Trauma Syndrome tend to suffer quietly and privately experience a compromised quality of life along with some social and occupational impairment of variable duration. However, after reading this book, readers should develop a better appreciation of the condition and its variable presentations, and should be able to understand the many ways there are to break free of the severe and persistent pain of a broken heart.

Chapter Two

The Love Trauma Syndrome

L
ove is one of the most wonderful emotions we can experience. Unfortunately, it can also be one of the most painful. The emotional pain of a broken heart can become manifest as a Love Trauma Syndrome. The syndrome exists as a discrete clinical entity with its own unique constellation of symptoms, which are described in this chapter.

Previously, love traumas were thought simply to precipitate other common psychiatric conditions, such as depression or "adjustment disorders." However, these generic psychiatric disorders are not adequate for capturing the unique character of the condition that occurs following a love trauma event. It is quite common that Love Trauma Syndrome is complicated by a variety of other psychiatric conditions, such as depression and substance or alcohol abuse.

An Example of Someone with Love Trauma Syndrome

One day I was asked to see a 30-year-old man in the emergency room. He was an alcoholic who had resumed drinking alcohol after 7 years of sobriety. When I met him he was staring at the floor. He was sobbing quietly. When I asked him what had happened, he just shook his head. "I feel terrible," he said through tears. "I started drinking again to see if it would make the pain go away, but it only made it worse."

He told me about his relationship with his girlfriend of 9 months, and how she was the "love of his life." "But obviously she doesn't feel that way about me, because she's dating other guys now," he said. I sighed and asked him to tell me more. He related to me how he thought everything was going well in the relationship, and how he had even planned to asked her to marry him. He had held off asking her now because he did not want to seem to be "rushing things." "I can't stop thinking about her," he cried. "I can't stop thinking about her and the other guy, you know, sleeping together." I handed him a box of tissues and he wiped the tears from his eyes. "I can't sleep at night anymore, and when I do I have nightmares of her with other men."

After letting him tell his story, I decided to educate him about Love Trauma Syndrome. I told him that the syndrome occurred when someone experienced a threat to a relationship with someone they loved very much. The person's response when first learning about the love trauma involves intense emotional distress. This distress includes feelings of sadness, fear, anxiety and hopelessness, and might involve physical reactions, such as feeling nauseated, shaky, dizzy, tired, even feverish. The emotional response might also include feeling "numb," "in a daze," or "spacey." He endorsed many of these symptoms. I then explained that people with Love Trauma Syndrome also had recurrent and intrusive thoughts about the love trauma, and maybe even had dreams about the situation. The syndrome commonly included difficulty with falling or staying asleep, at times feeling on the verge on tears, and difficulty concentrating. Again, the patient endorsed most of these symptoms. I spoke to him about treatment and follow-up for the condition, and the patient seemed less demoralized and upset. He was looking forward to starting treatment.

As I was writing up the case in the patient's chart at the nursing station, a nurse came up to me. "I heard you talking to that guy about Love Trauma Syndrome," she said. "You told him it shared many of the features of posttraumatic stress disorder." I nodded and said "Yes." "Is it the same in women?" she asked. "Yes," I replied. "Where can I read more about that?" she asked me, "'cause I've got a bad case of it too."

Love and Pain

John was a 65-year-old, recently retired man who came into my office with his head hanging down. He said he was very much in love with his wife and he was ashamed of the problem he was having with her. He could not believe that he was actually seeing a psychiatrist for the first time in his life but he said he had a problem he was unable to lick on his own. He was afraid that his problem would ruin his marriage and his happiness in retirement.

He told me that in 1968, while fighting in the jungles of Vietnam, his wife had a 3-month affair with a fellow math teacher at a local high school. John did not learn of the affair until 2 years later, when he stumbled across a love letter written by the man to his wife. The letter described some of the intimate details of their affair, and was signed Robert. John remembered one time when his wife accidently called him "Robert" while he was home on leave. John had met Robert a few years earlier at parties given by his wife's co-workers. He was ashamed to admit that he would have been better able to handle learning that his wife had been in a car accident and died than learning that she had the affair.

After learning of the affair, the relationship between John and his wife became quite rocky, but he stayed with her "for the sake of the kids." Through tears, John added that he still loved her, even after his discovery. His wife repeatedly asked him for forgiveness. "I remember those first couple of months after I discovered her affair. I was walking around in daze all the time. I was like a zombie. I was numb, and people used to ask me all the time if something was wrong. I used to lie and tell people it was Vietnam. But it was really what was going on between my wife and I."

Over the ensuing years, John said he seldom thought about her affair, and "things got better." They even had another child. "I thought I had gotten over it," John said. "I would tell other people who were in similar situations that they would get over it, and I truly believed that. But now something has happened that I can't explain. I can't stop thinking about it, and it happened almost 30 years ago! And I don't know what happened to suddenly bring it back on after all these years. Until a few months ago, I used to love 'oldies but goodies' songs on the radio. I had all these stations preset on my radio. But now I've changed all the presets, and listen to music I don't enjoy as much, or just listen to talk shows or the news. I avoid the 'oldies' stations because it makes me think more about my wife and Robert. I think about them sleeping in my bed together. I don't like looking at pictures of my wife from the sixties, even though she was beautiful. I avoid driving by the local high school where my wife worked. In fact, I don't like going by any school now."

After almost 30 years, John was once again increasingly thinking about his wife and her affair. He had intrusive thoughts and fantasies about his wife and her lover. "I am just looking for some peace," he said to me with his eyes beginning to tear up. "I was so looking forward to retiring, and now this. I just can't shake it, doc. I never thought I would come to see a psychiatrist. But here I am. I need help. I am miserable almost continuously. And I know it's absurd, because all this happened so long ago. But I feel like I did the day I found out about it. I feel like I'm going crazy."

John also described becoming "nervous all the time," and having difficulty falling asleep. "This is as bad as when I first got back from Vietnam," John said, before I knew anything about the affair. "Back then I used to have nightmares about 'Nam, and dream I was in combat, and that awful things were happening that I couldn't control. Now I dream of my wife when she was young. I dream about her and Robert. These dreams are as upsetting to me as my nightmares about Vietnam."

Upon hearing John's story, some people might be prone to advocate what mental health workers euphemistically call the "managed care solution for mental health problems"—that is, slapping the patient across the face while telling him "To get over it!"[1] However, such an attitude reflects a lack of appreciation for the potential severity and persistence of some cases of Love Trauma Syndrome. And it would be as effective as slapping someone with high blood pressure and telling them to lower it. It would not work.

People with the syndrome are often ashamed that they cannot recover on their own, which compounds their feelings of despair. Although most cases of Love Trauma Syndrome are short-lived, some can be quite persistent. Unfortunately, many people are quick to trivialize the notion of Love Trauma Syndrome. Additionally, John had repeatedly berated himself and tried to "get over it" on his own, but he could not shake his anguish.

Love Trauma Syndrome can be a complex and serious condition whose importance should not be minimized by laypersons, health care administrators, or mental health professionals. A slap across the face while telling them "to get over it" simply would not work for most people. It just intensifies the sufferer's distress and contributes to their feeling inadequate because they are bothered by something "they should be able to get over."

I noted that John had just retired from a job that occupied him for over 50 hours per week. Additionally, the last of his three children had just moved out of the house. I asked him if he thought, with his retirement, and with the kids out of the house, that maybe he was less distracted and was now able to think more about what happened 30 years ago. He nodded in agreement. However, this notion frightened him, as he loved his wife and was looking forward to enjoying his retirement with her. "I know she has been faithful to me since," John said. "When she had the affair she was young and it was difficult for her with my being in Vietnam. She didn't know for sure if I'd be coming back alive or dead in a pine box. She has been a wonderful mother to my children, and since then she has been a wonderful wife. I want to enjoy my retirement with her. I still love her. It would be ridiculous for me to leave her after 30 years. And I know I would be miserable without her."

Interestingly, John had experienced considerable emotional trauma during his combat in Vietnam. He had once been injured by a rocket powered grenade (RPG), and just barely escaped death. During combat he had witnessed the death of comrades. However, the patient said that the trauma of learning of his wife's affair was "worse than anything I went through in Vietnam." This was not the only time I had heard this sort of comment. John was in the throes of a relapsed Love Trauma Syndrome. Although the syndrome had been quiescent for decades, in its reemergence it was severe.

THE NATURE OF THE BEAST

The essential feature of Love Trauma Syndrome is the development of symptoms after experiencing a love trauma. Patients initially experience the love trauma as a "shock." What contributes to the sense of shock is that the love trauma event violates the person's desired *expectations* for the relationship, and assumptions of *safety* in the relationship. The shocked feeling is often associated with a sense of dread, fear, and helplessness similar to that described by people who have witnessed traumas where death (or the threat of death) occurred.

In Love Trauma Syndrome, the love trauma event is experienced as a severe stress and is traumatic in some way. By "traumatic" I mean that the person experiences significant emotional, psychological, or physical distress (e.g., racing heart, trembling, stomach upset, abdominal pain, nausea, diarrhea, "hot flashes" or chills) when first learning about the love trauma. The trauma involves someone the victim loves, typically very much.

Again, the trauma must be regarded as stressful. A stressful event is an event that overwhelms the person's ability to mentally process the event and to neutralize its ability to trigger anxiety, distress, and despair. Love trauma events evoke stress, and the person feels unable to control and prevent the events from happening.

The events which precipitate a Love Trauma Syndrome can be divided into Type I or Type II traumas. In Type I traumas, the events are unexpected and sudden, and the person feels completely overwhelmed by the incident.

In Type II traumas, the traumas are chronic or repetitive in nature. There have been, or are, a number of ongoing violations of the person's expectations for the relationship. For instance, in Type II love traumas, there have been repeated discovered infidelities by a marital partner, but the cuckolded husband or wife remains in the relationship. Love Trauma Syndrome occurs in the context of either Type I or II love trauma events.

The love trauma event (or events) induces fear, anxiety, and distress that generalizes to other triggers and cues not directly associated with the love trauma. The brain no longer accurately discriminates which environmental or internal mental triggers (reminders, cues) legitimately are associated with the love trauma memory and which cues are really innocuous and have no substantial connection to the love trauma. The innocuous cues become linked to the emotional distress and the dysphoric arousal related to the love trauma event through classical conditioning. Love Trauma Syndrome is also characterized by the subjective and internal experience of repeatedly "reexperiencing" the love trauma event.

In Love Trauma Syndrome, outside observers might not always understand why certain love trauma events are experienced as traumatic. The experience is personal and idiosyncratic. It is vitally important when assessing a person for Love Trauma Syndrome to assess the person's subjective meaning of the love trauma event and what the subjective (e.g., psychological and emotional) and objective (e.g., effect on social and academic/occupational) consequences have been. Some people do not experience any degree of Love Trauma Syndrome when a relationship dissolves. Some people are even glad when certain romantic relationships break up.

A love trauma is the result of a perceived threat to a *desired* love relationship. The greater the desire for the relationship to continue, the more severe the love trauma. The more "in love" someone is, the greater the risk of a resulting Love Trauma Syndrome if the relationship dissolves. The trauma usually involves relationships between lovers (straight or gay), but sometimes involves certain family members who were never lovers (e.g., between parents and children, or between siblings) or close friends.

The threat to the relationship might be in the form of a successful rival (as in the case of a romantic relationship), or might involve some other reason that the loved person withdraws from or rejects the patient. The withdrawal of the loved person could be because of sickness, death, suicide, or the need to travel or move to a distant geographic location.

The love trauma can represent a threat or damage to the *image* or representation that the patient has of their "loved person" (e.g., as available, loyal, devoted, loving, supportive). Such an image or representation might be destroyed after the discovery of an infidelity. I have also seen dramatic examples of Love Trauma Syndrome in men after the discovery of false paternity. In such cases, the images these men had of their relationships with their wives (e.g., that their wives had been faithful), children (e.g., that the children they loved were their biologic offspring), and of themselves are shattered. With about one third of all commercial paternity testing revealing that the man who thought he was the father is not, that is a lot of potential cases of Love Trauma Syndrome. If the images the man had of the relationship with his wife were already bad, the discovery of false paternity confirms or worsens the view. In most cases where commercial paternity testing takes place, the couple's relationship is already in crisis, and the confirmation of false paternity merely exacerbates an already problematic relationship. Commercial paternity testing centers should offer appropriate posttest emotional counseling to those who might need it. In such counseling, people should be asked questions to determine whether a Love Trauma Syndrome is present, and should be referred for more intensive therapy if necessary. With the current boom in commercial paternity testing, such counseling might be able to avert tragedies that could occur (e.g., assaults, murder, suicide) when the ensuing Love Trauma Syndrome is particularly severe and complicated.

Similarly, the acquisition of a sexually transmitted disease (STD; e.g., gonorrhea, genital herpes, crabs, syphilis, chlamydia, human papilloma virus, HIV, hepatitis B) leading to the discovery of an infidelity can be associated with the development of a Love Trauma Syndrome. Health care workers treating people with a STD need to be attentive to an emerging Love Trauma Syndrome in cases where sexual infidelity is involved. Such persons might need to be refered for approptiate counseling. At this time it is anyone's guess as to how many of the over 7 million newly diagnozed STD cases each year in the United States is complicated by a Love Trauma Syndrome. I have had numerous patients who discovered that their partners had been unfaithful after the patients were diagnosed with an STD. Many of these patients developed Love Trauma Syndrome, sometimes severe. Some even attempted suicide after the discovery.

The symptoms of Love Trauma Syndrome are outlined in the following list. Sometimes only some of the symptoms are manifest.

1. The person's response at the time of first experiencing or learning about the love trauma includes intense emotional distress. The distress could include fear, anxiety, hopelessness, tearfulness, shame, diminished feelings of self-esteem and self-efficacy, anger, or sadness. The emotional response might also involve feeling confused, distracted, shocked, numb,

dazed, or spacey. There might be dysphoric physical reactions, such as nausea, shakiness, dizziness, severe malaise, or even low-grade fever or feelings of feverishness or chills. Some people contain the distress by refusing to accept that the relationship is over and by denying that they are being cut off from the object of their affection. Others suffer a love trauma, but for some reason they do not initially experience significant distress. In these cases of delayed-onset Love Trauma Syndrome, the emotional and physical distress related to experiencing a love trauma might not be felt until sometime after the event has occurred.

2. The love trauma can be reexperienced in any of the following forms:

a. Recurrent and intrusive recollections of events surrounding the love trauma.

b. Recurrent distressing dreams related to the love trauma.

c. Recurrent distressing fantasies and thoughts related to the trauma. These can be experienced as obsessions.

d. Recurrent distressing emotions related to the trauma (e.g., jealousy, envy, anger, rage, yearning for revenge, anxiety, fear, apprehension, emotional "pangs," depression, emotional lability).

e. Intense emotional distress when exposed to cues (e.g., reminders, such as music) associated with the love trauma. The cue can be the remembered anniversary (e.g., month, date, year) of a love trauma event.

f. Physiological reactivity on exposure to cues (either external or internally generated) or reminders of the love trauma. The heart might race, the person might get butterflies in their stomach, or they might feel nauseated or dizzy.

g. A sense that the love trauma event is being relived (a "flashback").

3. There is avoidance of things associated with the love trauma, such as efforts to avoid thoughts, feelings, or conversations related to the trauma or efforts to avoid activities, places, or people that arouse recollections of the trauma. The development of avoidance of social situations should be clearly linked to the love trauma event(s).

4. There is an expectation that future romantic relationships will end in betrayal, disappointment, emotional pain or unhappiness. There might be pessimism about future relationships.

5. There is a diminished ability to experience loving feelings, fall in love; or a fear, apprehension, revulsion at the thought of falling in love

(e.g., "the thought of falling in love makes me sick"). If they do enter a relationship, they might want to remain somewhat detached from their partner (e.g., they do not want to "get too involved"). Once in a relationship, they might continually look for faults in their partner. Upon finding such faults, the partner's value is diminished, and the person can regard future loss of the partner as less important.

6. There is persistent or intermittent symptoms (not present or as severe as before the love trauma) of increased emotional arousal or aggression (the later can be directed "inward" or "outward"), including any of the following symptoms:

a. Difficulty falling or staying asleep.

b. Emotional lability, feeling on the verge on tears.

c. Increased possessiveness and "mate guarding" activities, and hypervigilance for potential rivals.

d. Anxiety, restlessness, or inner or outer trembling.

e. Difficulty concentrating.

f. Irritability and anger. The anger can be intense and erupt into rageful episodes and violence. The target can be the person they love who is snubbing them, the threat to their relationship (i.e., their rival), or accidental targets (i.e., people who happen to be around them when their rage erupts; or inanimate objects and acts of random vandalism).

g. A sense of "unreality" surrounding the love trauma event (e.g., feeling dazed, spacey, confused, "out of it," "out to lunch," "tranced out," distractable, or having memory problems).

h. A compulsion to pursue and "recapture" their love object by stalking, verbal intimidation, unwelcome phone calls, or violence. These compulsions can also be directed at real or imagined rivals for the person they love.

i. Preoccupation, agitation and guilt about not having done certain things to prevent the loss of the loved object, or about having done something to cause the loved object's loss. There is a preoccupation with somehow being responsible for the loss, and a sense of anxious regret for past actions (or lack of action).

Although the criteria for Love Trauma Syndrome described above have not been formally validated by rigorous research, the above list provide a guideline for the assessment of someone with suspected Love

Trauma Syndrome. Again, not all of the symptoms listed need be present for someone to be considered to have a Love Trauma Syndrome. Individual symptom severity, and the number of symptoms demonstrated, can be variable from person to person. Love Trauma Syndrome can appear in low- and in high-grade varieties. In medical parlance, "low grade" refers to a condition of lesser severity. For instance, when physicians speak of a low-grade fever, they are referring to a body temperature elevation only slightly above normal (but it is still a fever). People with lower grades of Love Trauma Syndrome are less distressed and impaired by their condition.

The listed symptoms apply to both men and women (both straight and gay). In all of the different forms of Love Trauma Syndrome, the nature, duration, and severity of the symptoms can vary from person to person. Some patients might be primarily hyperaroused (e.g., angry, irritable, and unable to sleep at night). Others might demonstrate predominately intrusive thoughts, memories, feelings, and fantasies, whereas still others experience more of an avoidance syndrome.

For instance, one patient of mine whose beloved 5-year-old son died of leukemia years earlier avoided anything that had to do with small children. When he saw a toy store he had sudden pangs of distress. He avoided going near playgrounds. He once began sobbing when he saw a picture of my 4-year-old son on my desk. He thanked me when I placed the picture of my son in a drawer. The practice of such avoidance limits the quality of life for many patients with Love Trauma Syndrome. (Note that some of the most profound cases of Love Trauma Syndrome involve parents whose children have died or left [e.g., run away] for some reason.)

The 4 A's of Love Trauma Syndrome

Instead of trying to remember all of the symptoms listed previously, it is sometimes easier to remember the major symptoms of Love Trauma Syndrome by becoming familiar with the "four A's" mnemonic. The four "A's" are arousal, avoidance, automatic remembering, and emotional anaesthesia.

As discussed previously, Love Trauma Syndrome typically includes a lot of emotional *arousal*. This arousal is associated with symptoms of anxiety, including feeling "on edge," apprehensive, hyperalert and hypervigilant, irritable, and always expecting the worst. Problems with sleeping (difficulty either with falling asleep or with staying asleep) is also evidence of hyperarousal (i.e., too much brain and body arousal).

The *avoidance* includes attempts to avoid exposure to any cues that remind the person of their love trauma. As the cues typically generalize to a whole host of innocuous and often everpresent cues (e.g., certain types of music, other couples or persons that remind them of their lost love), patients can become avoidant of social situations in general. As a consequence they can become less successful in their jobs and in other social relationships (e.g., they let friendships wither, especially when they are somehow linked to the lost object of their affection), and end up with less of everything that life has to offer. They might also have less interest in—or even avoid—sex. The "A" can also stand for *alone,* as these people often end up feeling alone and isolated. Because of their avoidance, their lifestyles can become restricted. These people who have suffered a Love Trauma Syndrome and avoid future romantic involvement often rationalize their avoidance by believing that future relationships would only end in emotional pain.

Some people actually become frightened at the idea of falling in love. One severe Love Trauma Syndrome sufferer told me that he "broke out in hives" every time he thought about having a loving relationship. "Love is for stronger people than me," this patient said. He later said that "even the thought of falling in love literally makes me sick."

Automatic remembering involves the intrusive thoughts and memories so common in Love Trauma Syndrome. Typically the brain activates memories that serve some need for the person. If you need to take a test, you need to access the memories associated with the material that you have learned. If you are going to ride a bike, you need to be able to activate your memory of how to ride a bicycle. However, sometimes memories seem to come out of nowhere, and the cues for the memories are not apparent. Although occasional automatic memories are not uncommon, in Love Trauma Syndrome the person becomes "flooded" with such automatic and intrusive memories and with thoughts associated with the memories. The memories generate unpleasant feelings and distress. They even intrude into sleep in the form of nightmares.

The Three "P's" of Love Trauma Syndrome

Emotional anaesthesia refers to the decreased ability of some people with Love Trauma Syndrome to be able to experience loving feelings in the future. They might report not knowing what love is, or a decreased capacity to fall in love.

The significance of someone's Love Trauma Syndrome is determined by considering the "three P's" of Love Trauma Syndrome: pervasive, persistent, and impairment. When you suspect that someone has the syndrome, you need to ask how *pervasive* and *persistent* the symptoms are and how much *impairment* the symptoms cause.

Problems with pervasiveness relate to the thoughts, feelings, and memories of the love trauma increasingly intruding into different aspects of both the conscious (i.e., while awake) and unconscious (i.e., while asleep, as in dreams) lives of people afflicted with the syndrome. Thoughts related to the love trauma become uncontained and increasingly pervade the victim's thinking.

Problems with persistence of the disorder relate to the fact that the distressing symptoms can last for days or weeks (in the case of "acute" Love Trauma Syndrome) to months, years, or decades (in cases of more "chronic" Love Trauma Syndrome). Persistence relates to the fact that the love-trauma-associated thoughts continually plague the person and are a source of continual worry, concern, and unhappiness. Some patients complain that they feel they will never get over the condition. Because the condition can be so persistent, they develop a sense of hopelessness about the prospect of recovery, and they feel helpless to do anything about it.

The symptoms often wax and wane over time, and patients are often disheartened when—after a period of feeling better—their symptoms return with full force. (The different possible courses of Love Trauma Syndrome are outlined in the following section titled "The Different Species of the Beast.")

Impairment refers to the fact that in order to be considered as having the syndrome, one's distress must be significant enough to cause some impairment in familial, social, academic, or occupational functioning. To borrow from the U.S. Army's recruitment slogan, the impairment must be severe enough that you are unable to "be all that you can be." The Love Trauma Syndrome-induced impairment can range from mild to severe. Slight impairment might result in a college student's falling behind in some of his or her schoolwork while still making passing grades. More severe impairment involves avoiding friends, being unable to complete tasks at work, or wanting to stay in bed for long periods of time during the day. The symptom severity must also be severe enough to diminish the person's life satisfaction.

Some people with Love Trauma Syndrome look better on the surface than they feel. They are able to "overfunction" even though they are experiencing considerable emotional distress. After a love trauma, some people will even work harder and appear to do a better job than before the trauma occurred. For some people, overfunctioning works to help them recover from a love trauma. For others, their overfunctioning eventually depletes their energy, and they "burn out" and become exhausted. They now have to contend with burnout, chronic fatigue, and a Love Trauma Syndrome.

Immediately prior to medical school, I was planning to marry someone with whom I was in love, but we broke up after she had an affair. I tried to deal with my Love Trauma Syndrome at the time by shifting my focus to my medical student studies. This strategy was at best partially effective, and probably the biggest mistake I made during my medical school career was not to have sought out counseling then. I would have been much more effective as a student, and much less depressed, had I undergone psychotherapy to help me process the pain of my love trauma. Interestingly, my girlfriend who had the affair also developed a Love Trauma Syndrome after we broke up. People who have affairs with others, which cause the dissolution of a relationship with someone else they love, can also develop Love Trauma Syndromes (sometimes severe ones). Their syndromes can be complicated by severe guilt, regret, and remorse.

THE DIFFERENT SPECIES OF THE BEAST

Acute Love Trauma Syndrome

There are many different varieties of Love Trauma Syndrome. There is an acute form, which occurs soon after the love trauma. This variety of Love Trauma Syndrome might occur soon after the breakup of an important relationship, after the discovery of an affair, or after a loved one's death or development of a sudden, serious illness. During this stage of the condition, people commonly characterize the way they feel as "shocked."

In addition to the shock associated with Acute Love Trauma Syndrome, the acute form of the condition is distinguished from the more chronic varieties by the presence of prominent symptoms of anxiety and what are called "dissociative symptoms." Dissociative symptoms include feeling "numb," "spacey," "like I'm in a trance," "zombielike," or "out-to-lunch." Dissociative symptoms also include the feeling that things seem "unreal," or feeling like you are "living in a dream." In fact, one of the most common dissociative complaints I hear from people who are suffering from Acute Love Trauma Syndrome is that everything around them seems "dreamlike"—life takes on the quality of a dream. People who experience love-trauma-related dissociative symptoms often use words such as "strange," "weird," "unreal," "shocked," or "surprised." They might also say that they "can't believe that this is happening to me." Other dissociative sensations that can be reported include a "sense of timelessness," feeling "distant" from your own emotions, and a sense that things are "slowed down" around you (often accompanied by a sense that your own responses are also slowed, or that you are now "slow to respond"). Patients with dissociative experiences might complain that "things look different" to them than they used to appear, or that they themselves feel different about who they are (e.g., "I have a different sense of who I am," or "I don't have the usual sense of who I am"). People with prominent dissociative symptoms might also complain of having problems with their memory, and have only partial recollection of events surrounding the love trauma.

An example of Acute Love Trauma Syndrome is a patient of mine whose wife had just left him for another man. The patient had experience with hallucinogenic drugs when he was younger. After his wife was gone, he said to me, "This feels weird, like I'm tripping. I can't believe that this is really happening. Things really seem unreal." He described the feeling as similar to feelings he had after "bad" LSD trips. The feeling lasted for weeks, and was especially prominent at night when he tried to sleep. He was experiencing prominent dissociative symptoms.

Some people feel physically and emotionally "sickened" after a love trauma event. This sickening is related to the intense stress of the love trauma. They might liken the sickening feelings in response to the breakup as similar to a hangover that you might experience the day after drinking too much alcohol. This physically sickened feeling can last for a long time, and can wax and wane in intensity. After a divorce, people can have what some experts refer to as a "divorce hangover." This hangover alludes to the emotional and physical sickening experienced after an unhappy divorce.

There are numerous different trajectories for the course of the symptoms of Love Trauma Syndrome. A simple acute form of the syndrome is illustrated in Figure 2.1. Here the symptoms intensify soon after the love trauma, but subside within a 6-month period. There are no long-term sequelae of the syndrome, and these people fully recover from their distress. The intensity of the symptoms over the course of the condition vary from person to person.

Chronic Love Trauma

More chronic forms of the syndrome are illustrated in Figures 2.2 to 2.4. In Figure 2.2, a more severe acute form of Love Trauma Syndrome is

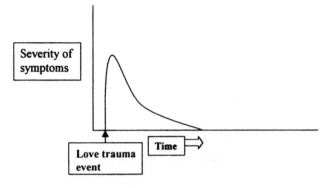

Figure 2.1   The acute Love Trauma Syndrome.

portrayed (compared to Figure 2.1), followed by a chronic syndrome of lesser symptom severity. In Figure 2.3, an acute form is followed by a period of almost complete remission of symptoms. This is then followed by a period marked by an exacerbation of symptoms. What triggers these exacerbations in people is often unknown to them, although symptom worsening is often associated with an emerging depression (sometimes subtle), other recent life disappointments (e.g., loss of a job), or the appearance of "reminders" of the love trauma (e.g., anniversary reactions).

Any stressful life change can also be associated with the reappearance of Love Trauma Syndrome. In the case of John presented earlier, his Love Trauma Syndrome began to reappear within the first 2 weeks of his longed-for retirement. In fact, the condition can be a manifestation of "Retirement Syndrome," where the person who is retiring experiences distress adjusting to their new, less hectic life. For many people, the sudden

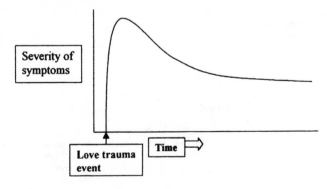

Figure 2.2   Acute followed by chronic symptoms of Love Trauma Syndrome.

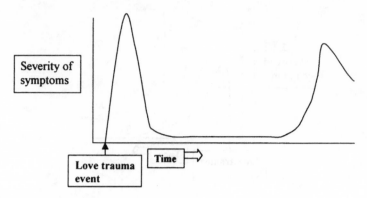

Figure 2.3 Acute followed by delayed symptoms of Love Trauma Syndrome.

reappearance of Love Trauma Syndrome is surprising, especially when the love trauma was long ago and the person feels that he or she had already reconciled themselves to the event.

In Figure 2.4, Delayed Love Trauma Syndrome, typically there is little in the way of an acute syndrome. An acute syndrome might have been present, but it was undramatic. There is a delay of months—maybe even years—before more profound and significant symptoms finally emerge. This "delayed onset" subtype of Love Trauma Syndrome can be surprising to people who did not believe they had love-trauma-associated difficulties.

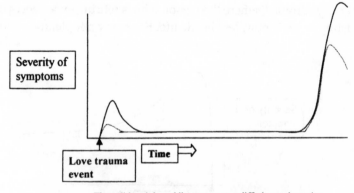

The solid and dotted lines represent differing trajectories . Note that for all cases of Love Trauma Syndrome, a wide range of varying severities of the condition are possible.

Figure 2.4 Delayed Love Trauma Syndrome.

In Love Trauma Syndromes with a rekindling of symptoms months to years after the love trauma event, the reactivation of symptoms often represents a "rethinking" of the love trauma. People might be on vacation, or have started retirement, or for some other reason have idle time on their hands. This spare time allows them to mentally pursue some of their love-trauma-related thoughts more than they could when they were busier. While they review the love trauma memory in their mind, the love trauma event becomes easier to remember, and it becomes more associated with dysphoric arousal. The original love trauma memories, now associated with brain hyperarousal, begin to link to other memories and environmental stimuli that previously had no traumatic associations. Formerly innocuous cues become potent triggers of dysphoric arousal and emotional discomfort. When the love trauma memory develops a greater number of associations (e.g., to present stimuli), the love trauma memory is strengthened and it is easier to recall the past trauma.

For instance, in the case of John described earlier in this chapter, when "oldies but goodies" music played on the radio he was reminded of his wife's affair decades earlier. Eventually, the music stimuli began to generalize, and he began to associate *any* music on the radio with his wife's affair. He either didn't listen to the radio, or he listened in pain. In the letters he read from his wife's lover, the man had referred to his wife as being "hot." John began to think of the affair every time he heard the word "hot"—even when he saw the word "hot" on the faucet of the shower.

The spreading of brain neural connections from love trauma memories to other nontrauma memories represents the malignant phase of Love Trauma Syndrome. It is often difficult to stop the spread of these connections and associations during this phase of the illness. There is also increased physiological arousal and anxiety associated with these increasingly intrusive love trauma memories.

DO YOU HAVE LOVE TRAUMA SYNDROME?

If you want to see if you have a Love Trauma Syndrome, take the following test. The Love Trauma Inventory (LTI) provides you with a sense of just how emotionally injured you have been by past love trauma events. Think about a love trauma (perhaps the most severe one you have ever experienced) and complete the following questions. When using the LTI, you can score with half-point increments if you'd like. Sometimes the best response is characterized by a response intermediate between two anchors (e.g., between 1 and 2 points, making the best response a 1.5). Choose the best response possible that describes they way you have felt over the past week. You don't have to choose the perfect answer—simply the choice that best reflects the way you feel or have felt. Then add up all of your responses to get a total LTI score.

1. *How much time do you spend thinking about the love trauma while you are awake?* (The "thinking" about the trauma can include images, thoughts, feelings, fantasies or perceptions related to the trauma.)

    a. Not at all. (0 points)

    b. Sometimes (less than 25 percent of the time). (1 point)

    c. Quite often (about 50 percent of the time). (less 2 points)

    d. Most of the time (at least 75 percent of the time). (3 points)

2. *How physically sickened do you feel when you contemplate the love trauma?*

    a. Not at all. There are no unpleasant physical sensations associated with my thinking about the love trauma. (0 points)

    b. Slightly sickened. There are some noticeable (but barely), usually fleeting physically distressing sensations, nervousness, or unpleasant arousal. (1 point)

    c. Somewhat sickened. There are definite sensations of physical distress, nervousness, and unpleasant arousal. The unpleasant sensations usually taper off in less than a minute or so. (2 points)

    d. Very sickened. There are profound sensations of physical distress, nervousness, and unpleasant arousal. They can last for minutes to hours. (3 points)

3. *How easy is it for you to accept the reality and the emotional pain of the love trauma?*

    a. Very hard to accept. I become very upset and feel like crying. I feel like I can't stand it. I can't believe it happened. (3 points)

    b. Somewhat hard to accept. I become upset and sometimes feel like crying. I can usually stand it. (2 points)

    c. Slightly hard to accept. I become upset only momentarily. I can stand it. (1 point)

    d. Not at all hard to accept. I do not become upset when I consider accepting the reality of the love trauma event. I have always been able to stand it. (0 points)

4. *If you scored at least 2 points on any of the first three questions* (i.e., questions 1, 2, or 3), *how many years ago was the love trauma?* (Add a point for each year up to 3 years. If more than 3 years, still score as a 3. If less than 6 months, score as a 0.)

5. *How often do you have dreams related to the love trauma?* (The dreams must be associated with unpleasant feelings or arousal.)

    a. At least one a week. (3 points)

    b. At least one every month or so. (2 points)

    c. At least one every 6 months. (1 point)

    d. No love-trauma-related dreams. (0 points)

6. *How easy is it for you to resist thoughts, feelings, and memories about the love trauma?* (When I say "resist," I mean how successful are you at getting the thoughts, etc., out of mind once they come on? For instance, can you successfully distract yourself with another activity, or think about something else?)

    a. I usually cannot resist the thoughts once they come on, and they last for minutes to hours. (3 points)

    b. I can resist them about half of the time, and they are rarely present for more than 10 to 20 minutes. (2 points)

    c. I can resist them most of the time, and they are rarely present for more than a few minutes. (1 point)

    d. I can resist them all of the time, and they are rarely present for more than a minute. (0 points)

7. *Do you think that you will ever get over your unhappy and sick feelings related to the love trauma?* (i.e., Are you hopeful about attaining a full recovery?)

    a. I do not think I will recover fully. (3 points)

    b. I am pessimistic about recovery. (2 points)

    c. I am somewhat optimistic that I will recover fully. (1 point)

    d. I am very optimistic that I will recover fully. (0 points)

8. *How frequently do you go out of your way to avoid contact with stimuli that remind you of the love trauma?*

a. I always try to avoid stimuli and cues associated with the love trauma. If I become aware of such a stimulus, I immediately and reflexively try to avoid more contact with the reminder. (3 points)

b. Only sometimes do I avoid stimuli and cues associated with the trauma. (2 points)

c. I seldom try to avoid stimuli and cues associated with the trauma. (1 point)

d. I never try to avoid stimuli and cues associated with the trauma. (0 points)

9. *Do you have difficulty falling or staying asleep because of unpleasant, anxious arousal related to thoughts and feelings about the love trauma?*

a. Almost every night I have sleep difficulties related to my thoughts, feelings, or unpleasant arousal about the love trauma. (3 points)

b. I occasionally have sleep difficulties related to my thoughts, feelings, or unpleasant arousal about the trauma. (2 points)

c. I seldom have sleep difficulties related to my thoughts, feelings, or unpleasant arousal about the trauma. (1 point)

d. I never have sleep difficulties related to my thoughts, feelings, or unpleasant arousal about the trauma. (0 points)

10. *How often do you feel like bursting out crying, or become angry or agitated, when you think about the love trauma?*

a. At least once a day. (3 points)

b. At least once a week. (2 points)

c. At least once a month. (1 point)

d. I never feel that way. (0 point)

Add up your score:
20 to 30 = A serious Love Trauma Syndrome. Professional help is advised, as the love trauma injury is probably having a major impact on your quality of life and your social, academic, or occupational functioning. (Note that some people can experience considerable psychological distress—with a diminution in their quality of life—but continue to function adequately.)
10 to 19 = Love Trauma Syndrome is present, but to a more tolerable degree. Professional help might improve your quality of life, or you might just want to talk to a good friend.

0 to 9 = Your Love Trauma Syndrome seems quite manageable and does not seriously impair the quality of your life.

However, as can be seen in Figures 2.1 to 2.4, the symptoms of Love Trauma Syndrome can fluctuate over time. Scores on the LTI can fluctuate from hour to hour, day to day, week to week, month to month, or year to year.

Other Ways of Measuring the Severity of Love Trauma Syndrome

Another way of assessing the severity of Love Trauma Syndrome is to ask the patient about the "penetration into consciousness" of their love-trauma-related thoughts. You can ask the person, "What percentage of the time that you are awake do you think about the love trauma?" Anything over 5 to 10% of the time suggests a severe Love Trauma Syndrome. Alternately, you can ask the patient "How many minutes or hours a day do you think about the love trauma?" People who are spending over an hour a day distressed with their love trauma thoughts might also have a serious syndrome. The love trauma of these people has significantly penetrated into their consciousness. Some people prefer using a Subjective Distress Scale (SDS), where they rate the pain of their Love Trauma Syndrome on a graduated scale of 0 to 10 (0 being no distress and 10 representing extreme distress).

Some people will describe their love-trauma-related thoughts as being in the back of their minds all day. "Even when I watch T.V.," one Love Trauma Syndrome victim recently told me, "I am often distracted from the program by my thoughts and feelings about my wife's affair." Her affair had occurred 9 years earlier. "It's always in the back of my mind," he said.

You can ask patients to graph the daily or even hour-to-hour change in their percentage of penetration into consciousness of the love-trauma-related thoughts. On a scale from 0 to 100 on the y-axis, as a function of time on the x-axis, patients are asked to estimate the percentage of penetration into consciousness. Figure 2.5 is an example of such a graph. Alternately, some patients like to graph the severity of their symptoms on the 0 to 10 SDS scale. Patients should also be asked to list triggering events if they can be identified.

Sometimes I have patients draw circular diagrams of how much of their daily thinking is made up of love-trauma-related thoughts, feelings,

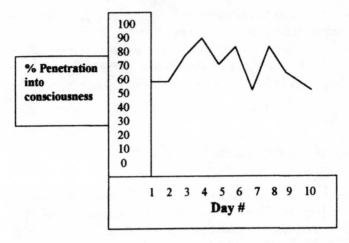

Figure 2.5   Percentage of Love-Trauma-related thought penetration into consciousness.

and memories. Such "bubble diagrams" are illustrated in Figure 2.6. Each circle representing the totality of conscious thoughts for the entire day is the same size, and the person is asked to draw another circle inside illustrating how much time during the day their thinking has been preoccupied with love-trauma-related thoughts. The diameter or area of the circles that the patient draws can be used to quantify the amount of intrusion they are experiencing in much the same way that a 100 mm visual analog scale is used.

If the person feels that most of their waking thoughts are tainted with love-trauma-related material, then the inner circle that they will draw is almost the size of circle provided. If the person is only thinking about the love trauma from a few seconds a day, then the person would place a small dot in the circle. If the person has no thoughts related to the love trauma, then they would put an "x" outside of the circle, and leave the

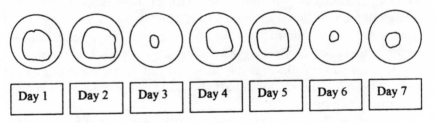

Figure 2.6   Sample "bubble diagrams" for a week.

inside of the circle blank. I also ask them to write down some of the prominent cues, or triggers, for their symptoms that they remember. This "cue diary" can be used in future therapy sessions designed to try to diminish their reactivity to these problematic stimuli.

When Love Trauma Kills Future Love

Most people who experience a love trauma continue to seek loving relationships. However, for some people with Love Trauma Syndrome, there can be diminution in a desire for future romance. They lose the desire to love again. Their capacity for intimacy is reduced or disappears. An example of this is a 77-year-old man I interviewed a few years ago. After fighting in World War II, the patient fell in love with a woman who initially described herself as separated from her husband. He said that this woman "was the love of his life." She lived in Texas with her 7-year-old daughter, and he lived in another Western state. After she returned to Texas, she kept calling him, asking him for money so that she could "get a divorce and move out to live with him." The patient ended up sending her thousands of dollars.

After several months he began to wonder if she would ever come. He says that he was so in love with her that he would do whatever she asked, and he never questioned her requests for money. He kept sending her money, but she never came. He later found out that she and her husband had gotten back together and had conspired to get as much money from the patient as possible. He felt betrayed and decided to never be deceived by a woman again. He never married or became involved with another woman. He remained preoccupied with intrusive thoughts about her for decades. During our second session together, the patient showed me the diamond ring he had bought for her decades earlier. When he opened the case to reveal the beautiful diamond ring, he began to sob uncontrollably. Many Love Trauma Syndrome victims remain bitter and angry about the whole concept and emotion of "love."

Love Trauma Syndrome-Induced Social Withdrawal

Love trauma can induce a withdrawal from future love interests, or can cause a social withdrawal from people in general. This generalized social withdrawal can be temporary or long lasting. It can happen even to people who were previously outgoing and sociable.

Love Trauma Syndrome victims can "disconnect" from the attachments they had in the outside world prior to the love trauma and withdraw into themselves. This is just the opposite of what is best for these patients. Clinicians, families, and friends of these patients need to remain vigilant for this sort of social constriction. These patients often withdraw from their social environment and cannot verbalize why this withdrawal is occurring. They might not be aware of its connection to their love trauma. In fact, they often are not aware that the social constriction is happening. Sometimes these patients will use alcohol or other mind-numbing substances in an attempt to self-medicate the pain of Love Trauma Syndrome, and in service of their withdrawal from their surroundings.

Love Trauma Syndrome can cause withdrawal from people one cherishes most. I have worked with men and women who, after a romantic breakup, have not seen their children, grandchildren, or other family members for long periods of time—sometimes for decades. This is because visiting their family worsens their Love Trauma Syndrome-associated pain and distress. Their love trauma memories, thoughts, and feelings become activated by painful reminders and cues of the lost love. This can happen because they see the resemblance of their lost loved ones in their children, or when they visit their families they see pictures of their lost loves (sometimes with a new mate). Rather than deal with the pain, they withdraw from their family.

Love trauma is often associated with a lot of humiliation and shame, which worsens social withdrawal. This can be especially true of men who find it difficult to accept a lessening of their social standing in the eyes of their friends and relatives (however this certainly also occurs in women). I have also had patients who have refused to return to visit their families, children, old friends, and neighbors because they felt ashamed of having been defeated in love, and having to "face" their family members, friends, and acquaintances again.

Unwanted Memories

Love Trauma Syndrome is a disorder of remembering too much. One of the most common symptoms of Love Trauma Syndrome is recurrent and intrusive memories of the love trauma event. In more severe cases of Love Trauma Syndrome, these recollections are accompanied by intense emotional distress and physical upset. The physical upset can include a wide variety of bothersome symptoms, including pounding heart, accelerated heart rate, elevated blood pressure, trembling, shaking, sweating, chills or hot flashes, choking feelings, nausea or abdominal distress, fatigue, dizziness or light-headedness, chest pain or discomfort, or other aches and pains. The physical upset can cause a generalized sense of malaise and result in the patient "feeling sick."

In Love Trauma Syndrome, the brain wants you to remember and review the love trauma events (so you won't make the same mistakes again). But the memories are associated with intense apprehension—so much so that you fear that they might overwhelm you. The memories cause considerable arousal and distress, and some people describe being afraid of being "sucked into" the memory. They fear they might go crazy, lose control, become intensely angry, or break down and cry.

This results in what is often referred to as the "push–pull" of traumatic memories. The memories are intense and one wants to review and to process them. However, the pain associated with the memories is so great that the memories are pushed away, pushed out of consciousness. Sometimes they are pushed away so completely that there is incomplete conscious memory of the event(s). These incomplete memories can later suddenly intrude into conscious (or into dreams) and overwhelm the person. This can happen days, weeks, months, years, or even decades after the trauma. This results in the *paradox* of love-trauma-related memories—you want to remember, but at the same time you don't want to remember (because the memories hurt too much). Hence the push–pull.

Whereas some people might have varying degrees of "photographic" memory for visual material (e.g., books, scenes), some people have very detailed and enduring memories of more emotionally laden events. As a geriatric psychiatrist, I have worked with a large number of older patients and have had the benefit of watching the course of Love Trauma Syndromes. I have been amazed at how some patients can provide me with an incredibly detailed blow-by-blow description of love trauma events from 50 years earlier! Some of my most enduring cases of Love Trauma Syndrome have been in people with this sort of heightened—almost photographic—memory of love trauma events. They can sometimes tell me what the other person was wearing—even when the event was decades earlier. Having such a good memory has its down side—it makes it more difficult to "conveniently" forget love trauma memories. Other non-love-trauma-related memories are often recounted in a much more impressionistic and less detailed manner.

Sometimes memories or memory elements of the love trauma intrude upon sleep in the form of love-trauma-related nightmares. These nightmares are associated with considerable distress during the dream. The distress persists after the person awakens and when the dream is recalled. Some patients describe repetitive dreams that night after night recreate the trauma. The patient John, whom I described at the opening of this chapter, described a repetitive dream where he saw his wife as she appeared in the 1960s, sitting naked by the side of the bed and smiling. Initially John thought she was smiling at him, but her lover Robert, also naked, suddenly appears and lies on top of her. He was amazed that although he had never witnessed her actually being unfaithful to him, his mind had been able to synthesize such a scene. Repetitive love-trauma-related nightmares (called "stereotypic" nightmares), where the material and sequence of dream events is exactly (or almost exactly) the same from dream to dream, usually is an indication that the Love Trauma Syndrome is of greater severity than cases that lack such nightmares.

Flashbacks

As described previously, Love Trauma Syndrome is characterized by unwanted and intrusive memories of the love trauma. These intrusive recollections can be so complete in recreating the images, feelings, and thoughts associated with the original trauma that the person feels as if some aspect of the event is recurring. Such complete and intrusive recollections of the love trauma are called *flashbacks*. Some flashbacks can be so intense and complete that the patient becomes temporarily disoriented and they believe for a moment that they are reliving the trauma. There is a continuum of how complete, intense, and lengthy a flashback can be.

These intrusive memories and flashbacks can be triggered by some reminder of the original traumatic event. For instance, one woman who returned home from work unexpectedly one afternoon heard the bed in her bedroom rhythmically creaking. She also heard coital moaning, and discovered her husband in bed with her best friend. For a few years after the event, when she heard a creaking sound she often had a flashback of the bedroom scene she witnessed that afternoon. She also had flashbacks when she heard moaning, or something that sounded like moaning.

Although flashbacks can have triggers, they often occur spontaneously in the absence of a clear trigger. Some love-trauma-related events can feel as if they happened yesterday (or are happening again now in the form of a flashback)—even though the traumatic event might have occurred years or decades earlier.

Unwanted Fantasies

Fantasies related to the love trauma are common in Love Trauma Syndrome. The brain has a remarkable ability to "fill in the blanks" when it needs to do so. It represents one of the more dangerous and malignant aspects of Love Trauma Syndrome, as it can become uncontainable. It can make you feel like you are going crazy. Indulging in these fantasies expands the love trauma and exacerbates the Love Trauma Syndrome. Some Love Trauma Syndromes are the result of imagined love trauma. Many cases of Love Trauma Syndrome are exacerbated by these fantasies, and they can actually fuel the syndrome.

One patient of mine found another woman's panties on the floor of her boyfriend's sportscar. When she confronted her boyfriend, he admitted to having had sex with a co-worker in his car. What upset her the most with her Love Trauma Syndrome were the fantasies she had of her boyfriend and his co-worker having sex in the car. "I just can't get them [the fantasies] out of my mind," she told me. "I sometimes feel that I'm going insane. I am miserable constantly." These fantasies ended when she fell in love with another man a few months later.

Avoidance of Love-Trauma-Related Stimuli

People with Love Trauma Syndrome often avoid situations, thoughts, and feelings that somehow remind them of the trauma. For instance, John described going out of his way to avoid listening to "oldies but goodies" songs on the radio. When such songs came on the radio, he quickly switched to another station, and he often had to listen to music of which he was less fond. He removed his wedding picture from his bureau because "it reminded me of the way she looked in the 60s, and whenever I looked at it I was reminded of her and Robert." To avoid driving by the local high school where his wife and Robert worked together, he actually would drive out of his way and take a more circuitous route. "I feel like an idiot doing this," John told me. "But it's a way of keeping me more comfortable."

Another patient of mine who had an affair with his secretary left a good job and moved to another state. This was because his wife, who had discovered the affair, insisted that they start over. This new start was an attempt on her part to remove as many of the stimuli as possible that would remind her of his infidelity. The few times I saw her it was clear that she was suffering from Love Trauma Syndrome.

By avoiding triggers, patients prevent the activation of their love-trauma-related and anxiety-provoking memories. The symptoms of Love Trauma Syndrome can wax and wane for many years, often being exacerbated after exposure to cues that remind the patients of the trauma. Some patients' lifestyles become constricted as they try to avoid many love-trauma-related cues. I have had patients who had difficulty finding any environment that was completely devoid of cues.

Another type of potent cue to trigger and exacerbate Love Trauma Syndrome-related symptoms are *anniversary reactions*. I have seen dormant Love Trauma Syndrome awakened in the context of an anniversary of a love trauma event. One patient of mine became depressed and anxious every April, and then again in September. Her association was that in April, she had broken off with a man whom she hoped to marry, and later that month had an abortion. September was the baby's due date. Ten years later, her depression became particularly acute on the 10-year anniversary of her breakup and abortion.

LOVE HURTS

Usually, the more "in love" you are with someone, the greater the potential for Love Trauma Syndrome should things not work out. If the person with Love Trauma Syndrome remains in love with the person who hurt them and rejected them, then it is more likely that the syndrome will be persistent. If the person experiencing the syndrome can fall out of love with the other person, the syndrome usually dissipates. A patient with Love Trauma Syndrome often feels motivated to try and "fall out of love" with the person who caused them the love trauma. They try to devalue the person they formerly loved, and to focus on the negative aspects of the relationship so they can adopt a "good riddance" attitude.

If a person remains in love with the person who caused their Love Trauma Syndrome, the pain of the syndrome becomes persistent. Many relationship breakups and divorces are caused by the attempts of a traumatized partner to leave the source of their pain. I have had patients who precipitously left their partners of many years after a love trauma without spending much time considering the pros and cons of leaving. They just wanted to get away from the pain. They quickly devalued their partner, and some quickly become involved with others. However, some people with severe Love Trauma Syndrome spend their lives never allowing themselves to commit to others again, never allowing themselves to fall in love, in part to defend against experiencing a repeat of their Love Trauma Syndrome pain.

Chapter Three

Why Are Love Traumas So Traumatic?

OUR BRAIN'S SECRET

The reason love traumas can be so traumatic can be found in our brain. Our brain has a secret. It is dedicated to propelling our genetic material (i.e., our genes) into the future. As the psychiatrist Randolph Nesse and his colleague Kent Berridge recently wrote, "the brain was not designed to benefit individuals, but their genes" (Nesse and Berridge, 1997). That is our brain's hidden agenda—to get those genes into perpetuity. The brains of both men and women know what sort of behaviors are needed by partners to best ensure that our genes are successfully propelled into future generations, and our brains continuously monitor the environment to determine how we are doing in this regard. We are happy if our brains "think" that things are going well for their secret plan (even if in reality it is not). If our brains "think" that things are not going well for this hidden agenda, we are made to feel unhappy (even if in reality things are going well).

The brain's neural circuitry ("wiring" if you will), and the brain's neurochemistry, allow us to be feeling, thinking, and behaving beings. With all of the amazing things that the brain does, its primary purpose is to help us generate offspring and have offspring that will survive into their reproductive years. Ideally, our offspring will have offspring of their own, and our genetic material (i.e., our genes) will be sent on its way into posterity.

Emotions—both pleasant and unpleasant—are highly evolved brain and body mechanisms that motivate the execution of certain behaviors that serve to promote the survival of our genes into future generations. We have evolved with brain mechanisms that assess dangers to our genetic material automatically, beneath our conscious awareness.

Any threat to a loving relationship that compromises the realization of our brain's secret goal will cause emotional distress in at least one of the parties. Our brain's "alarm systems" will be activated, and we will feel unhappy. For instance, rivals who might steal away our desired mates are not taken lightly by our brain. Threats to our children, the vehicles of our genetic material, can be devastating to us emotionally. Threats to one or both of our parents, either through illness, death, separation, or divorce, are also experienced by the brain as a potential threat to our genetic material. Our parents are our greatest protection, and the loss of either one or both of our parents places us in tremendous danger in the ancient ancestral past in which we—and our brains—evolved.

You love people who assist you in your brain's secret goal. You hate those who want to thwart that goal. Your brain judges the severity of a traumatic experience based on how serious the threat is to your genetic material (and the threat to its being successfully passed on into future generations).

When you are in love with someone, no matter what your intentions (or abilities) are at the time of having children with that person, your brain registers that person as an important ally in its attempt to realize its secret goal. You are in love with that person because your brain—whether rightly or wrongly—has established that, for some reason, the person you love would be a good partner in bearing offspring. Your brain is often tricked into falling in love by good, "healthy" looks. Maybe it was something they said, or some sign of intelligence, problem solving ability, compassion, empathy, and support they demonstrated. Or maybe they were bold, exciting, funny, or demonstrated easy access to resources (e.g., they were rich) or had lots of committed allies (i.e., they had devoted friends and family). It might have been something in the way they looked at you, or the way they kissed or touched you, that subconsciously suggested to your brain their reciprocal desire to mate and raise offspring with you, and to remain with you through the effort. They also probably showed (at least initially or for sometime thereafter) a desire and willingness to ally themselves with you.

Whatever the reason(s), your brain was impressed with their being good mates and allies in your struggle to get your genes into the next generation and beyond. And the more your brain "thinks" (note that your brain's decision making process typically is beneath your awareness) that the person will be a good reproductive partner (who you hope will also be able to successfully help you raise your offspring to reproductive age), the more your brain "locks on" to the person, and the more romantically "in love" with that person you will be. The more "locked on" to the person you are, the more vulnerable you are to a case of Love Trauma Syndrome should a threat to the relationship develop.

Any threat to that love relationship is not taken lightly by our brains. Loss of the anticipated future reward of getting our genes successfully ensconced in the next generation with our chosen partner can be almost unbearable for our brains. Serious threats can be traumatic. The brain activates certain emotions (e.g., jealousy, rage) to try to counteract the threat. Even if conceiving a child is impossible, the brain does not understand this (e.g., in the ancient ancestral environment in which we evolved, there was no birth control). If the couple has no childbearing potential—for example, it has been lost by employing contraceptive technique, or because of disease, accident, or age, or because the couple is gay or lesbian—the brain still has the same hidden agenda. Although the brain can be remarkably brilliant and capable (e.g., it solves calculus problems, figures out ways to get people to the moon, regulates your breathing, heart rate, digestion, endocrine functioning, etc.), it can also be quite stupid. It does not fully understand—or care—that actual reproduction with a desired partner is impossible. It does not register this fact deep down in the emotional parts of itself (i.e., the limbic system). The brain will continue to interpret a threat to a romantic relationship with the same degree of distress as it would if you could actually bear offspring with the desired partner. The brain centers that support the Love Trauma Syndrome experience remain active beneath our level of awareness even when our conscious brains know that we cannot reproduce. For the brain, sexual attraction, romantic desire, and sex equals reproduction, whether or not it is possible.

Therefore, although a life-threatening event is traumatic, so is any event that potentially thwarts the brain in its secret objective. During a love trauma, you might not be witnessing or experiencing a serious threat to your personal survival, but your brain sees a serious threat to the survival of your genes—even if you do not consciously perceive it in this way. The brain understands that anything that compromises its secret objective is tantamount to death—and is hence quite traumatic. The loss of a loved one, including children, by any means, be it voluntary or involuntary separation, or through serious injury, illness, or death, can be the ultimate trauma. Our brains want to guarantee the perpetuity of our genes. Unfortunately, our brains are much less interested in our happiness. As

Edmund O. Wilson wrote in his now classic book *Sociobiology*, "Love joins hate, aggression, fear, expansiveness, withdrawal, and so on, in blends designed not to promote the happiness of the individual, but to favor the maximum transmission of the controlling genes" (Wilson, 1975). And our brains will make us quite unhappy until we fix things to be in accordance with the way our brains want them to be.

Our brains also know one can better raise children if both parents are around to help out in the effort. If one parent is wooed away, or for some other reason leaves the joint parenting effort, it can be traumatic for the remaining parent and children. The emotion of *love* is important for our survival, or more specifically, the survival of our genes into posterity.

Our brains are "wired" for the capacity to love and be attached to someone else. When someone loves you, you usually have access to the assistance of other people who are related to and who love the person who loves you. The importance of a love attachment for successfully raising our young is better understood by considering the way of life of our ancestors as they evolved from ground apes on the savannahs of Africa a few million years ago. The young of our primate ancestors needed more and more attention for longer periods of time (e.g., years) before they would be able to care for themselves. Being "unattached" and not having someone who loved you (and access to other allies) meant that you and your offspring would have had fewer allies to help you obtain food for yourselves. You also would have had fewer allies willing to help care for your young. If you felt ill or were somehow weakened, you would have had less assistance, making it far more likely that you and your offspring would not survive. Without someone to help you keep alert for predators and enemies, you would have felt less secure. You would have had to spend more time being vigilant for danger and less time foraging for resources, such as food, if you had been by yourself. You would not have had the early warning of danger that a strong ally could have provided. Someone who loves you is a very valuable resource indeed—for both you and your offspring. Your brain knows it, and reacts very strongly when this resource appears threatened.

The Persistence of the Love Trauma Memory

When you experience a love trauma, it changes your brain functioning. Your brain processes the context in which the love trauma occurred, and stores the *memory* of the trauma. Usually, the more aroused and upset you were at the time of the trauma, the more your brain and body secrete substances such as adrenaline. These substances enhance the formation of the memory and contribute to the *persistence* of the memory. These brain substances also diminish the ability of the brain to *forget* and inhibit the processes associated with "convenient forgetting" and ignoring of painful memories. The brain seizes the trauma and records every detail of the event in its attempt to keep a record. It does not want the trauma repeated again.

Love trauma memories have an impact on your future behavior. The more profound the trauma was felt, the more physiologically aroused you were at the time the memory was made; the stronger and longer lasting the memory of the event will be; the more aroused you will be when the memory is *triggered* by cues; and the greater its ability will be to "sicken you" in the future (i.e., make you feel depressed, anxious, weakened, negative, "limited" in your abilities, or otherwise physically or emotionally "unwell" or "sick").

The severity and duration of your initial upset at the time of first experiencing the love trauma is often a gauge of how severe and enduring your Love Trauma Syndrome will be. The initial distress is often a good measure of the degree of psychological and physiological arousal you were experiencing. Some patients will even develop a low-grade fever, their heart will race, and they will feel profoundly physically sick. The more intense your emotional response when you were first traumatized, the stronger the conditioned response to reminders.

Your brain automatically (beneath your awareness) rates the importance of memories in terms of their relevance to your survival—and the survival and *successful* propagation of your genes into future generations. The more important and traumatic the event is rated, the greater the degree of brain arousal, and the greater the likelihood of developing a serious Love Trauma Syndrome. This system of storing memories is designed to keep your most important memories available to you at all times and to keep you alert and wary of future events that would again place you at risk. Memories that are regarded as important for survival (or for the survival of your genes) are linked with a physiological state of hyperarousal and cause a state of "too much memory" (technically referred to as *hypermnesias*).

However, when the love-trauma-related brain arousal is very excessive or chronic, the love trauma can become associated with symptoms of *dissociation*. During dissociation, there is a *disruption* of the usually integrated functioning of the mind and body. Memory systems can begin to break down, and there is a breakdown of the person's normal sense of who they are and of what the world is. When the dissociation becomes profound, there can be a disruption of normal memory processes, and the love trauma memory can become very distorted, or even partially or totally obliterated.

These dissociative brain mechanisms can disconnect the person from reality by disconnecting their memory systems. After all, our sense of reality is supported by our brains' memory systems. We *remember* what is real and what is not real. To disconnect from reality, we need to disconnect some of our memory systems. When this happens, we develop amnesia for the traumatic event.

However, when we become amnesic, this does not mean that we have not stored the memory somewhere in our brain. In fact, it appears that extremely traumatic memories can be stored in a place in the brain where we cannot get *conscious* access to them. However, these memories can still affect our behavior.

Raising the Love Trauma Memory Profile

Because of the intense central nervous system arousal associated with a love trauma memory, the brain begins to *separate* the love trauma memory from the context of one's total memory. The love trauma memory becomes separated and fragmented from other memories, and becomes very important to us. The tremendous brain arousal and activation associated with these traumatic memories contributes to the brain's becoming fixated on them and becoming less able to focus and process other non-love-trauma-related memories (see Figure 3.1). The hyperarousal raises the love trauma memory onto a "mental pedestal" for continuous contemplation and examination.

Because of the reinforcing brain arousal associated with the love trauma memory, there is less convenient forgetting of the love trauma. Instead, there is more such forgetting of other nontrauma-related material, as this material is regarded by the brain as being less relevant for the survival of your genes. It is almost as if one's life story becomes rewritten and distorted. The love trauma memory begins to loom and achieve dominance, as other lifetime memories are conveniently forgotten (e.g., brain connections for these memories are withdrawn).

Another useful analogy is to consider love trauma memories intrusive to other memories in a manner similar to malignant cancer cells. Malignant cancer cells invade and destroy good, healthy, noncancerous tissues in the body. Likewise, love trauma memories (and associated feelings,

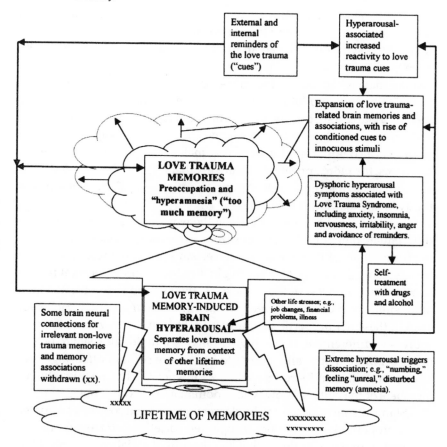

Figure legend:  = memories in brain storage

⬆ and ⚡ = brain-associated arousal ("hyperarousal")

XXX = Withdrawn brain neural connections for irrelevant non-love trauma memories and memory associations. Withdrawal of brain connectivity mediated by high state of neurophysiologic arousal related to the love trauma memory.

External and internal reminders of the love trauma ("cues")

Hyperarousal-associated increased reactivity to love trauma cues

Expansion of love trauma-related brain memories and associations, with rise of conditioned cues to innocuous stimuli

LOVE TRAUMA MEMORIES Preoccupation and "hyperamnesia" ("too much memory")

Dysphoric hyperarousal symptoms associated with Love Trauma Syndrome, including anxiety, insomnia, nervousness, irritability, anger and avoidance of reminders.

Self-treatment with drugs and alcohol

Some brain neural connections for irrelevant non-love trauma memories and memory associations withdrawn (xx).

LOVE TRAUMA MEMORY-INDUCED BRAIN HYPERAROUSAL Separates love trauma memory from context of other lifetime memories

Other life stresses; e.g., job changes, financial problems, illness

Extreme hyperarousal triggers dissociation; e.g., "numbing," feeling "unreal," disturbed memory (amnesia).

LIFETIME OF MEMORIES

Figure 3.1 *The disturbance of love trauma memories in Love Trauma Syndrome (or how love trauma memories are placed on a "mental pedestal" of hyperarousal for continuous contemplation).*

thoughts, and secondarily elaborated memories) can become intrusive and destructive of healthier, non-love-trauma-related memories, thoughts, and feelings. In Love Trauma Syndrome, the love trauma memories become intrusive and impair the patient's ability to concentrate and carry out normal memory and thinking functions. Patients with Love Trauma Syndrome sometimes describe themselves as becoming forgetful. Some will describe themselves as feeling as if they are going crazy.

Love Trauma Syndrome in the Ancient Ancestral Environment

In the ancient ancestral environment in which humans developed, Love Trauma Syndrome and the constellation of symptoms and complications of the syndrome played an important role in social regulation. We have evolved as social animals who want to maximize our access to a healthy mate whom our brains register as being sound and able to help us propel our genes into future generations. We also try to maximize our access to resources, such as food and other material supplies, needed to feed and protect ourselves, our mates, and our offspring. Good access to resources is also important for attracting mates. The greater your access to resources, the more appealing you are to others. The higher ranking males and females in a group—or the group "alphas"—usually get first pick of the available mates and resources.

In cultures where there is little in the way of material possessions to differentiate higher ranking people from lower ranking ones, higher ranking individuals often have access to certain *nonmaterial* resources of the tribe, such as tribal secrets. They might also have more important roles in sacred ritual services. In these societies, the ranking differentials can be quite subtle and difficult to recognize by the casual observer. However, even in these nonpropertied cultures with little in the way of material resources to differentiate status, higher ranking individuals seem to be able to attract more mates, and appear to have more sex and offspring. They have more allies and stronger alliances in general. The people who are members of the culture know who is dominant and who is not.

Status distinctions tend to be clearer in propertied societies compared to nonpropertied communities. Propertied societies also have more pronounced status competition. Whatever the type of social group, only a few individuals end up at the top of a social hierarchy. We cannot all be alphas. The rest occupy varying degrees of less dominant and subordinate positions.

We have evolved with brain mechanisms that try to maximize our social positions and access to the wealthiest, healthiest, and most fit mates and love interests, but facilitate withdrawal from competition over desired mates and over dominance when losing seems inevitable. These brain mechanisms help "put us in our proper place." This "automatic" brain response to defeat—or predicted defeat—is sometimes referred to as the Involuntary Subordinate Strategy (ISS). The ISS is a "neuropsychophysiological mechanism deeply rooted in our phylogenetic [evolutionary] ancestry."[2] Giving up on a preferred mate and accepting a lower social position in the group if necessary is protective for one's survival. It allows the defeated to cease their efforts to overcome a superior dominant and still remain a part of the group. It also helps maintain social order and harmony.

Thus, in the ancient ancestral environment, there were two possible responses to a love trauma secondary to competition from a successful rival (or to the situation where your love interest wanted to leave you for another). You could have defended your rights to access to the desired mate, or surrendered those rights. If you chose to defend your rights, you would have mounted a ferocious *intimidation display*[1] designed to intimidate your rival or mate into submission—if not an outright physical attack of him or her. The more your intimidation display conveyed a sense of asymmetry of strength in your favor, the more likely your opponent, or mate, would cede to your desires. Intimidation displays also served to erect barriers to competition or to desertion, and reflected a readiness to fight should those barriers not be respected. The intimidation display was designed to diminish the will of the opponent to fight, and to cede defeat before the onset of a fight.

This is one of the reasons why people with Love Trauma Syndrome can feel so physiologically aroused and angry. Their bodies are being prepared to mount a credible and ferocious intimidation display. This angry and aroused response was important in our ancient evolutionary past. If you chose to defend your rights, there would be increased demands on your heart (reflected by an increasing heart rate and blood pressure) to provide an increased availability of blood and oxygen to your possibly soon-to-be fighting muscles and brain.

Alternatively, the brain might be pessimistic about your chances for victory over a rival or for retaining your desired mate, and would be more apt to surrender. If you engaged in a fight for the person you loved, you might be defeated (e.g., the object of your desire might choose in favor of your rival, or your rival might physically overcome you). In the context of defeat in love, the emotional distress of Love Trauma Syndrome can help a person internalize that they have lost and can inhibit the expression of further intimidation displays or attacks against a successful rival.

In the ancient ancestral environment in which we evolved, such internalization of defeat played an important protective role for both individuals and social groups. The bridling of aggressive instincts in the context of defeat or inevitable loss served to help the person *act* the defeated role. Weaker rivals who were unable to be restrained by defeat and ceased their intimidation display and fighting would have had reduced reproductive success. This is because they would have been annihilated by their betters.

The ability to have one's aggressive instincts bridled and surrender one's love interest to a better rival gave an individual at least some chance of surviving and ultimately having offspring (albeit with less desired and probably less healthy and fit mates). Such bridling of aggression kept our ancestors out of fights that they could not win, and helped the probable loser surrender before it was too late. Additionally, the bridling forces often needed to be maintained to prevent one from wanting to rechallenge one's rival. The victors would have tolerated the individual remaining in the group only if their potential as a rival had waned, and they could be relied upon to be a useful ally in the future. Bridling of aggressive instincts in the context of being defeated in love enhanced the harmony and strength of the social group by diminishing the conflict between group members. The loser, however, typically remained miserable.

When you are successfully restrained by the sickening effects of something like Love Trauma Syndrome, your desires for resources are diminished. Your wanting less in this bridled condition diminished the likelihood of your getting into conflicts with others, and make you less of a competitive threat. For instance, in depression, sexual interest wanes and can disappear completely. Hence, the depressed person is less likely to become involved in competitive struggles over mates. In the ancestral environment, your betters tolerated your presence when you were depressed because you were no longer a sexual rival.

The Sexual Brain Bond

The scientific literature now supports the notion that when sexual activity is involved in romantic relationships, these relationships are strengthened by certain brain changes that occur at the time of sexual activity and orgasm. Hence, threats to these bonds, or to the breaking of these bonds, become even more traumatic.

For instance, some experts believe that the secretion of oxytocin at the time of orgasm (and other brain substances as well) further solidifies the romantic bond, and makes it more traumatic when these bonds are threatened or broken. The role of substances such as oxytocin secreted at the time of orgasm in the strengthening the bonds between mates has been most clearly demonstrated in certain nonhuman animals (e.g., the prairie vole *Microtus ochrogaster*) (Young, Wang, and Insel, 1998; Wang, Hulihan, and Insel, 1997; Insel, 1997).

The hormone vasopressin has also been shown in animal studies to facilitate bond formation. In certain animals, when the brain effects of oxytocin and vasopressin are blocked, the social bonding with only a single mate is blocked, and the animals engage in promiscuous (non-single partner) mating. Interestingly, when monogamous animals are compared to nonmonogamous animals, there are clear differences in the numbers of oxytocin and vasopressin receptors in the animals' brains. We can only speculate that human swingers have lower numbers or sensitivities of these brain receptors.

Other brain substances are also involved in bond formation. For instance, the neurotransmitter dopamine is involved in the experience of reward and pleasure, and is also prominently secreted in the brain during sexual activity. Dopamine also seems to be involved in the strengthening of social bonds with a mate. Dopamine happens to be the brain substance that mediates the rewarding properties of all substances of abuse, such as the addictive drugs cocaine, heroin, and nicotine. Like the intense distressing withdrawal symptoms experienced by addicts who stop their use of an addictive substance, withdrawal from a person whom you love is associated with tremendous distress. This distress seems to be heightened if the person from whom you are being withdrawn has been a valued sexual partner.

However, we all know that the brain changes associated with sexual activity and the formation and maintenance of a romantic bond do not guarantee the long-term success of relationships. Some people are not interested in maintaining longer term relationships with their sexual mates, and they successfully overcome any brain changes that might encourage them to do otherwise. These people typically are able to inhibit their becoming attached to their sexual partners by not allowing themselves to fall in love with them. Simply put, if you are able to prevent yourself from falling in love, you will not develop Love Trauma Syndrome.

LOVE TRAUMA SYNDROME AND STRESS

Love trauma is a type of stress called *defeat stress*. In the brain, the love trauma-related defeat stress induces the sickening feelings associated with the Love Trauma Syndrome. These sickening feelings make the victim feel weakened and emotionally upset. Love trauma is a type of stress that can change a person's sense of overall potency. After a love trauma there is often a malignant spread of excessive negative self-evaluations. That is, love-trauma-related defeats can *generalize*. Failures in the area of love can spread to feeling inadequate in other areas as well. Love Trauma Syndrome afflicted persons become vulnerable to making negative generalizing statements like "I'm not appealing to anyone," "I'm not good at anything," or "I'm a failure and a loser."

Cues for triggering symptoms of the Love Trauma Syndrome can also generalize. While a favorite song associated with a lost love might initially trigger symptoms, eventually the cues can generalize to all music being able to trigger symptom exacerbation. There is often a flashpoint in the course of Love Trauma Syndrome where there is a *malignant generalization* of the cues to encompass a wider and wider range of cues, resulting in greater amounts of avoidance of stimuli, overall social constriction, and misery.

Indeed, the changes in brain chemistry that occur with love trauma appear not to be specific to sickening you in the area of love interests alone. Brain changes triggered by love trauma can spill over and affect other areas as well. Love trauma victims can begin to view life through a "negative filter;" they see only the "down" side of everything. "Life sucks" was the repetitive response of one college student whose girlfriend had just broken up with him.

I have seen college students who, although they were doing well academically before their Love Trauma Syndrome, suddenly begin to perform poorly. One student who had been a straight "A" math student began to fail her exams. "I'm not good at anything," she said to me. "I can't even hold on to a boyfriend." Her Love Trauma Syndrome-related feelings of being defeated affected a wide range of her thoughts and feelings about herself.

Self-Esteem and the Love Trauma Syndrome

As already alluded to previously, Love Trauma Syndrome can be devastating to people's self-esteem. When a mate rejects his or her partner, the partner's self-esteem can plummet. Some experts regard your sense of self-esteem as representing your perceived resource holding potential (RHP). This RHP includes your brain's sense of how well you can hold on to your mates. This includes your sense of how well you could hold on to them in the face of challenges from rivals. The loss of a loved one for some reason, including a successful challenge from a rival resulting in a love trauma, can reduce your perceived RHP and self-esteem. For instance, being a victim of an infidelity can be devastating to your RHP and your self-esteem.

Your RHP is "calculated" in the emotional part of your brain (called the limbic system). Many of the calculations are made automatically beneath your awareness. It often requires careful psychotherapy to "make conscious" the underpinnings of a person's RHP and of their self-esteem.

The brain attempts to defend self-esteem, because a decrease in self-esteem is associated with a constellation of brain changes designed to foster submissiveness, decreased access to environmental resources, and a decrease in the likelihood of one producing gene-bearing progeny. Sometimes, however, after experiencing the loss of love (a form of "social defeat"), the brain is unable to prevent a fall in self-esteem. Along with the decrease in self-esteem occurs a cascade of brain changes associated with the correlates of diminished self-esteem (e.g., depression, sadness, and anxiety). Indeed, as already discussed in this chapter, Love Trauma Syndrome, and its interaction with neural circuitry that supports our sense of self-esteem, played an important role in social regulation during our evolution in the ancient ancestral environment.

Love Trauma Syndrome and Infidelity

Relationships work best when partners can help maintain and bolster each other's sense of RHP and self-esteem. Having sex with someone usually bolsters one's self-esteem. The brain usually registers the sex act as a victory, and increases the person's sense of RHP and of self-esteem. Being able to have sex with someone means that you have been accepted and honored by them. Your status is regarded as adequate to be their sexual partner. People willingly have sex only with those for whom they have high regard. We tend to feel much better about ourselves when we are involved in sexual relationships. The experience can be profoundly rewarding.

However, when your partner has sex with someone else, this tends to have the opposite effect on your RHP and your self-esteem. Your sense of

RHP and self-esteem plummets when your mate mates with someone else. Your brain experiences the infidelity as a defeat (i.e., a social defeat, a "defeat stress"). The discovery of an infidelity can have a profoundly sickening effect on people as their brain adjusts them to a new and reduced sense of RHP and self-esteem. Their sense of power and potency is diminished.

Sexual liberation has increased our freedom to engage in sexual activity with others, but it has also increased the amount of love trauma as people are hurt when their mates choose other sexual partners. In a sexually liberated culture, Love Trauma Syndrome comes with the turf. Not everyone who participates in the culture will get the syndrome, but many will.

I have had combat veterans tell me that the sickening feelings they experienced from learning that they had been cuckolded was more intense than the sickening feelings they experienced related to combat-associated traumas and defeat. One decorated Vietnam veteran described to me experiencing intense humiliation upon discovering that his youngest daughter was not his biological offspring. His daughter was the offspring of a man with whom his wife had an affair while he was on active duty in Vietnam. He could not understand, after having gone through so much trauma in Vietnam, how the humiliation of this discovery overshadowed any pain he had ever experienced in his life. "I thought I had been through the worst," he said. "But I guess I was wrong."

When Someone Has Both PTSD and Love Trauma Syndrome

Some people can suffer from both a PTSD related to a traumatic event that involved a physical threat or injury to themselves or loved ones, and Love Trauma Syndrome related to a loss of love. People with PTSD are considered to be *stress sensitive*, and typically have exaggerated emotional and physiological responses to subsequent stressful experience. Hence, persons with PTSD are more prone to developing Love Trauma Syndrome in the context of a love trauma. They are susceptible to the most severe forms of Love Trauma Syndrome. I have seen people with PTSD commit suicide, or contemplate murder, in the context of a love trauma.

One example of a patient with a combination of PTSD and a Love Trauma Syndrome was a woman who had been raped by three men who entered an open back door of her house. When her boyfriend entered the house through the front door, the rapists fled out the back. Both the woman and her boyfriend had an acute PTSD. Both were very upset when they first came to the emergency room. They were seen in individual and couple's counseling for a few weeks, but the boyfriend eventually left what had already been a fragile relationship. Even before the rape, he had been on the verge of leaving. When he did leave, she developed a full-blown Love Trauma Syndrome in addition to her already severe case of PTSD. She eventually recovered from both conditions and found an understanding and supportive boyfriend.

Chapter Four

When Depression Complicates
Love Trauma Syndrome

For some patients, Love Trauma Syndrome is associated with considerable depression. Love trauma can represent a significant defeat for people, and the experience of such defeat can trigger depression.[1] Depression is associated with a sense of loss—not only the loss of love—but also the loss of self-esteem. Precipitous drops in self-esteem commonly accompany Love Trauma Syndrome. When the Love Trauma Syndrome becomes associated with significant depression and suicidal ideation, it can signal the emergence of a particularly lethal form of the condition. A broken heart can literally completely break a person. It can even kill them.

There is a whole spectrum of different types and degrees of depression that can be triggered by a love trauma. Some of the depressions are low grade, whereas others are of a higher grade. When psychiatrists describe a depression as low grade, they regard the depression as being of low severity—a minor depression. Such minor depressions can precede more severe, or higher grade and more serious depressions, although some patients remain parked in a low-grade depression for years, maybe decades.

Classic Depression

Classic depression (or *typical* depression) is a syndrome where the patient complains of sadness and depression, as well as a constellation of other symptoms. Some classic symptoms include insomnia (i.e., difficulty initiating sleep or staying asleep), feelings of agitation and restlessness, and decreased interest and motivation. Other important symptoms associated with classic depression include feelings of worthlessness and guilt, decreased energy, tiredness (or tiring easily), decreased memory and concentration, and changes in appetite for food and sex. One of the most serious symptoms of classic depression is *suicidal ideation*—or simply the desire to be dead. Love Trauma Syndrome can progress into different varieties of depression associated with significant suicidal ideation.

The following is a list of symptoms associated with classic depression to help you gauge if you or someone you know has become depressed with the variety of depression in the context of a Love Trauma Syndrome. Two of these symptoms indicate at least a minor depression. The presence of five or more of these symptoms suggests a more severe depression (e.g., a major depression).

1. A depressed or sad mood most of the day and nearly every day.

2. Decreased interest in activities. There is also a diminished ability to experience pleasure during these activities.

3. A "significant" weight loss not in the context of dieting. Alternately, there might be weight gain, but this is less common. (Many researchers and clinicians regard a weight change of more than 5% of body weight in a month as significant.)

4. Insomnia (too little sleep) or hypersomnia (too much sleep) almost every day.

5. Feeling or looking slowed down or agitated and restless.

6. Bothersome tiredness and loss of energy nearly every day.

7. Feeling worthless almost daily, or feeling overly guilty.

8. A noticeable decrease in your ability to concentrate, think, or focus your attention nearly every day. There might be an increase in indecisiveness.

9. Recurrent thoughts of dying or suicidal ideation. The suicidal ideation might or might not include a specific plan for committing suicide.

Stuck in a Lower Mood Register

Our brains regulate certain body functions. For instance, our brains try to control our blood pressure and body temperature and try to keep these parameters within some normal range. If our blood pressure goes too low, there are problems (e.g., we get dizzy and lightheaded). Likewise, if blood pressure goes too high, there are other problems (e.g., we sustain potential damage to our arteries). Our brains try to control the fluctuations in our blood pressure and keep it in a normal range.

Similarly, there is a normal range for our mood, and a normal "up-and-downedness" of mood. Sometimes people wake up in the morning feeling energetic, clear headed, and optimistic. On other mornings they might wake up feeling tired, fuzzy-headed, and down. Patients with depression tend to stay stuck in a lower register of mood, where their mood is predominantly down and depressed. In this lower mood register they primarily feel sad and distressed.

Sometimes the timing of their mood fluctuations is quite predictable. For instance, I have patients whose moods "cycle down" every other day. On one day they feel relatively well, and can go about their business without difficulty. The following day they might feel depressed, anxious, and overcome with dread. They usually cannot identify about what it is they are feeling depressed or anxious. They just feel like "something bad" might happen, but they don't know what. On these days they cannot go about their business without difficulty, and sometimes they don't even have the courage to leave their homes. They might not even be able to watch television or to read because they are so overwhelmed with their anxiety. However, the following day they feel better, and they repeat the up-and-down cycles on subsequent days. People might meet criteria for depression in the mornings, but less so in the afternoon. They might have symptoms of a severe depression on one day, and a minor depression the next.

Love trauma events can precipitate a shift into a lower register of mood and mood cycling. After a love trauma, people have fewer good days and more bad days. (see Figure 4.1). They might develop more

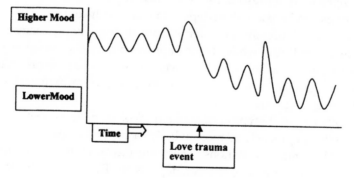

Figure 4.1   *A shift into a lower register of mood cycling after a love trauma.*

prominent *diurnal variation,* where they feel much worse in the mornings than they do in the afternoon or evening.

Love Trauma Syndrome and Atypical Depression

Love Trauma Syndrome can progress into what are referred to as "atypical" manifestations of depressive disorder. One type of atypical depression is called a *masked depression.* In a masked depression, patients might even deny feeling depressed. I have had many patients who were on the verge of tears, or actually crying, deny that they felt depressed. Other people can have what is sometimes referred to as a "smiling depression"—these people have many of the symptoms of depression described above, but are quite capable of smiling. This is also a form of masked depression. Some patients will actually cry and smile at the same time, and still deny that they are depressed. Such individuals are less successful at fully masking their depression.

Other variations in the presentation of depressive disorders include persons who do not identify themselves as feeling depressed, sad, blue, or "down in the dumps"—but rather complain of feeling "empty," "blah," or as if "life does not have meaning anymore." Depression is sometimes manifest as a loss of previously held beliefs and convictions about religion, God, morals, relationships, friends, work and country. "I have faith in nothing now," one patient recently told me. "I feel devoted to nothing and no one," he later said. Another common refrain of such patients is "I have nothing to live for anymore." Some depressed people focus on feeling "let down"—even betrayed—by institutions they had been committed to (e.g., the church, military, government, school, company)—and they appear more angry than depressed. Many depressed patients complain more of nervousness and anxiety than depression. Hence, it should be noted that persons with a depressive disorder will not always identify themselves as being depressed! And while classic depression is most commonly associated with a decreased appetite (and weight loss), some patients will complain of an appetite increase, especially for sweets or carbohydrates (with an accompanying weight gain).

Another type of atypical depression involves patients who complain less of feeling depressed and more of body "aches and pains" and other uncomfortable somatic sensations. These are the "somatic depressions"—which can also be a type of masked depression. The focus of the patients' complaints are more on feeling physically sick, unwell, or tired than on feeling depressed. If they see a doctor, they might describe complaints of simply "feeling sick"—although complete medical evaluations do not reveal any reasons for their sick feelings. Other symptoms commonly associated with atypical depressions might include increased appetite, overeating (hyperphagia), weight gain, and sleeping too much (hypersomnia).

Leaden paralysis is another atypical symptom of depression. In leaden paralysis, patients are not actually paralyzed, as all the nervous inputs to their bodies are intact. But for some reason, their bodies and extremities feel heavier, and it seems to take more effort for them to move. One patient of mine with leaden paralysis described it as feeling that the earth's gravitational pull on her was getting greater and greater, and it was becoming harder for her to move. "It just takes so much more effort for me to move and do things," she complained. The opposite of leaden paralysis are feelings of buoyancy, which typically are experienced when people feel the opposite of depressed—i.e., they feel euphoric, gay, and "lighthearted." During buoyant periods people feel as if the gravitational pull on their bodies has been reduced, and they feel light—sometimes almost as if they could float. During such buoyant periods movements of their body feel effortless.

Some researchers and clinicians regard a depressed person's ability to temporarily feel better in response to a positive life event as an important aspect of atypical depression. In more "typical" depressions the depressed mood is more sustained, and more typical depressives do not enjoy substantial mood elevation in the context of positive life events. For instance, one "typical" depressed college student I saw experienced no change in his mood upon graduating. "I can't remember the last time I felt happy about something," he said.

Other symptoms that can accompany atypical depression and further complicate Love Trauma Syndrome include muscle pains, headaches, stomach upset, and pelvic pain. Such symptoms can be especially intense when the patient's Love Trauma Syndrome is exacerbated.

Although some patients with atypical depressions deny having thoughts of suicide, they can eventually end up killing themselves. The impulse to kill themselves can come on suddenly and unpredictably. Even on the day of their suicidal act, patients with certain types of atypical depression might deny any suicidal ideation. Suicidal thoughts and behaviors are the most dreaded outcome of Love Trauma Syndrome. There is no more sad and dramatic end for someone with Love Trauma Syndrome than suicide. The reader should remember that suicidal ideation and behavior can be seen in *both* typical and in atypical forms of depressive illness.

Rejection-Sensitive Varieties of Depression or "Thin Skin Syndrome"

Another type of atypical depression is called *rejection-sensitive depression*, or *rejection-sensitive dysphoria*. This is a common form of depression seen in the context of someone with a Love Trauma Syndrome. People with rejection sensitivity usually have a lifelong pattern of sensitivity to interpersonal rejection and criticism. They are more likely to have been phobic of social situations and have been overly concerned that something was "wrong" with their body or physical appearance. Patients with this type of atypical depression experience overwhelming feelings of distress and discomfort when they feel rejected, snubbed, or criticized by others. The dysphoria refers to intense unpleasant feelings experienced in the context of rejection.

It has been hypothesized that "social brain circuits" in the limbic system of our brain mediate our feeling bonded to others. When our sense of connection to others is threatened, these brain circuits trigger alarms (e.g., in our amygdala) resulting in dysphoric mood. People prone to rejection sensitive varieties of depression are thought to have a greater degree of instability in their social brain circuits.

These brain circuits evolved to help monitor and maintain our attachments to others. In the ancient ancestral environment in which we evolved, being involved in relationships with others meant that we and our offspring had a better chance of surviving into the future. Even today, when members of aboriginal tribes are studied, those people with less social affiliation are more likely to die when they get sick. Their offspring are also more likely to suffer a similar fate.

We have brains that are wired to feel uncomfortable and unhappy when certain important social relationships are threatened—because maintaining these relationships once meant the survival of ourselves and of our loved ones. Some people, by virtue of the DNA that they have inherited and the differences in their social brain circuitry, are more sensitive to feeling upset in the context of social disruptions than others.[2] People with rejection sensitivity sometimes protect themselves from experiencing their rejection sensitive dysphoria by remaining relatively isolated and withdrawing from relationships as a defense. People with rejection sensitive dysphoria are particularly susceptible to the development of Love Trauma Syndrome after a love trauma event.

When a loved partner withdraws from or rejects someone with rejection sensitivity, the person with rejection sensitive dysphoria mounts a wide range of *distress displays*[3] designed to either reintegrate them back into the alliance or to punish the person who has rejected them. For instance, people with severe rejection sensitivity might engage in suicidal gestures to regain the attention and concern of their lost partners. They present themselves as willing to die if they cannot maintain their desired relationships. They might also be willing to injure or even kill those who do not respond to their distress.

Additionally, people with rejection sensitivity often try to heighten their attractiveness to others in an attempt to keep the loved partner from leaving. This attempt at being more attractive can sometimes have unpleasant consequences. For example, a rejection sensitive teenage girl might have unprotected sex with her boyfriend to maintain the relationship.

Treatment for Love-Trauma-Syndrome-Associated Depression

The good news about patients with depression (and the anxiety and nervousness often associated with depression) is that when they take antidepressant medications, they feel better. They might continue to cycle from time to time, albeit in a "raised register" (see Figure 4.1). They have fewer down days, and when they have such a day they are not as down as before being on the antidepressant. Anxiolytic medications can reduce the anxiety symptoms associated with the syndrome. Psychotherapeutic interventions for the treatment of depression are outlined in chapter 9.

The Antidepressants

Medications known as *antidepressants* represent a number of different medications useful for treating depression, depression associated anxiety, and panic disorder related to Love Trauma Syndrome. The antidepressants that were initially available to clinicians were the tricyclic antidepressants (such as amitriptyline [Elavil] or imipramine [Tofranil] and the monoamine oxidase inhibitors (such as phenelzine [Nardil]). Newer antidepressants include fluoxetine (Prozac), sertraline (Zoloft), paroxetine (Paxil), citalopram (Celexa), buproprion (Wellbutrin), nefazodone (Serzone), venlafaxine (Effexor), and mirtazapine (Remeron). Other antidepressant agents that are sometimes used include methylphenidate (Ritalin) and dextroamphetamine (Dexedrine).[4]

New and equally effective antidepressants periodically become available. Naturally occurring phytotherapeutic agents (e.g., extracts of St. John's Wort, *Hypericum perforatum* [*Hypericaceae*]) have been demonstrated in preliminary studies to be as effective as conventional antidepressants (and often without the side-effects associated with the more conventional antidepressant medication). Sometimes patients respond better to one agent than to another. At this time, psychiatrists are unable to predict which antidepressant will be best tolerated and most effective for a particular patient. Finally, antidepressants are often combined with an antianxiety agent such as those described in the following paragraphs.

Manic and Hypomanic Responses to Love Trauma Syndrome

Some patients with Love Trauma Syndrome experience what is called *mania* or *hypomania*. Whereas most people become depressed in the context of defeat, some develop the opposite response, often to the point of clinical hypomania or mania. The symptoms of hypomania and mania are the mirror image of depression. For instance, patients with depression have low-self esteem, whereas those with hypomania/mania have high self-esteem. People who are depressed usually suffer from feelings of low-energy and fatigue, whereas those with hypomania/mania feel full of energy. Patients with depression are pessimistic, whereas individuals with hypomania/mania are optimistic.

It has been hypothesized that for some patients the hypomania or mania is a compensatory response to their defeat. A case example illustrating how this might be so is a patient with manic depression whose wife became increasingly ill and died. Before her death he seemed to be becoming depressed. In fact, before her death his wife described him as in a "pitiful state, walking around crying and mumbling to himself all the time." A month later, at his wife's funeral, he had to be taken out of the funeral home because he had become manic. At the funeral, the patient proclaimed that his wife would have wanted everyone to have a "good time." He danced around her coffin before being whisked away.

Psychiatrists call such manic transformations at the time of a loved one's death *funeral mania*. I have seen bereaved people thrust themselves into affairs powered by varying degrees of funeral mania. The usual love-trauma-associated grief seen after the death of a loved one is replaced in these patients with sometimes hypomanic or frankly manic cheerfulness.

The criteria for a manic episode include the following:

1. *Euphoric, overly cheerful, or irritable mood.* Some of these patients will describe themselves as feeling high. People who try to thwart their wishes are often the targets of irritability and anger.

2. *Unusual self-confidence, inflated self-esteem, or grandiosity.* They can even have grandiose delusions (e.g., believe that they are entertainment superstars or heads of state—when in fact they are not). They can believe that they possess extraordinary talents, skills, or powers.

3. *Decreased need for sleep.* They might report feeling rested after only a few hours of sleep. I once had a manic patient go 4 days without any sleep before I saw him. I asked him if he felt tired. He just shook his head.

4. *Overly talkative.* Their speech can be loud and rapid. They tend to interrupt others.

5. *"Racing thoughts."* These patients typically have the sensation that their thoughts are racing. When they speak, they skip from topic to topic (a form of speech psychiatrists call "flight of ideas"). The logical flow of ideas during speech begins to break down, and the topics discussed are often only superficially related to each other. For instance, one patient with symptoms of mania was describing to me a problem he was having with a junior office colleague. The patient switched to a discussion of the colleague's abilities as a tennis player, then to a discussion of where the colleague went to college. After a brief talk about the college, the patient when on talking about how colleges today "were not operating up to the same standards" that they used to. He then switched to talking about the important role computers play in modern education, and how he has been unable to feel comfortable working with a computer. Then he asked me where I went to college. When a patient is engaged in flight of ideas, the ideas expressed are often only tangentially connected (this is sometimes called "tangential speech"). They can also be very funny and entertaining, and their flight of ideas can include numerous jokes and puns.

6. *Distractibility.* These patients are drawn to attend irrelevant stimuli. For instance, when you are trying to discuss their problems, they switch the subject to something irrelevant (e.g., a discussion of how they dislike the tie you're wearing).

7. *Excessive involvement in social, occupational, academic, or sexual activities.* They often take on multiple new ventures in each of these arenas of activity.

8. *Excessive involvement in pleasurable activities.* They may become unfaithful to their partners, or stop going to work to pursue activities that they find more pleasurable (e.g., golf, going to the beach). Spending sprees are

common. I once had a patient buy an airplane, luxury car, and over $100,000 in stocks in one day. He completely drained his and his wife's life savings doing so. These patients ignore the painful consequences of their actions.

To meet the criteria for mania, you need to have symptoms consistent with those listed in Item 1, and any three of the features listed in items 2 through 8 (although you need to meet four of the features if the only symptom you have from Item 1 is irritability). Hypomania is a less severe form of mania. However, even with hypomania people can get into trouble in their personal relationships and on their jobs. For instance, because of their propensity to challenge others, it can be difficult for people with hypomania to compromise and successfully negotiate. People who always want to get their way can be a problem for others. In couples therapy, it is not uncommon for the hypomania of one or both of the partners to be a cause of conflict between them.

Similar to people who are manic, those who are hypomanic suffer from a diminished perception of risk and a minimization of potential onerous consequences. It is for this reason that people who are hypomanic, like those who are manic, are more likely to get into trouble in general. One classic problem for those who are manic and those who are hypomanic is their tendency to get overly involved in pleasurable activities without regard for adverse consequences. They might ruin their marriages by impulsively becoming romantically involved with others. By the time they realize what they have done, irreversible damage has been done to their marriage.

A patient I met several years ago provides us with a good example of how a Love Trauma Syndrome can precipitate dramatic forms of mania. The only reason this patient (we will call him Michael) came to see me was because his longtime friend (we will refer to him as Peter) pleaded with Michael to see me. Peter was a former patient of mine. Peter thought that something was wrong with Michael's behavior, but Michael did not agree that he needed to see a psychiatrist. In fact, Michael told me that things had never gone so well for him. He came to see me only to appease his good friend. "I thought I'd just drop by and chat for a bit" was what Michael said to me.

Michael was 25 and had a youthful, handsome appearance. His thick. jet-black hair was moussed and neatly combed back. He was clean shaven and dressed neatly in casual clothing. He smiled broadly and appeared happy, animated, and energetic. Michael explained to me that he had finally "discovered" himself a few months earlier. He had just finished writing a screenplay, and was on his way to Los Angeles to sell it for "a few million dollars." When I asked him what made him think that his screenplay would sell for such a large amount of money, Michael said, "Oh, wait to see the movie, you'll see." He went on to explain how some movies made "hundreds of millions of dollars," and that people who made movies were willing to pay large amounts of money for a "winning screenplay."

Michael told me he had quit his job as an airport rental car agent in a major New England city, and that he had just stopped over at his friend's house in Washington, D.C. on his way to the West Coast. Michael had just broken off a 2-year relationship with a woman named Suzanne whom he was scheduled to marry. Just prior to the breakup, Michael and Suzanne had brought their parents together for dinner, during which wedding plans were discussed. The evening after the dinner, Suzanne told him that she wanted to call the wedding off, and thought that it would be best to break off their relationship. Within 2 weeks, she left for the West Coast to embark on a singing career. He showed me a picture of Suzanne, who was quite beautiful. Michael smiled the whole time while he related this story to me, and concluded that it was "all for the best," and he was "looking forward to becoming involved with other women." In fact, Michael claimed to have become quite a "pick-up artist." He said that he no longer wanted to feel "tied down" to one woman.

Michael gave me permission to talk to his friend Peter. Peter told me that Michael had arrived at his apartment 2 days earlier, and that Michael did not seem to need sleep. Peter went on to say that at about 1:00 a.m. of the first night that Michael stayed at the apartment, Michael started calling people to whom he had not spoken in years. Michael called to inform his old friends about his upcoming move to California and about the movie deal. When Peter asked Michael to stop making phone calls at so late an hour, Michael started to shout at Peter to leave him alone. He told Peter that "it was none of his business." Michael instructed his friend to go sleep, and that he would speak softly on the phone to not keep him awake. What seemed to finally stop Michael's phone calls was his inability to find certain phone numbers or to get an answer to his calls at so late an hour. Peter said that Michael's belligerence that night was uncharacteristic of him. He also had seen the screenplay Michael was talking about—it was only 20 pages long and poorly developed. Peter was worried about his friend's state of mind.

When I asked Michael about his decreased need for sleep, he described sleep as a "waste of time." "There's too much to do and too little time to do it," he said. When I asked Michael if he felt tired, he said no. "I just don't need sleep anymore," he said. He did not look tired, and he was animated and quite the chatterbox. He ultimately left my office refusing further workup and treatment, but agreed to call me if he changed his mind.

What Goes Up Usually Comes Down

When patients like Michael cycle up into a hypomanic or manic state, it is often followed by a period of depression. This is illustrated by describing what happened next to Michael. At the conclusion of my meeting with Michael, I told him that I thought he had a manic condition, perhaps precipitated by the breakup with his fiancée. His response was, "Suzy did a favor for both of us." I told him that he needed psychiatric treatment. I asked him to consider inpatient psychiatric hospitalization. He refused my offer for inpatient treatment, and I asked him to consider letting me treat him as an outpatient. He thought that he did not have a psychiatric problem, and he refused my offer. Since I knew he was going to Los Angeles, I gave him a list of a few places he could go for treatment there should he change his mind. I strongly recommended that he follow up with treatment.

To this day, I still don't know why I telephoned Michael at his friend's house a few days later. Perhaps it was because I was concerned about his need for treatment, and I thought that if I kept calling him that I could "soften him up" and he might reconsider his need to see a psychiatrist. When Michael answered the telephone, I could tell from the sound of his voice that he had changed and that something was wrong. I remember feeling frightened. His voice was slow, and he spoke in a monotone. He teeth were chattering. He sounded distant and spooky. I asked him how things were going, and there was a long pause before he responded. "I guess not very well," he answered. "How so?" I asked. "The light came out of the ceiling." "What?" "The light came out of the ceiling and fell on me." "How did that happen?" I inquired? Again there was a long pause. "I tried to hang myself," he said matter-of-factly. In an instant I was flying through my files trying to find his friend Peter's address so that I could get the police there quickly. "Where's Peter?" I asked, stalling for time. "He's at work." Michael paused, and then said, "He's going to be angry." "Why?" "I broke his hair dryer," Michael said. "How did you break his hair dryer?" "I put it in the bathtub . . . in the water."

I didn't need to hear much more. When the police and the fire department personnel finally got to Peter's apartment, they had to break down the door to get in. They found the light fixture from which Michael had tried to hang himself on the floor with a noose tied to it. The bathtub was full of water with a hairdryer in it. He had tried to electrocute himself in the bathtub. Michael had also swallowed every pill in Peter's medicine cabinet, and had cut deeply into both of his wrists. Michael was in intensive care for 3 days before he could be transferred to a psychiatric unit.

When I first saw Michael on the psychiatric unit, he was slumped in his chair with a downcast gaze. He was disheveled and unshaven in his hospital pajamas. He was expressionless and still. His bare arms were black and blue from where the intravenous infusions had been placed in his arms, and he had thick bandages on both of his wrists. A total of 50 stitches were required to close his wrist lacerations. "I'm worthless rot," he said slowly and softly. "What?" "I'm worthless, stinking, filthy rot!" he said getting louder with a slight quake. "I'm a no-good shit!" he spat out. "Suzy was right to leave me. She knew. She discovered what a shit I was, and ran as far away from me as she could. She knew. Go talk to her." He cried pitifully with his head hung low. I was shocked by his sudden transformation.

Although I knew that Michael had manic–depression, I was surprised by the rapidity with which he had cycled down. While I sat talking with Michael, I was thankful for the shoddy construction that allowed the light fixture to fall to the floor under Michael's weight. You could still see the rope burn on his neck where the rope had tugged on his skin before the fixture fell out of the ceiling.

For most of us, after a love trauma event, our up-and-down swings in mood are not as dramatic as Michael's. People with a personal or a family history of cycling mood disorder, or cycling bipolar mood disturbance, are more prone to these dramatic cycling reactions after a love trauma. Their mood might go way up, but forces within their brains are quick to pull them down from their up position. It works like gravity, keeping them close to earth. This downward pull keeps their hypomanic/manic tendencies in check.

Dysphoric Mania in Response to a Love Trauma

Love-Trauma-associated hypomanic and manic reactions can also be of the dysphoric type. *Dysphoria* refers to a wide range of intense unpleasant feelings experienced in the context of the love-trauma-related defeat or loss. People with dysphoric mania commonly have distressing and upsetting "racing thoughts" about the love-trauma-related event. They often feel agitated and experience an increase in their activity. They look and act manic, but they also feel depressed.

For instance, one such patient of mine with a Love Trauma Syndrome following the breakup with a longtime girlfriend became very agitated and nervous. To deal with the agitation he exercised so much that he lost 30 lbs in one month. Additionally, people with dysphoric mania or hypomania, instead of experiencing a decrease in sexual libido, might have an increase in their sexual interest. In essence, dysphoric mania is depression and mania/hypomania combined.

This dysphoric mania is also referred to by psychiatrists as "mixed bipolar disorder." Again, in this condition patients demonstrate both clinical-grade depression and hypomania/mania simultaneously. Beginning mental health practitioners often are surprised that both conditions (i.e., depression and mania) can be present at the same time in the same patient. Novice clinicians tend to think that depression and mania would "cancel each other out." In fact, mixed bipolar disorder represents at least one third of bipolar patients seen by psychiatrists. Although it is initially difficult for people to understand how a person could be happy and sad simultaneously, it happens all the time, and you can detect it if you listen to your patients carefully.

Treatment of Love-Trauma-Syndrome-Associated Hypomanic and Manic Reactions

Mood stabilizers are a class of medications used for the treatment of hypomanic and manic conditions. The medications decrease manic/hypomanic excitement, and prevent future cycles of mania/hypomania alternating with depression or depression-related sickening syndromes. Mood stabilizers include medications such as lithium and anticonvulsants such as valproic acid (e.g., Depakote) and carbamazepine (Tegretol). Newer mood stabilizers that seem effective but are still under study include gabapentin (Neurontin), lamotrigine (Lamictal), and nimodipine (Nimotop).[5] Antidepressant medications alone can worsen mania/hypomania, and can increase the rapidity and frequency with which patients cycle between manic/hypomanic states and depression.

Love-Trauma-Syndrome-Associated Anxiety

Although Love Trauma Syndrome is most commonly complicated by depression, it can also be complicated by anxiety, panic, phobias, and a wide range of psychosomatic conditions. This is because Love Trauma Syndrome is associated with considerable brain hyperarousal, which is often experienced as feelings of anxiety. Whereas the dominant theme in patients with depression is a sense of defeat and loss, the dominant theme in patients with anxiety is *danger* and fear of some dreaded outcome. It could be that they feel that their relationship with someone they still love is in danger, or they fear of the loss of love, or they fear being unlovable. It could also be the fear of being hurt in relationships, or the fear of having some terrible disease that would make their lives all the more miserable.

Patients with Love Trauma Syndrome often describe feeling nervous and jittery all of the time, even when they are not possessed by love-trauma-related thoughts and recollections. One patient described feeling like he was always "trembling inside." He also described "laying awake in his bed all night," often unable to get thoughts of his unfaithful girlfriend out of his mind. His anxiety persisted for months after the love trauma event.

Another patient of mine who learned that her husband had an affair described constantly feeling "on edge." She returned to smoking cigarettes after years of not smoking. She also lost her appetite. "The one good thing about this whole ordeal, Dr. Rosse," she said to me, "was that I was finally able to lose those 20 pounds I had been trying to lose for so long. This is probably the best weight loss program I've ever been on," she laughed. Some patients in the throes of a Love Trauma Syndrome become "keyed up" and describe an increase in blood pressure or a racing heart.

The symptoms of anxiety in Love Trauma Syndrome can be particularly problematic, and some of the anxiety symptoms overlap with the symptoms of depression. If you have at least three of the following symptoms, you are reaching levels of problematic and serious anxiety:

1. Persistent anxiety and worry.
2. Feeling on edge, restless, agitated, keyed up, and unpleasantly aroused.
3. Tiring easily. Persistent fatigue.
4. Problems concentrating, or the "mind going blank."
5. Irritability.
6. Muscle tension.
7. Difficulty falling asleep or staying asleep. The sleep that is obtained is unsatisfying, and then you wake up still feeling tired.

Other symptoms commonly associated with anxiety disorder include "feeling shaky" and trembling. Patients with anxiety disorder can have problems with muscle aches and soreness. They might feel like they have a "lump in their throat" and have the sense that it is difficult to swallow. Many patients complain of having to urinate frequently, or complain of having diarrhea or nausea.

Panic

Another type of anxiety condition that can begin to occur in the period after a love trauma is called *panic disorder*. In panic disorder, patients have what are called panic attacks. The brain hyperarousal associated with Love Trauma Syndrome can facilitate the experience of panic attacks. I have seen patients have their first panic attacks in the weeks following a love trauma event. The panic attacks themselves are severe anxiety attacks that seem to come out of nowhere, and are not necessarily associated with thoughts, feelings, or memories of the love trauma. Interestingly, the appearance of the panic attacks often distracts the person from thinking about their love trauma.

The symptoms of a panic attack can include the following:

1. A racing or pounding heart.
2. Profuse sweating.
3. Trembling and shaking.
4. Smothering sensations.
5. Choking sensations.
6. Chest pain or discomfort.
7. Nausea or abdominal distress.
8. Dizziness, lightheadedness, or feeling unsteady or faint.
9. Feeling unreal ("derealization") or detached from oneself ("depersonalization").
10. Feeling that you are going crazy.
11. Fearing that you are going to die.
12. Numbness or tingling sensations in your skin or body.
13. Chills or hot flashes.

If you experience at least four of these symptoms within a 10-minute period (and there are no other medical reasons why you might be experiencing these symptoms), you might be having a panic attack. If you have less than four of the symptoms, it is considered a *limited symptom panic attack*.

In both panic and anxiety states, there is often an accompanying desire to escape and retreat to an area of perceived safety. Panic disorder represents the activation of the brain's "alarm" systems, which drive the patient to seek safety. In such patients, their desire to escape and retreat to safety is associated with the development of agoraphobia. Such people tend to feel safest at home, and they can become "homebound." Their lifestyles become restricted as they no longer venture out of their houses for years. This homebound state is called *agoraphobia*, and for many agoraphobics, leaving the relative safety of home becomes an intolerable risk. The brain of the agoraphobe is more interested in keeping them safe than happy.

In agoraphobia, patients acquire fears of being in public places, crowds, elevators, bridges, tunnels, aircraft, subways, or buses. When they are in these places, patients with agoraphobia (called *agoraphobes*) experience anxiety and an intense desire to escape to a place of safety. It is thought that a common element of these agoraphobic fears is some unconscious perception of being vulnerable (e.g., to attack or humiliation) with limited opportunity for escape. One panic-ridden and agoraphobic patient of mine developed his disorder after the breakup of a long-term relationship. He only felt comfortable in the safety of his home. As soon as he got into his car to drive to the store, or to a friend's house, his arms felt so weak that he could not turn the wheel of his car. He was also afraid that as soon as he drove a few blocks away from his house he might have a bout of diarrhea and would not be able to get to a bathroom. He told me he felt "pinned down to his house." He broke off relationships with people who lived "too far" from him because he was afraid of venturing off to their houses. His brain was more interested in keeping him safe than happy.

When Depression and Anxiety Are Mixed

Both anxiety and depression can be serious complications of the Love Trauma Syndrome, and are commonly present at the same time. Both conditions are linked to the brain hyperarousal associated with Love Trauma Syndrome. When symptoms of anxiety or depression become significant, or begin to impair a person's ability to perform academically, socially, occupationally, or as a family member, it is important that the person seek professional assistance with their condition. Finally, suicidal thoughts and ideas are never to be taken lightly.

Antianxiety Agents in the Treatment of
Love-Trauma-Syndrome-Related Anxiety

A number of antianxiety agents, such as lorazepam (Ativan), ox-
azepam (Serax), alprazolam (Xanax), and diazepam (Valium) are useful in
the short-term management of the anxiety associated with Love Trauma
Syndrome. Some patients feel quite agitated, aroused, and upset and are
unable to fall asleep at night and perform academically or occupationally.
These medications can provide patients with the short-term relief they
seek. As all of these substances are addictive, they should be used with
caution, especially in people with addictions to other substances, such as
alcohol or cocaine. They should never be considered as curative of the condition. They are merely "band-aids" that temporarily diminish some of the
symptoms of anxiety. But unlike band-aids, there is little real healing that
occurs during treatment with these antianxiety agents.[6] The antidepressants described earlier typically are best able to treat and remedy anxiety,
panic, and phobic reactions with the fewest side-effects—albeit their effects are not immediate, and sometimes take weeks to become realized.
The term "antidepressants" is perhaps unfortunate, as these medications
can have powerful antianxiety, antipanic, antiobsessive-compulsive, and
antiphobic properties. Some of these medications are also useful in the
treatment of posttraumatic stress disorder. Hence, the usefulness of "antidepressants" is not limited to the treatment of depression. And as will be
described in chapter 9, antidepressants can be useful in patients with prolonged and severe Love Trauma Syndrome, a condition which shares
many features of the anxiety, depressive, obsessive-compulsive, and posttraumatic stress disorder syndromes.

WHEN DEPRESSION RECRUITS A LOVE TRAUMA

Depression is related to what experts call defeat stress. In the brain,
defeat stress sets up considerable restraining influences on future behavior. This includes the induction of sickening, which weakens the person and
makes them feel less up to task of challenging others. The saying "once
beaten, twice shy" is a good expression for what happens after defeat. Defeats are "setbacks" that change our internal sense of potency and our ability to hold onto loftier hierarchical positions. The brain's response to
defeat is protective, and keeps us from rechallenging others (e.g., rivals for
mates) we have little chance of overcoming.

We have evolved with brain mechanisms that try to maximize our social positions—doing so also increases our access to mates. Your brain knows that the higher your social position, the more likely you will be to have more mates and more offspring that survive into their reproductive years. Simply put, people of higher social standing tend to have more offspring. Statistics from all over the world show that such individuals have more money and greater access to resources—and the resources to which they have access are of higher quality. For instance, they consume more calories and have greater access to safe drinking water. They have more doctors and live longer. When they give birth, it is more often attended to by trained health personnel, and consequently they have lower infant and maternal mortality rates. Access to resources means life for you and for your descendants.

As great as it is to feel dominant, our brains also have evolved mechanisms that facilitate *withdrawal* from dominance struggles (e.g., for mates) where losing seems inevitable (the ISS discussed in chapter 3). These brain mechanisms "put us in our place." Giving up and accepting a lower social position in the group if necessary is protective. It allows the defeated to cease their efforts to overcome a superior dominant and still remain a part of the group.

When the brain wants you to feel beaten, it can "recruit" past defeats and traumas to help you feel beaten, depressed, and sickened. When we talk of sickening here, we are not just referring to feeling physically sick, "sick to your stomach," or nauseated. Sick feelings involve a large constellation of feelings of "unwellness." Your brain can sicken you in many different ways, and people often experience multiple forms of sickening at a time.

The purpose of feeling sick is to pin you down, to keep you from challenging others whom you have little chance of beating. Sickening feelings can include feeling nervous, anxious, depressed, tired, and weak. Sickening can also involve the experience of different types of physical pain (e.g., musculoskeletal pain or headaches). Depression often recruits other sickening feelings due to concurrent physical problems. For instance, if you have arthritis—even a minor case—depression can recruit the pain and amplify it. I have seen patients who experience their arthritic pain only when they were feeling down and anxious.

Depression commonly precipitates a Love Trauma Syndrome by triggering love trauma memories. This serves to deepen the depression. The overall sense of defeat is augmented. Love traumas often represent the greatest defeats of our lives, especially since they are linked to the brain's desire to send your genes into posterity. Love traumas typically represent what the brain regards as the ultimate defeat—the thwarting of your chances of genetic propagation.

Psychosomatic Reactions in Love Trauma Syndrome

Love Trauma Syndrome is often associated with the precipitation or exaggeration of various psychosomatic conditions. A *psychosomatic condition* involves physical symptoms that are generated (or exacerbated) in the patient's mind. The person feels as if they are afflicted with a physical illness. When physicians evaluate the medical bases of these patients' physical symptoms or complaints, they cannot find evidence of disease—or sufficient evidence of disease—to explain the severity of the patient's symptoms.

Psychosomatic disorders include the so-called neurasthenic syndromes. *Asthenic syndromes* are characterized by a profound loss of mental and physical energy and strength. These can be prominently associated with a Love Trauma Syndrome. In the past, people suffering from severe nervous and physical exhaustion after a psychological trauma were thought to be suffering from neurasthenia.

People afflicted with neurasthenic conditions experience pervasive tiredness and fatigue easily. They also typically complain of a wide range of other symptoms besides fatigue, such as muscle aching, dizziness, painful menstruation, headache, crampy diarrhea, or symptoms of prostatic inflammation enlargement (e.g., prostatic pain, pain and burning on ejaculation, urinary frequency, burning on urination). Neurasthenic conditions include fibromyalgia, chronic fatigue syndrome (CFS), chronic headache, primary dysmenorrhea, chronic prostatitis, and irritable bowel syndrome (IBS). These syndromes often occur together in the same person.

Other neurasthenic conditions include a variety of affective spectrum disorders. Affective spectrum disorders include major depression and other clinical and subclinical depressive disorders, mixed anxiety and depressive syndromes, panic and anxiety disorders, and chronic headaches and migraine.

These psychosomatic conditions recruited by Love Trauma Syndrome often include an exacerbation of chronic pain conditions. These patients experience more pain in various parts of their body. Some of these patients attribute their increased pain to their "arthritis acting up," but their flare-up is temporally related to their love trauma.

Love Trauma Syndrome and the Immune System

Evidence of immunologic dysfunction has been reported in people who have experienced a disruption in a relationship with someone they love. Some of the immunologic changes increase the person's predisposition to experience "allergic" reactions to even minor immunologic challenge (e.g., trivial quantities of allergens, such as dust, pollen, etc.). These patients can have chronic complaints of allergy symptoms, such as a runny nose, nasal congestion, postnasal drip, and seemingly unexplained skin reactions such as itchiness or hives. Sometimes the triggers for their allergic reactions cannot be identified. The compromised immune states of people with Love Trauma Syndrome might even be associated with diminished immune function and compromised resistance to infectious illnesses and cancer. With our love relationships intact, our immune system functions better—and is better able to resist infection and the growth of nascent tumor cells.

Love Trauma Syndrome and the Autonomic Nervous System

Love Trauma Syndrome can also be associated with changes in autonomic nervous system functioning. The autonomic nervous system is responsible for controlling many "automatic" physiological functions of our bodies, such as the regulation of heart rate, breathing, blood pressure, digestion, blood sugar, temperature, and sleep. For instance, changes in autonomic nervous system functioning can cause dizziness, lightheadedness, gastrointestinal distress, nausea, upset stomach, constipation, and diarrhea. Love-trauma-precipitated changes in autonomic nervous system arousal can result in changes in blood pressure, blood sugar, and sleep.

After a love trauma, the brain can alter autonomic functioning in a way that causes you to feel sick. For instance, when some people are faced with an overwhelming stressor, they faint. I have seen fainting spells—or complaints of lightheadedness—develop in the context of a love trauma. The faint is mediated by the autonomic nervous system, which provokes a precipitous drop of blood pressure, thus compromising the supply of blood and fresh oxygen to their brain. Love-Trauma-Syndrome-associated increased anxiety and hyperarousal can also cause increases in blood pressure and pulse rate.

Obsessive–Compulsive Responses to Love Trauma Syndrome

Some patients with Love Trauma Syndrome develop obsessions. *Obsessions* are thoughts, ideas, feelings, or impulses that repetitively and disturbingly force themselves into the patient's consciousness. Most commonly, the obsessions are related to disturbing thoughts and fantasies related to their love trauma. The obsessions might also revolve around violent themes, including suicidal or homicidal ideas.

Some patients develop compulsive behaviors. *Compulsions* are repetitive acts that the patient feels he or she must complete. The compulsive acts represent an excessive response to the realistic demands of the environment. Classic compulsive acts include repetitive hand washing and checking (e.g., of doors to make sure they are locked, of stoves to make sure they are turned off, of guns to make sure they are not loaded, or of furniture to make sure it is clean). Compulsive acts can also include repetitive mental activities, such as the repeating of certain number sequences or prayer. Some people compulsively hoard things that they are unable to throw or give away. They become "pack rats," and their whole apartment or home can become a storage center for these often useless things. Other people might compulsively hoard money and become quite miserly and stingy.

One patient began to hoard in his apartment things largely related to his childhood and young adulthood after his wife of 20 years left him. This included newspapers and magazines he had accumulated during their "happy years" together, and nonfunctioning household appliances such as a refrigerator, air conditioners, stereo equipment, radios, and clocks. He admitted that he still loved her, and hoped that she would one day return to him. He still held onto this belief after she moved out of the country and married another man. When he came to see me, he had so many boxes in his apartment that he could no longer get out of his front door. He had begun to exit and enter his apartment through a window. This plan was not acceptable to his landlord, who gave him 2 weeks to clean out his apartment.

His hoarding behavior was only minimal when he was living with his wife, but occupied the majority of his time since his wife left. He was paralyzed in his ability to organize his apartment and throw useless items away, and made list after list of things he had to do "in order to get organized." He often simply rearranged things into ever more compact accumulations of junk. On a number of occasions he was unable to sign his divorce papers because he could not find the papers that had been mailed to him among all the other papers and materials he had accumulated throughout the apartment. "I want to sign them," he would say with frustration, "but I just can't find them." After he was forced to clean out much of his apartment (or be evicted), he became depressed, and required over a year of psychotherapy and treatment with antidepressants before he began to recover. He admitted to being grief stricken over "missing" his "stuff."

When Love Trauma Syndrome Drives You Crazy

While Love Trauma Syndrome can become complicated with a wide variety of psychiatric and psychological disturbances—such as depression, anxiety, panic, psychosomatic conditions, obsessions and compulsions, antisocial behavior, and substance abuse—it can also make some people psychotic. When someone becomes psychotic, the person has difficulty differentiating reality from fantasy.

One patient of mine came home early from work one afternoon and found his wife of 10 years in bed with his best friend. Over the next several hours his speech became more difficult to follow, and he began to discuss his belief that his friend was an alien implanting his wife with "alien seed." He appeared confused at times and would intermittently break down and cry. After crying for a few moments, he would suddenly shift from a sad affect to a more euphoric one, laughing uncontrollably. He was finally brought into the hospital after he walked through and shattered a sliding glass door, which left him with a number of lacerations on his arms (some of which required suturing). When asked why he walked through the glass, he said "I don't know if I want to go on living." But he later described walking through the door "as an accident," and did not have full memory of the event. "I don't remember ever even seeing the door," he told me.

Another example of a person becoming psychotic in the context of a Love Trauma Syndrome was John, who fell in love with a fellow college student, Leslie. They dated for a semester. John believed the relationship was strong and monogamous—until he discovered that Leslie had also been sleeping with another man who was working at a nearby gas station and was not attending college at the time. After a few arguments, Leslie broke off the relationship with John. When I spoke with John a few weeks after the breakup, he had a severe Love Trauma Syndrome, along with the delusional belief that he had contracted AIDS from Leslie. His HIV test was negative, but he insisted that not enough time had elapsed for it to turn positive. Later, Leslie also tested negative, but John was still convinced that the AIDS virus lurked within them both, and was also in her new boyfriend (the person from whom John thought Leslie first caught the virus). After a few months on a low dose of an antipsychotic medication, coupled with psychotherapy for his Love Trauma Syndrome, John's belief that he was infected with the AIDS virus gradually subsided.

Some people with a Love Trauma Syndrome might develop a psychotic condition called erotomania. In *erotomania*, people become convinced that someone is in love with them when in fact they are not. There might never have been a romantic relationship with the person to begin with, or it might never have been as serious as the patient believes it was.

People with erotomania can continually bother the objects of their affection with persistent letters, cards, flowers, gifts, and unwelcome visits and telephone calls. Some people with erotomania become involved in elaborate surveillance of their partners. They are often willing to come into conflict with the police in their desire to pursue their love objects. Certain people with erotomania also develop the delusion that their love object needs to be "rescued" from some imagined danger; this delusion often justifies the stalking and surveillance.

Some people remain obsessed with former lovers and are unable to let go of the relationship. They can develop erotomanic delusions that their former lovers are really still in love with them. Such people might also stalk their former mates and become murderously angry when their affections are not reciprocated. Psychiatrists often treat such delusional, angry, and homicidal individuals with antipsychotic medications to help these people attain better reality testing and to better control their rage.

It is not uncommon for people who become psychotic in the context of a Love Trauma Syndrome to develop delusions of jealousy. They become convinced that there are rivals for their romantic interests and mates, or that their partners are being unfaithful. Such intense jealousy can continue years after a love trauma. Patients with Love Trauma Syndrome complicated by delusions of jealously sometimes need to be treated with antipsychotic medications. When appropriately treated, the patients, and the people around them, become more comfortable. The patient becomes less controlling and possessive.

Chapter Five

The Varieties of Human Love Trauma Response

Different Styles of Response

People can be divided into two different categories based on their responses to a stress such as a love trauma. They can be classified as *internalizers*, that is, they tend to keep their psychological responses to a stress to themselves. They become depressed, anxious, unhappy, or pessimistic. Internalizers are likely to have a neurotic disposition, and regard their relationship problems as being the result of their own personal inadequacies, or "their own fault." Although internalizers might look sad or nervous, their distress is usually a private affair, perhaps known to only their closest friends and family members.

Then there are the *externalizers*; people who react to stress by "acting out" and angrily blaming others. The distress of externalizers is not a private affair—they let others know that they are unhappy (and often make others unhappy as well). Externalizers generally regard their relationship problems as being other people's fault—not their own. They are often demanding and feel "entitled," and become angry with those who have not given them what they feel entitled to.

Internalizers might also feel resentful and angry, but they generally try to keep these feelings to themselves. Internalizers are more likely to hurt themselves than they are to hurt others in response to a love trauma. Externalizers are willing to hurt others—either emotionally or physically—in retaliation for perceived wrongs.

Internalizers usually can be differentiated from externalizers by the intensity of their expressed anger. Internalizers typically direct their anger inward and are overly critical of themselves. Rather than being angry at others, they more frequently become depressed and anxious. Externalizers are angrier, harsher, and more critical of others. They have more problems controlling their tempers. Externalizers are more likely to throw tantrums and become violent. They are more likely to be aggressive, challenging, resentful, and demanding, and are more likely to fight, steal, destroy property, and threaten others. They are also more likely to engage in a full range of self-injurious behaviors (as well as behaviors designed to hurt others). On the other hand, internalizers are more likely to be depressed, moody, unhappy, anxious, and have psychosomatic problems.

Internalizers tend to feel miserable in response to a stress, while externalizers are more likely to make others feel miserable. Classically, internalizers suffer in silence; externalizers declare their distress to the world. At their worst, internalizers might think about suicide, or even commit suicide. At their worst, externalizers might think about injuring or murdering others.

In my clinical experience, I have found that in general men are more likely to be externalizers, whereas women are more likely to be internalizers. There are certainly exceptions to this rule, and it is probably best not to make generalizations regarding gender differences here. To complicate matters further, some people have a behavioral style that represents a combination of internalizer and externalizer types.

TWO PATHS

People who develop Love Trauma Syndrome essentially have two paths to choose from. These are illustrated in Figure 5.1. They can choose to engage in primarily *healthy* coping behaviors; or go down a potentially more destructive and dangerous path in search of relief from their distress, and engage a variety of unhealthy maladaptive coping responses. Healthy responses promote healing from a love trauma, whereas unhealthy responses tend to cause more problems and complications for the person.

There is a wide range of healthier responses to a love trauma event, including the appropriate grieving over the loss of love, maintaining positive thinking and self-evaluation (e.g., "I am an intelligent and thoughtful

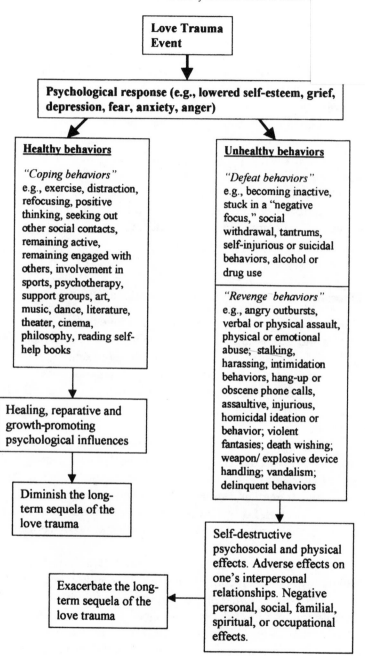

Figure 5.1   Healthy versus unhealthy behavioral responses to a love trauma.

person"), maintaining an optimistic attitude ("I will recover from this painful experience"), and developing a more philosophic and religious outlook on life (e.g., "Change in life is inevitable and I must learn to adjust to these changes, even when they are profound," and "My Higher Power will help me through this"). Other healthier activities include nourishing one's social support system and friends, exercising, and becoming involved in various recreational, community, religious, and learning experiences.

Unhealthy responses include morbid preoccupation with the love trauma event, anxiety, depression, low self-esteem, harsh and overly negative self-evaluation, social withdrawal, suicidal ideation, and revenge and "payback" fantasies. Other less healthy responses to a love trauma include becoming angry and blaming others for one's misfortune, acting on one's revenge or violent fantasies, vandalism, and engaging in other risky activities (e.g., joining gangs, "road rage").

Direct and Indirect Expressions of Emotional Distress

One type of response to a stress such as a love trauma involves direct recognition and expression of the many feelings one has in response to the loss of love. Such direct (and usually healthier reactions) include controlled expressions of anger, disappointment, sadness, dismay, surprise, shock, disbelief, hurt, and jealousy. These expressions can be in the form of discussions (often intense) with others, or writing, art, dance, or music—even exercise.

Indirect responses to a love trauma involve acting out of one's feelings rather than directly recognizing, expressing, and dealing with the emotions. Instead of recognizing and discussing your hurt, disappointment, and anger over being snubbed by a loved one, you demonstrate via actions how you feel. For instance, you break things in your apartment, you drive your fist through the wall, you get drunk and drive your car in a reckless "I don't care" manner.

Direct, healthy expressions of feelings tend to promote healing. Indirect, unhealthy acting out complicates one's life and makes it more difficult for one to become aware of their problems and address them in more constructive and meaningful ways. People who engage primarily in acting out behavior tend to become imprisoned in a vicious cycle of misery—not only for themselves, but for others around them. Some people are able to directly express their dysphoric emotions, but act out as well.

The Energy Locked Up in Love Trauma Syndrome

Love Trauma Syndrome generates a lot of emotional and physical energy. One patient of mine likened the syndrome to a "psychic hurricane." As previously discussed, Love Trauma Syndrome represents a state of neurophysiological overactivation and hyperarousal. Although the energy can manifest itself as anxiety, irritability, poor sleep, and anger, it can be harnessed and directed into more positive and healthy pursuits. These can include exercise, weight training, academic pursuits, the development of new interests in art, science, computers, sports, entertainment, and leisure activities—just to name a few.

However, the energy can be used to do harm to yourself and to others. This is the greatest danger of Love Trauma Syndrome. Some Love Trauma Syndrome victims will release the energy locked up through committing violence against others—and not necessarily just those who have hurt them. There can be many innocent victims of someone's Love-Trauma-Syndrome-related violent outbursts. For instance, I had one college student as a patient who, after an unhappy breakup with his girlfriend, got drunk and proceeded to vandalize over 20 cars parked in the dormitory parking lot. "I just had so much rage in me," he said. "I wanted to make everyone feel just as unhappy as I did. I didn't know what to do with all the anger. Destroying the cars made me feel better, at least at the time."

This case also illustrates how alcohol and drugs can disinhibit people to act on their more unhealthy and violent responses to a love trauma. Because of this, people with Love Trauma Syndrome should avoid the use of such substances, especially if they have a history of becoming violent. Alcohol and drug abuse increases the likelihood that the energy of Love Trauma Syndrome will be released in violent, unhealthy, and unproductive ways.

One of the goals of dealing with a Love Trauma Syndrome is to try to capture and control as much of the energy as possible, rather than letting the energy take control of you and throw you around. An example of someone who was able to do this was a physician colleague of mine whose husband had abandoned her for a younger woman. For the first few weeks after her husband left, she was depressed and tended to wallow in self-pity. The only time she became animated was when she described her anger and rage toward her husband for deceiving and leaving her.

When I suggested getting involved in an exercise program, she claimed she was too tired and exhausted to do so. I pointed out to her that when she was angry she seemed quite energized, and that she could put the energy to good use by exercising. She was about 30 pounds over-weight, and for years she had been engaged in a battle to lose this weight. However, she had never found the time or the energy to main-tain a regular exercise program. Now, however, she hit the treadmill en-ergized by her Love-Trauma-Syndrome generated anxiety and anger. Within 3 months she had reached her weight goal and she looked great. She even confessed to me that there were times at the gym when she felt too exhausted to continue exercising. "But all I have to do is think of him [her husband] with her [his new lover] and I get all the energy I need to carry on."

Indeed, Love-Trauma-Syndrome-associated arousal and energy gen-erates a lot of sweat in exercise gyms across the country. However, there is a danger that some people will exercise too much. Such individuals can lose excessive amounts of weight, do damage to their joints, and not exer-cise in a wise and healthy fashion. In such cases the exercise becomes an unhealthy response to a love trauma.

Determining When a Response to Love Trauma Syndrome Is a Problem

How does one determine if the emotional response to a love trauma is a problem? After all, a certain amount of dysphoria and unhappiness is appropriate for someone who has just experienced a breakup or loss of someone they love.

You can determine how problematic an emotional response to a love trauma is by considering the "4 D's" mnemonic. The 4 D's are duration, severity of distress, extent of disturbance to social and occupational func-tioning, and the destructive effects on the person's life and their physical and mental health. A problematic response to a love trauma is reflected by an excessive duration of the dysphoric response. However, one can never define exactly what an appropriate duration of a dysphoric response to a love trauma event for a particular patient should be. It varies somewhat between patients and relationships. For instance, it might not be unrea-sonable for a dysphoric response to the breakup of a relationship of 10 years to last up to 6 months. Dysphoric responses of longer than 6 months to a year suggest a problem.

Of course, one cannot just consider the duration of the dysphoric response—one needs to also consider the severity of the distress, and its severity should decrease over time. Although some distress is to be expected after the breakup or the loss of a prized romantic relationship, severe symptoms of anxiety, depression, anger, or insomnia will markedly compromise a person's quality of life. If the distress is so intense that it causes a disturbance in social and occupational activities, this is also a problem that needs to be addressed, especially if the dysfunction is persistent and fails to improve over time. Finally, destructive attempts to cope with the love trauma, including the use of illicit substances of abuse or of alcohol to numb yourself to the pain, are a sure sign that unhealthy Love Trauma Syndrome responses are present. Assaultive and homicidal ideas are more likely to be carried out when someone is intoxicated with drugs or with alcohol. Violent acts are never an appropriate response to a love trauma.

Years ago a friend of mine in college became upset when she saw her boyfriend flirting with another woman at a party. She got into her boyfriend's sports car and wanted to "mess it up somehow." While she was driving down the highway at over 80 miles per hour, she had the impulse to crash the car. She jerked the steering wheel and flipped the car into the medium strip. This friend survived the accident with minor injuries, but the outcome for herself—and possibly others on the road—could have been much worse. She brought up this story to me when I was casually discussing Love Trauma Syndrome with her. "Yeah," she said, "It can make you do crazy things you never thought you would do. I can't imagine what came over me to make me flip that car over. But I just wanted to get back at that jerk [her boyfriend at the time] in a way that I knew would hurt him. I guess I didn't care what it might do to me."

Self-Injurious and Suicidal Behavior

Both internalizers and externalizers can engage in self-injurious or suicidal behaviors. People can have fantasies about such behaviors, and some actually act on their fantasies. Self-injurious or suicidal behavior represents a serious complication of Love Trauma Syndrome.

Self-injurious behaviors include self-mutilation involving superficial wounding (e.g., cutting) or burning (e.g., with cigarettes) of the skin. Amazingly, many people who engage in such self-injurious behaviors describe feeling no pain when they are inflicting the wounds on themselves. It is thought that in these people, their brains' stress response involves the secretion of certain stress neurochemicals (e.g., endorphins, endogenous benzodiazepines) that anaesthetize them to their self-inflicted pain. These people describe feeling relief from tension and dysphoria during and after attempting to injure themselves (e.g., rubbing a broken glass bulb up and down their forearms). Self-injurious behavior can facilitate the development of dissociative phenomena (as described in chapter 3) that can help people numb themselves to their Love-Trauma-Syndrome-related pain. Importantly, self-injurious behaviors can leave the person permanently scarred, disfigured, or emotionally or physically impaired. Using a cost–benefit analysis, the benefits derived from self-injurious behaviors never outweigh the risks (i.e., costs). If you think otherwise, you need to see a therapist.

Psychiatrists differentiate self-injurious behavior from suicidal behavior. In self-injurious behavior, the person says that they want to hurt themselves, but are not interested in killing themselves. Someone who is suicidal has the desire to die. Importantly, up to 80% of people with a history of self-injurious behavior end up trying to kill themselves at some point. Self-injurious behavior is often considered as part of a continuum with suicidal ideation (see Figure 5.2).

For both self-injurious behaviors and suicidal ideation, there is a continuum of ideation and behavior from *passive* to *active* (see Figure 5.2). During passive ideation, the person only contemplates injuring or killing themselves. They fantasize about these behaviors but have little to no intention of acting on their fantasies.

When they develop a plan to hurt themselves, and decide to act on the plan, the ideation has become active. People with a Love Trauma Syndrome can find themselves anywhere along the spectrum depicted in Figure 5.2. If you do find that you are somewhere in this spectrum, you should seek professional mental health care immediately. I have seen people in

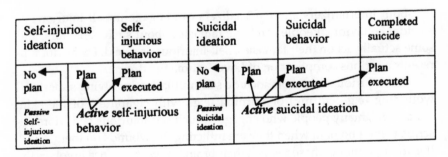

Self-injurious ideation		Self-injurious behavior	Suicidal ideation		Suicidal behavior	Completed suicide
No plan	Plan	Plan executed	No plan	Plan	Plan executed	Plan executed
Passive Self-injurious ideation	*Active* self-injurious behavior		*Passive* Suicidal ideation	*Active* suicidal ideation		

Figure 5.2 The self-injury/suicide spectrum.

the throes of a Love Trauma Syndrome kill themselves. This is a dangerous way of escaping from the pain of a love trauma. Interestingly, most people who attempt suicide have thought about it for less than 1 hour. Hence, most suicide attempts are impulsive acts that have not been carefully considered. However, some suicides are contemplated over much longer periods of time.

People in the midst of a Love Trauma Syndrome might unexpectedly kill themselves. Usually, however, they emit clues that suicide is on the horizon. People need to be alert to these clues. One clue is when someone says they feel they would be better off being dead. Another clue is when someone threatens suicide. Any such threat should be taken seriously, and the person should see a mental health specialist. It is a mistake to minimize a person's suicidal threat. People with a past history of suicide attempts are at greater risk of trying to do so again. Another clue is when an unhappy and depressed person starts giving away a lot of their possessions. They might be making preparations for their death. I learned about this last clue the hard way.

When I was in medical school, I went to dinner at my friend Michelle's house. Her mother had just separated from her father. Michelle had explained to me that her father had been having an affair with an office co-worker for the past year, and that he was now planning to marry this other woman. At dinner was my friend Michelle, her mother (whom I had known for several years), and another friend of mine named Paul. Michelle's mother seemed sad, but she could periodically offer a brief smile and she did not seem uncharacteristically melancholy.

Michelle's mother was preparing to move out of the house that she, Michelle, and Michelle's dad had lived in for 15 years. Her mother offered me certain items, such as a lamp, small pieces of furniture, and books, explaining that she was not going to have room in the apartment into which she was moving for all these things. Both Paul and I left the house that evening with a carload of her possessions that she was giving away. Michelle had commented several times over the course of the evening that "Mom's been giving everything away."

The next day Michelle, Paul, and I went to an art museum in the city. When we returned to Michelle's house later in the day, police were outside of her house. Michelle's mother had committed suicide by taking an overdose. I was too early in my medical school studies to know that Michelle's mother giving things away in the context of her being depressed over her husband's leaving her was a warning sign that she was about to commit suicide. The event contributed to my wanting to become a psychiatrist and wanting to prevent similar tragedies.

Assaultive or Homicidal Responses to a Love Trauma

Some people afflicted with a Love Trauma Syndrome believe the only way of dealing with their pain is to injure or destroy the object of their unrequited affections. Luckily, most people with a Love Trauma Syndrome only have fantasies of carrying out their injurious or murderous plans. These fantasies, plans, and acts designed to injure or destroy others are some of the most serious complications of Love Trauma Syndrome.

Some patients might kill the object of their love, and then kill themselves (homicide–suicide, or dyadic death). It has been estimated that at least two thirds of homicide–suicides are related to "jealous love." Men more commonly commit homicide–suicide. In fact, when men murder their wives or lovers, an estimated one fourth will go on to kill themselves. For women who kill their husbands or partners, fewer than 3% then kill themselves. In someone with a severe Love Trauma Syndrome, it is important to elicit whether they have fantasies or plans to commit homicide, suicide, or a combination of the two. As guns are the murder/suicide weapon of choice, people with a Love Trauma Syndrome should have their access to such weapons eliminated.

In the "Medea Syndrome," people who feel betrayed in a relationship seek revenge against the person who offended them by harming their joint offspring. In the Greek myth of Medea, Medea obtains revenge against her husband, the adulterous Jason, by killing the two sons they had together. Although Medea was a woman in the Greek myth, the Medea Syndrome can occur in men and in women. However, although both men and women kill their children and can suffer from Medea Syndrome, statistics suggest that women commit the majority of neonatal and child homicides. It is not known how many of these murders have elements of a Medea Syndrome in the context of someone with a Love Trauma Syndrome. In the ancient ancestral environment, Medea Syndrome-motivated murders might have been a way for a parent to "cut their losses" with an unreliable (e.g., cheating) mate.

In the Greek myth, Medea escaped and lived on after committing the murders of her children. However, many times such tragedies end up as homicide–suicides—that is, the parent who kills their children frequently takes their own life as well. It is estimated that 30% of women who kill their children then kill themselves. For men who kill their off-spring, the number who then commit suicide is higher—somewhere between 40–60%. Sometimes people who have fantasies of killing their children kill themselves first in order to prevent themselves fro.n acting on their homicidal ideas. Others might kill pets jointly owned and raised by the partners. People who are having Medea-like homicide fantasies usually are in considerable emotional distress and are always in need of psychiatric help. Finally, some people might simply kidnap or otherwise make their children less available to the mate against whom they seek revenge.

Just as there is a spectrum of passive to active ideation for self-injurious and suicidal thinking, there is an equivalent spectrum of thoughts and behaviors for the desire to injure others (without the intent to kill) and for the desire to kill others. This spectrum has the desire to inflict injury on others on the left side of the spectrum, and the desire to commit homicide on the right. Just as with self-injurious and suicidal ideation, anyone who finds themselves contemplating hurting others needs to see a mental health professional immediately.

One person who would have benefited from seeing such a professional is Luke Woodham. He is the 17-year-old who shot and killed two classmates—his ex-girlfriend Christina Menefee, and her friend Lydia Dew. Woodham said his primary motivation was revenge against Menefee, who broke up with him a year earlier. The college coed Tatiyana Tarasoff was killed by a boy who was spurned by her. He remained obsessed with her for many months and ultimately acted on his fantasies to kill her. The "Unibomber" Ted Kaczynski is said to have begun contemplating his reign of terror after being spurned by a woman with whom he was in love at his place of employment. The case of Kaczynski illustrates how the homicidal targets of people with Love Trauma Syndrome might not be the person who snubbed them, but innocent bystanders. People with Love Trauma Syndrome can take up terrorist or criminal causes as a vehicle for them to act out their aggression born of a Love Trauma Syndrome. The desire to hurt others in response to a love trauma is more fully described in chapter 7.

By injuring or destroying the person whom they love, they simultaneously express their anger and desire to obtain control over their love interest. The expressed anger also punishes the person who has rejected and hurt them. The retaliation against the offending party might be swift, or carried out over a lifetime of subtle attacks and deprivations.

Dissociative Responses to a Love Trauma

As already described, people can have a range of dissociative responses to a love trauma. The continuum of dissociative responses ranges from feeling mildly shocked to experiencing profound dissociation. This profound dissociation might be associated with some degree of psychotic experience (e.g., auditory or visual hallucinations). During dissociation, the brain processes reality differently, allowing the phenomena of dissociation and psychosis to be realized.

Stressful experiences of all types, not just love trauma, can precipitate various forms of dissociation and even psychosis. At certain thresholds of high arousal and stress, different neurotransmitter systems in the brain become activated, and a person can begin to dissociate. They begin to feel spacey and "out-of-it," and things take on a dreamlike quality. As described earlier, dissociation involves a disruption of the normally integrated functions of consciousness. These functions include your memory, your sense of self, and your perception of the world around you.

This dissociation enables us to deal with some of the more awful things that life has to offer. Intense stress is thought to "autoinduce" dissociation in many people. During periods of dissociation, the normal processes involved in making a memory are disturbed. For instance, children who are sexually abused by adults or by parents are thought to sometimes dissociate to the point that they cannot retrieve the memories of the sexual abuse. Dissociation-inducing brain substances secreted during severe stress seem to interfere with memory formation (and memory processes in general).

It is thought that dissociating during a traumatic event lessens the painful impact of the trauma. Not having access to the memory of very traumatic events diminishes the sickening processes that would occur if the memories were clearer. It enables the person to function in a cruel environment over which they have no control over (albeit disconnected from parts of themselves).

Dissociation provides a protective function. With some degree of dissociation, people can still function despite being under significant amounts of stress. For instance, I have patients who were going through difficult times in their lives, such as dealing with an unwanted divorce. These patients have described to me how "unreal" things seemed to them. They described a range of dissociative symptoms, including feeling that life had taken on a "dreamlike" quality. I have found that for many of these patients the dissociation diminishes the shock of their circumstances.

One patient with a Love Trauma Syndrome provides us with an example of more severe dissociative responses. This young woman's husband of 5 years left her for another woman. She had two young children and felt unprepared to deal with life and parenting on her own. She described herself as being "under a lot of stress."

Two weeks after her husband left, she had to go out of town on a business trip and leave her children with a friend. Her husband was out of town and unable to care for the children in her absence. She was very apprehensive about her trip, and, up to the last minute, almost cancelled it. Even before her husband left her, jet travel had always made her nervous. However, she felt safer when flying with her husband.

While she was at the airport waiting for her flight to depart, she noticed that tears were coming out of her eyes. She began to hear her husband's voice telling her "it's all right, honey, it's all right." She lost track of time and of where she was. When she closed her eyes, she saw a "lattice" design and other geometric patterns. She began to hear a buzzing sound in her ears and felt as if she was "popping" out of her body. She became very frightened at the notion that she was leaving her body, and she thought that she might be "dying" or going crazy from all the stress.[1] She immediately went back home, and made the trip a few weeks later when her husband was able to care for the children and the patient was able to travel with her friend. But she still had occasional periods—especially when she was under stress—where she complained of feeling "weird." "I call these my Twilight Zone feelings," she said to me.

Defense of Self-Esteem

One of the reasons that there is so much psychic energy involved with the Love Trauma Syndrome is because the mind works very hard to preserve self-esteem after a love trauma event. If self-esteem falls, the person will be less able to function effectively. Many responses to a love trauma represent attempts to defend self-esteem. Some people are more successful than others in the ways they consciously or unconsciously cushion themselves against the love trauma-induced blows to their self-esteem. In general, the more fragile the person's self-esteem is to begin with, the less successful they will be in coping with a love trauma event. Defenses can be healthy, adaptive, and constructive ways to maintain self-esteem. However, some defenses are unhealthy, or *pathologic*—that is, defense of self-esteem "at any cost"—including hurting or destroying those who have offended our pride (pride is used here in a fashion synonymous with self-esteem) or hurting ourselves. And why would our brains want to so vigorously defend our self-esteem? To understand this, we must first understand what self-esteem really is.

As previously discussed in chapter 2, some experts regard your sense of self-esteem as representing your perceived RHP. Your RHP is your brain's sense of how much in the way of resources you can secure and retain (not just material resources, but also "social resources" in the form of mates and allies). This includes your sense of how much you can obtain in the face of challenges and other dangers, and your sense of how well you can hold on to resources (and your mates) in the face of challenges from rivals (and other dangers). We have evolved with brains that fiercely defend against drops in self-esteem. Why? Because in the ancient ancestral environment, drops in self-esteem would have diminished your sense of confidence and courage, which would have resulted in your feeling less able to access resources from the environment. This ultimately would have translated into diminished survival potential for you and your offspring.

Thus we have evolved as social animals who try to maximize our self-esteem. This maximizes our sense of power, and thereby increases our ability to access resources in the face of competition (which is ubiquitous). These resources are necessary for our survival, and for the survival of our offspring, kin, friends, and allies. Resources, including food and shelter, are necessary for the survival of our genetic material into future generations. (Additionally, the more resources you have, usually the more attractive you are to potential mates.)

The psychological and behavioral mechanisms we use to protect ourselves from experiencing drops in self-esteem are called *defenses*. They are "automatically" activated when we experience a potential drop in our self-esteem. The drops in self-esteem secondary to a love trauma event can be particularly precipitous.

These defenses served an important function in our evolutionary past. For instance, in our ancestral environment, dramatic drops in self-esteem would have been associated with a significant decrease in RHP. That is, you would have felt much less competent to "hold your own," and more likely to surrender. Again, this would have resulted in your feeling less able to access resources from the environment, which ultimately would have translated into diminished survival potential for you and your offspring. Decreased self-esteem means diminished future success for our genes.

People go through all sorts of mental contortions to avoid the full internalization of humiliation, defeat, and subordinate status that erode their self-esteem. Like our body's defense mechanisms that destroy invading microorganisms, the mind uses mechanisms of defense to keep out "toxic" views of events that would poison our self-esteem. These can include verbal and physical attacks against those who have caused the love-trauma-related humiliation.

One classic defense against a drop in self-esteem is to provide yourself with *success fantasies* ("fantasy thinking"). In these fantasies you can be successful in your endeavors (e.g., love, sex), and provide your brain the opportunity to experience the brain changes associated with victory and success. These "refueling" fantasies mitigate against the effects of defeat. These fantasies can be healing and allow a temporary propping up of self-esteem.

When the fantasy activity is extensive, it suggests a need to shore up flagging self-esteem. Additionally, these fantasies can be problematic for some people who begin to mistake their private fantasies for reality. I have seen patients after a love trauma give up some of their hold on reality so they can spend as much time as possible in their self-indulgent fantasies. They can become angry or even violent when others do not corroborate their imagined successes. Some people spend so much time in this sort of fantasy that they miss the opportunity to improve their life situations. In such cases, the defensive fantasy becomes a substitute for action, and can become corrosive to their long-term success and happiness in life and in love. However, most people who engage in periodic success fantasies are able to differentiate reality and fantasy, and do not let their fantasies get out of hand. They can use these fantasies as temporary props to their self-esteem.

If it is so important to maintain our self-esteem, why have our brains evolved with the capacity to experience a fall in self-esteem? Indeed, there are basically two ways of dealing with defeat. As discussed previously, we can defend ourselves from fully internalizing the defeat, thereby minimizing the extent of our sickening and suffering. Alternately we can accept the defeat and allow the subsequent sickening to occur. In the latter instance our brains' strategies to defend our self-esteem fail.

In fact, although we have evolved with brains that try to maximize our self-esteem, our brains do so only when they feel it is safe. Our brains are more interested in our safety than our happiness. We settle into a social status and a matching self-esteem position that our brains regard as the best we can do. We try to do better only when our brains tell us it is safe to do so—we retreat from our status positions when our brains tell us that it is no longer safe to do otherwise.

However, the fracture of our self-esteem and retreat from a social status position comes at a cost. For instance, intact self-esteem is important for our physical health. Low self-esteem causes an unhealthy physiological state. People with low self-esteem are more likely to be sick, and when they get sick, they remain sick for longer periods of time. They have more impaired immune function and higher levels of abnormal and unhealthy blood fats. They also have higher blood levels of the stress hormone cortisol, greater degrees of atherosclerotic blood vessels, and their body chemistry is more likely to promote abnormal thickening of blood vessels in and around the heart that leads to heart disease and heart attacks.

Pathological Defense of Self-Esteem

Hence, threats to our love interests are met with automatic brain responses. These responses are designed to protect our self-esteem. As described previously, intact self-esteem is important for our psychological and our physical health. Falls in self-esteem not only hurt us emotionally, but also physically. Some defenses are healthy and adaptive responses to the loss of love, whereas others represent pathologic and maladaptive responses. The question is, will the response prove adaptive and further future intimacy and communication (i.e., be a healthy response)? Or will it activate thoughts and behaviors that will diminish intimacy and create conflict (i.e., sacrifice intimacy for the sake of self-esteem)? Pathological responses represent an unhealthy, pathological defense of self-esteem—defense of self-esteem regardless of the destructive cost to ourselves or to others. Some people find it difficult to disengage from their destructive behaviors because they are simply unwilling to accept any diminishment in their self-esteem and pride.

An example of pathological defense of self-esteem in the context of a love trauma is illustrated by the following case example. My patient was a 20-year-old man who was attracted to a young woman in his neighborhood. He had approached her on a number of occasions, and he believed that she liked him. However, she began dating another man. The patient was so enraged by his defeat in love that he planned to murder her new boyfriend, and maybe her as well. My patient could not accept that she had chosen this other man over him.

When I first discussed the negative consequences that would befall him should he murder her, he replied, "I don't care. I can't live with this pain. She was the best. I just want to get even." When I pointed out that she and her boyfriend had done nothing wrong, he insisted that she had "led him [the patient] on," and she deserved to be punished. He also believed that her new boyfriend knew that my patient was romantically interested in her, and he needed to "respect that" and "keep away from her." Initially, I could not get this patient to see how maladaptive his thinking and his plan of action were, but luckily he did agree to be admitted to an inpatient psychiatric unit. There he was able to accept the insult to his self-esteem, and to grieve her loss as a potential girlfriend when he was finally discharged from the unit he was smiling, unable to believe that his emotional reaction to her dating someone else could be so intense. My patient appreciated being in the safety of an inpatient unit so that he was protected from acting upon his assaultive desires. "You win some and you lose some," he later told me.

His anger and revenge fantasies protected his self-esteem. They allowed him to not have to fully accept the blow to his pride. He felt that there was nothing wrong with him—it was the object of his affections and her new boyfriend that were in the wrong. Because they were wrong and worthy of blame, he felt that they should be punished. Indeed, anger often has antidepressantlike effects in that it can protect self-esteem. It is also one of the advantages of blame—you do not have to accept fault or responsibility for the failure in love. You are protected from experiencing the fall in self-esteem and subsequent depression. As the old saying goes, "Pride goes before a fall." With our pride damaged, our brains become ready to accept defeat. We are ready to fall—both in our sense of self-esteem and sense of social status. However, pride also goes after a fall. Once sickened by the loss of love, our self-esteem and confidence are further eroded. People need adequate self-esteem and confidence to carry on in the world with any success. Those who feel defeated are unhappy, lack self-confidence, and achieve less.

Anger can serve a "retrorocket" function designed to reverse any further diminishment of a person's social position and self-esteem and to prevent further descent into depression. These people have gone as low as they are willing to allow themselves—their anger in the context of depression represents their turning from retreat to "stand their ground."

For instance, one depressed patient whose wife had an affair had become continually angry, which interfered with reconciliation efforts with his wife. In a couples session, when we were discussing his anger, he spit out in a fit of rage, "What do you want me to do, become some prostitute willing to submit to any indignity, any humiliation, just to achieve harmony?" "She doesn't give a damn about my pride," he said, pointing to his wife, "but I sure as hell do."

Note that a person's sense of social position is intimately linked to their self-esteem. People who perceive themselves as having a greater RHP (i.e., greater self-esteem) have more confidence and tend to feel that they can take command of higher social positions (and take charge of a larger resource domain). People with higher self-esteem are quick to defend their higher status, and they have little tolerance for people who challenge them. They are quick to try to reestablish their influence over challengers—sometimes aggressively so.

When such aggression is directed at profligate mates, it represents an attempt by the injured party to reassert their status and control and protect their self-esteem. Sometimes people will direct their retrorocket aggression against themselves. When they do so, they can become transiently suicidal. Such individuals would rather be dead (or think about being dead) than accept a lower status and self-esteem than they already have. They might even act on their suicidal ideas.

Antidepressants, Anger, and Self-Esteem

Interestingly, when people with irritability and anger attacks are given more "lift" with antidepressant medication, the irritability and anger attacks often disappear. Under the influence of an antidepressant, the brain adopts a higher threshold for the expression of irritability and anger. Antidepressants also allow people to feel less desperate about their social standing and self-esteem, and decrease the likelihood of their lashing out at others. Antidepressants seem to restore the brain centers that help support improved and higher self-esteem.

One patient of mine was depressed and angry all of the time. He was in a relationship where he felt he was chronically being put down and "not appreciated." He admitted that he was always looking for ways to get into fights with his partner. He had a problem with premature ejaculation, and he felt inadequate to "meet her needs." This sexual problem significantly contributed to his low self-esteem. He was concerned that his girlfriend regarded him as an inadequate lover, and would seek out other men to satisfy her sexual needs.

However, after only a few weeks on the antidepressant Zoloft (sertraline), he told me,

> *She doesn't annoy me the way she used to. Before I was on the antidepressant I felt like I had to always defend myself against her. I felt like I was always under attack. I felt unappreciated. But her behavior hasn't changed. I feel like I've changed. I don't know what it is, but I'm not nearly as defensive as I used to be.*[2]

Excessive Loss of Self-Esteem After a Love Trauma (or Pathologic Vulnerability of Self-Esteem)

For each of us, the neural circuitry and neurochemistry underlying our sense of self-esteem is slightly different. In the context of a threat to our self-esteem—for example, after a love trauma—some of us are wired to be more aggressive in retaliating against the threat than others. Some of us are more likely to want to defend our self-esteem at all costs. However, others are wired to surrender quickly, and experience an excessive loss of self-esteem.

It should be noted that different people respond differently to similar love traumas. The decision of whether to defend your self-esteem or to accept defeat and a decrease in self-esteem is made deep within the emotional parts of our brains (our limbic systems). Our limbic systems' "settings" for defending our self-esteem or for accepting defeat probably are based on a combination of genetic endowment (i.e., the genes we inherit from our mothers and our fathers) and experience (i.e., what we have learned from the environment).[3] Some of us are simply born with a predisposition to be bolder and less likely to experience low self-esteem, regardless of the defeats we endure. But note that "predisposition" does not mean "predetermined." By learning and by force of will people can overcome their predispositions.

After a love trauma, it is not uncommon for people to experience some temporary decrease in their self-esteem and to have some negative thoughts about themselves. However, for some people, their self-esteem plummets and negative self-evaluations and memories predominate. As discussed previously, they begin to view the love trauma experience and their life through a "negative filter," and they only see the downside of things. This is especially true for people who already have a tendency toward negative self-evaluation; that is, they tend to view themselves as inept, inferior, unappealing to others, or defective in some way. They are more prone to see themselves as inadequate to the task (whatever that task might be, including being a good mate). Their low self-esteem is based on their negative evaluations of their abilities. They might remain in unsatisfying and problematic relationships because they lack the confidence that they can do better. After the failure of a problematic relationship, such individuals can develop a severe Love Trauma Syndrome even when everyone around them (e.g., friends, relatives, colleagues) believes that the breakup was for the best.

People with low self-esteem are quick to access memories that corroborate their sense of defectiveness and lower self-esteem. They have diminished access to memories that might heighten their sense of esteem and of worth. They seem more invested in providing support for their sense of defectiveness and negative self-evaluation than in improving their self-image. They are pessimistic and view their actions as likely to meet with failure. These negative-prone individuals sicken easily—both emotionally and physically. This sickening breaks their spirit to want to defend their self-esteem.

One straight "A" college student developed a Love Trauma Syndrome after his girlfriend of 7 months left him for another boy. This other boy apparently had more time to spend with the girlfriend than did my patient. She told my patient, "You're no fun." My patient experienced a dramatic drop in his self-esteem. He became depressed and saw himself as inadequate. "Is someone who gets straight "A's" with a full load of courses inadequate?" I asked him. His response was, "What's the use if I can't keep a girlfriend? I'm doomed to be unhappy, because in order for me to get good grades I have to study too hard and I have no time to have fun. I'm not really all that smart. I'm an overachiever. Whatever I do in life I'll have to work too hard, and I'll never have a satisfying relationship with anyone, because there will be no time for fun. There will always be men out there better than me, and they [the women] know that. I might as well give up and resign to be alone and unhappy no matter what I do."

Low self-esteem is also highly correlated with feeling depressed. Depression is associated with a reduced appetite for food. Some depressed people decrease their caloric food intake and lose large amounts of weight. In the ancestral environment your decreased desire for food would have diminished your competitive struggles over food resources. Your weight loss would have made you a physically less-threatening challenger. In general, victors in romantic competitions would have been more likely to tolerate your membership in the group when you used less of the group's resources and appeared to be less of a threat. It would also have been useful for defeated people to want fewer resources in the ancestral environment because they would have had their access to resources limited by the victors anyway.

But as can be seen in the previous example, sometimes people, after a love trauma, experience a drop in self-esteem that appears out of proportion to the seriousness of the love trauma event. Whereas some people resist accepting any diminishment of their self-esteem, others accept too much.

"To Be or Not to Be"

After a love trauma event, your brain decides whether to defend your self-esteem (i.e., "to be") or to let it plummet (i.e., "not to be"). Your brain will let you defend your self-esteem when it feels that it is safe to do so, and when you have a chance at being successful in your efforts. If your brain sizes up the situation and views the situation as hopeless, it lets your self-esteem take the hit. Whatever position your brain takes in the context of a defeat such as a love trauma, the initiation and maintenance of either position requires a lot of brain neurophysiological arousal. The energy and arousal required to support both positions are born of the Love Trauma Syndrome. The energy is used to either bolster you so that you can defend yourself, or to keep you down, so you will submit and surrender.

When you take an angry stance in defense of your self-esteem, your anger is preparing your brain and your body to fight. Anger is preparation for fighting (whether or not you really intend to fight). Fighting emerges out of the steam of anger. When you become angry, you breathe faster to augment your blood oxygen to service your increased muscular and brain metabolism. Your heart beats faster to get more of this oxygen-carrying blood to your muscles and your brain. Blood pressure increases to flush more blood where it is needed in your body. If and when you fight, your muscles and your brain will need more oxygen. Your angry brain wants you to be ready just in case. It mobilizes your brain's and your body's energy to be available should it be needed for a fight.

Simply put, the purpose of anger is to prepare your body to mount an intimidation display, or to physically attack someone if there is an inadequate response to your attempts at intimidation. The angrier you feel, the more physiologically aroused you are, and the more your body is readied to be a formidable fighting force.

Interestingly, if your brain chooses to accept an excessive hit to your self-esteem and allows you to become depressed and anxious, this is also a neurophysiologically aroused state (even though you might feel tired and weak). The brains of people who are depressed display evidence of central nervous system activation. For instance, the brain pumps out large amounts of stress hormones that keep the brain activated. Evidence of this hyperaroused brain state is reflected in the sleep problems of people with Love Trauma Syndrome. They feel too aroused to be able to fall asleep or to stay asleep. This aroused state is dysphoric, and people search for relief from this unhappy and unpleasant state.

Looking for Relief in All the Wrong Places

The pain associated with Love Trauma Syndrome can be intense. As described in the previous chapter, this pain is usually associated with a threat to one's self-esteem. Some people fall into the trap of drug or alcohol addiction, or some other type of addictive behaviors (e.g., gambling, compulsive sexual activity) while searching for escape from the hurt of Love Trauma Syndrome. The hope of many people who use these addictive substances or engage in addictive behaviors is that they will be able to overcome—or somehow obscure—the pain of a broken heart.

It has been demonstrated that stress and ensuing emotional distress, which typically is quite profound in Love Trauma Syndrome, makes people more impulsive and decreases their concern about risk. These two characteristics, that is, impulsivity and decreased perception of risk, increase the likelihood that someone will become a drug addict, addicted to alcohol, or begin to engage in other risky, unhealthy, and pathological behaviors.

As the Love Trauma Syndrome victim becomes more impulsive, they can rush into action without fully thinking about the consequences of their actions. For instance, they lose their concern about becoming addicted to alcohol or drugs. "What does it matter, anyway?" they might say to themselves. Some people can become obsessed with weapons of destruction, such as guns or bombs. Ted Kaczynski, the Unabomber who killed and maimed his victims with increasingly deadly bombs over an 18-year period, reportedly began his reign of terror after being rebuked by a woman with whom he had become obsessed at work.

Drug Addiction

Becoming addicted to drugs occurs in two stages. The first stage is a period of drug experimentation. Love Trauma Syndrome victims are vulnerable to wanting to engage in drug experimentation despite warnings that they might become addicted. Unfortunately, after they have experimented with the drug, the unconscious "emotional" memory of the drug intoxication automatically begins to drive cycles of future drug use. During the period of experimentation, the addictive drug gets its hooks into them. They then move into the second stage of drug use—addiction. During this stage, the patient loses voluntary control over their drug use. I have had numerous people tell me that if they had not been miserable with a broken heart they would have never begun experimenting with drugs. "I did it just to try to feel good again. I never thought it would make me feel worse. I didn't think I could feel any worse."

One crack addict told me about how he had resisted cocaine use for years. He was a hard working, industrious man who had problems with shyness and depression. His girlfriend had recently started dating someone else. His friends told him that crack cocaine would help him "get over her." "I was in pain," the patient said. "I was willing to do anything to take the pain away." He went over to a friend's house and finally gave in and took his first hit of crack cocaine. He fell back on his friend's bed, and he knew from that point on that he was in trouble. He knew he would not be able to put cocaine down easily in the future. The euphoria was beyond anything he had ever known. Besides the cocaine-induced euphoria, he felt confident, and even enjoyed his newfound freedom. "It made me excited, like I didn't need her, that I could do better." However, his initial enthusiasm about the high was replaced within months by misery. Amazingly, the despair he felt did not diminish his cravings and urges to use more cocaine. He remained a crack cocaine addict for the next 10 years. His cocaine use in crack houses was associated with his having unprotected sex and eventually contracting the HIV virus and developing AIDS. "When I was high I didn't care about anything," he told me. "When I wasn't high I knew that I should use protection. But I didn't think about it when I was high."

Alcohol Use

In my clinical practice, one of the most common causes of people becoming addicted to alcohol, or relapsing to their alcohol addiction, is a broken heart. For instance, one patient, a once well-respected scholar at a local university, took up drinking alcohol heavily at age 46 after he discovered that his wife, 15 years his junior, was having an affair. He told me that the pain of this discovery was "unbearable." "I heard that you could drown your sorrows in alcohol," he said to me. "By George, they were right!" By the time I met him 10 years after the onset of his heavy alcohol use, he was a shell of the man he once was. He had lost his teaching position, and was divorced and living alone, separated from his children. Now, in addition to his severe Love Trauma Syndrome, his condition was complicated by severe alcoholism.

Another patient returned to heavy alcohol use after 15 years of sobriety when she discovered that the man she had fallen in love with would not reciprocate her love. She was involved in a 12-Step program and had regularly attended Alcoholics Anonymous meetings during her 15-year period of being sober. Her reinitiation of sobriety occurred after her Love Trauma Syndrome was addressed.

Promiscuous Sexual Activity

As described previously, research has shown severe emotional distress, as is typical in Love Trauma Syndrome, makes people more impulsive and decreases their concern about risk. They can become bolder with an "I don't care anymore" attitude and do things that they never would have otherwise done. Some people with Love Trauma Syndrome throw themselves into multiple sexual relationships in an attempt to overcome their pain. Often they become sexually involved with others to prove to themselves that they are sexually attractive, which mitigates some of their Love-Trauma-Syndrome-associated drop in self-esteem.

Although impulsive and risky sexual involvement with others might temporarily improve one's self-esteem, it ultimately can result in further cycles of repeated Love Trauma Syndromes and further lowering of self-esteem. Some people try to inflict Love Trauma Syndrome on others in an attempt to deal with their own love traumas.

People involved in this sort of promiscuous sexual activity after a love trauma event are often looking for another love object to fill the void left by their previous lover. Their choices of partners are often not carefully considered. People afflicted with Love Trauma Syndrome will often devalue the importance of "love" in a relationship, and look to sexual encounters alone as a means to emotional fulfillment. They feel that sex without love is the ideal. However, many are not able to live up to their ideal, and they end up falling in love with partners who were not carefully considered and who are inappropriate.

Rebounding and the Sleeping Beauty Syndrome

Some people with Love Trauma Syndrome instinctively know that one of the best ways of getting over a love trauma is to fall in love with someone else. When you are successful in this endeavor, this typically cancels out a Love Trauma Syndrome. Hence, people suffering from the syndrome seek—and sometimes too quickly—accept substitutes for their lost love. In their desperate attempt to diminish the Love-Trauma-Syndrome-associated pain, they might not carefully consider the merits of their new loves. They simply want to replace their lost love object as quickly as possible. This can sometimes inhibit a useful period of grieving the lost love, and can mask a Love Trauma Syndrome. However, it should be noted that many successful relationships have been forged on the rebound, and rebounding is not always unproductive.

In fact, in patients with a severe Love Trauma Syndrome associated with profound sickening (e.g., depression, anxiety, psychosomatic illness), involvement with someone else can quickly restore them to their normal state of emotional and physical health. I have called this the "Sleeping Beauty Syndrome," after the story of the poisoned and sickened princess who is quickly revived to good health by a kiss from the man who loves her (and whom she loves). Although the designation "Sleeping Beauty Syndrome" might imply that this phenomena occurs mainly in women, this is certainly not the case.

For instance, the most dramatic case of Sleeping Beauty Syndrome I ever saw was a man who was thoroughly sickened, depressed, and racked with chronic lower back and shoulder pain after the breakup of a relationship with a woman whom he loved. About 6 months after the breakup, the kiss from another woman who was interested in him (and in whom he was interested) completely restored him. He was no longer depressed, and his chronic pain completely disappeared. When he first told me about the experience, and the fact that his physical pain completely disappeared after the kiss, he kept shaking his head telling me that "You won't believe me, Dr. Rosse." In fact, it was the patient who could not believe the power of one kiss! He eventually married his rescuer, and they lived happily ever after.

However, for both men and women, gays and lesbians, sometimes this search for the "magical kiss" can escalate into promiscuous sex. The search for relief from a bad case of Love Trauma Syndrome by way of kissing and sex often results in compound cases of Love Trauma Syndrome.

Compound Love Trauma Syndrome

Some people who are in the throes of a Love Trauma Syndrome feel so lonely and are in such pain that they impulsively enter other problematic relationships. They do not carefully consider the merits (and demerits) of their mates. These people are often somewhat dissociated and numbed with an "I don't care attitude" (see Figure 6.1). This attitude makes them more prone to become involved in relationships with riskier partners (see chapter 10 for descriptions of certain types of "high risk" partners).

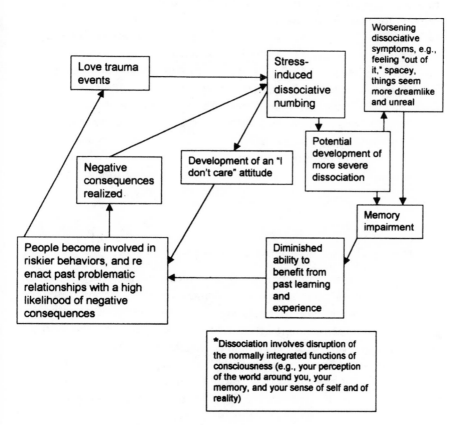

Figure 6.1 *The dissociation-potentiated vicious cycle of love trauma events.*

If the dissociation is severe enough, it can interfere with their normal memory functioning. Memories of what they learned from their past problematic relationships are not completely accessible. This impairs their judgement, which is based on experience and past learning. They are less able to "learn from their past mistakes," and to benefit from what they have learned. These Love Trauma Syndrome victims often reenact their past problematic relationships.

In compound Love Trauma Syndrome, acute and chronic forms of the syndrome become superimposed on each other. When their current relationships disintegrate, their acute Love Trauma Syndrome becomes added to their chronic Love Trauma Syndrome related to past romantic failures.

Another common form of compound Love Trauma Syndrome occurs in a person who has been unfaithful to their partner. The unfaithful party often is (or was) in love with the person with whom they had the affair. Now that the adulterous relationship is threatened (or broken off), the person who was unfaithful typically is brokenhearted about the loss of their other love. Often the adulterer stands to lose (and often eventually does lose) both people with whom they were in love. The adulterer's love traumas can include the complete or partial loss of the partner to whom they were married or somehow committed, the loss of easy access to their joint children, and the loss of the loved person with whom they were having the affair. Some of the most difficult cases of compound Love Trauma Syndrome I have ever treated were people with these multiple losses in the context of having had an adulterous affair. They lost all of the people they loved most.

Pleasure From Pain—Sexual Masochists and Sadists

I have seen a number of people develop interests in sexual masochism and sadism after experiencing a love trauma. As described above, patients with Love Trauma Syndrome often describe some degree of dissociation. At times the dissociation can be quite profound, and the person's normal sense of pain can become altered. This dissociation prepares their brains to experience pain differently than they might ordinarily if they did not have a Love Trauma Syndrome. Dissociated people display insensitivity to physical pain, perhaps making them more able to experience the euphourigenic aspects of sadomasochist sex. Sometimes, this love-trauma-induced dissociation facilitates some people's entry into sexually masochistic or sadistic behaviors, another set of dangerous ways to deal with a love trauma.

The endogenous analgesia systems work more robustly in some people than in others. When pain is inflicted upon certain individuals, it can acquire a pleasurable quality—especially in the context of sexual activity when brain pleasure centers are already activated. This is the case for the sexual masochist, for whom pain—coupled with the sexual activity (or the prospect of sexual activity)—can become pleasurable and euphoria inducing. In someone with a Love Trauma Syndrome associated with significant levels of dissociation, the pain inflicted during sexual activity can become less unpleasant, and perhaps even take on a pleasurable quality.

This is because when sexually stimulated, endogenous euphorogens and other pleasure-inducing substances are secreted. Inflicting pain augments the secretion of these pain-suppressing and euphoria-inducing compounds, making the pain that is being administered tolerable. It also imbues the painful experience with a sense of pleasure and euphoria. This is why some people engage in sexual masochism. However, such experiences can be quite dangerous for the practitioners of sexual masochism, and can result in their accepting mutilating physical injury and even death.

Conversely, for some people their Love-Trauma-Syndrome-associated dissociation facilitates their perpetrating sadistic sex. They become numbed to inflicting pain, and they can begin to find the infliction of pain on others—in the context of sexual activity (or the prospect of it)—pleasurably arousing. People who are significantly dissociated lose their normal inhibitions against hurting others, and they might accidently inflict serious injury even though their intention was not to do so. In their dissociated states, some people with Love Trauma Syndrome might become willing to do anything to hold on to a partner. This can include involvement in very risky sexual masochistic or sadistic behaviors.

Other Risky Behaviors

In fact, people with Love Trauma Syndrome are more prone to becoming involved in all sorts of risky behaviors. These can include risky sports activities (e.g., mountain climbing, bungee jumping), and worse yet, participating in sports in a manner beyond their skill level. They become much more prone to physical injury.

They can become involved in risky behavior in all spheres of activity. For instance, I have seen patients make impulsive financial investments or business decisions after a love trauma. These people became emboldened by an "I don't care attitude," and hoped that tremendous success in another sphere of activity would counter the depression that they felt secondary to their love trauma. Some emboldened lovesick people can become involved in a "cycle of destruction," and they abuse their bodies and financial health. One patient went on a gambling spree and lost over $300,000 after a breakup with a girlfriend. The money represented his life savings. Another raced his car down a rural highway at 4:00 a.m. He was clocked by the police as going over 180 mph (it was a Ferari). This patient ended up spending a night in jail, and paying a hefty fine. He is lucky he did not end up getting into a fatal car accident.

ADOLESCENTS AND LOVE TRAUMA SYNDROME

The pain of Love Trauma Syndrome can be quite overwhelming for adolescents. Adolescent narcissism and propensity for fragile self-esteem make this population of boys and girls particularly vulnerable to Love Trauma Syndrome. Many adolescents have difficulty dealing with unrequited love and a broken heart, and Love Trauma Syndrome is ubiquitous among teenagers and young adults. It can affect their academic performance adversely and impair their ability to interact with peers and family. Some serious problematic behavior in adolescents and in young adults is secondary to Love Trauma Syndrome.

Adolescents, and even preadolescents, can be driven to murder in the context of Love Trauma Syndrome. For instance, as described earlier, in March 1998, two junior high school boys—ages 13 and 11—opened fire on a crowd of their fellow students and killed four girls and a teacher. The 13-year-old had recently broken up with his girlfriend, and the day before the killings, he reportedly told others that he "had a lot of killing to do."

I remember once walking across the campus of a large university at 2:00 a.m. Another college student (who was quite drunk) approached me with his friend. He insulted and threatened me without any provocation on my part. He threw the first punch and we began to fight. I knocked him to the ground (this was relatively easy to do as he was quite intoxicated) and when I was on top of him he began to cry. "Why did she do this to me," he sobbed. He became limp and just put his face into the grass. "She's probably with him right now," he sobbed. "Why?" he called out. "Why me?" He told me that his girlfriend had broken off with him earlier that evening and had gone off with someone else. I spoke to him of my own experiences with

Love Trauma Syndrome (of course I did not call it that at the time) and he calmed down. He later thanked me and we parted as friends.

Turning to Delinquency

Some adolescents suffering from the pain of love trauma turn to delinquency to help shore up their flagging self-esteem. Delinquency is often a part of a pathological defense of self-esteem. Many of these adolescents are caught up in a vicious cycle of rejection from their families, from school, and from peers. Rejection by someone they love only compounds their sense of low self-worth. Love-Trauma-Syndrome-afflicted youths can engage in criminal activity to reobtain a sense of their potency and shore up their flagging self-esteem. I have seen Love-Trauma-Syndrome-afflicted youths end up in jail within days of their love trauma event. They are often ashamed of their loss, and act out their Love-Trauma-Syndrome-related anger and pain by resorting to illegal delinquent activities (e.g., vandalism, reckless driving, driving under the influence of alcohol).

Love-Trauma-Syndrome-afflicted youths might join gangs to help them deal with their fears of rejection. Being accepted into a gang can restore the self-esteem of teenagers who have suffered a love trauma event. Gangs can also serve "mate guarding" functions who intimidate, and at times even retaliate, against "outsiders" who try to romantically access either women or men considered within the gang's province.

These gangs carve out psychopathic niches for themselves that have disastrous consequences for those around them. People in the gang are taught that they are "predators"—anyone outside gang membership is "prey." They become desensitized to having loving feelings for others, and by falling out of love with those who have hurt them, their Love Trauma Syndrome dissipates.

Gang members often lose touch with the more "caring" side of themselves. They will tell you how participation in gang activities slowly changes the way they think and feel. One teenager who had joined a gang told me, "I became hard. Real hard. There was no love left in me." Without the capacity for feeling love, he was insulated from the pain of love trauma.

Some more desperate and psychopathic Love-Trauma-Syndrome-afflicted adolescents and young adults turn to a preoccupation with firearms (or some other explosive force) to help them recapture a sense of power, control, and pride. Such people regard firepower as a way of intimidating rivals and of punishing those who have hurt them. The use of guns is a particularly dangerous way to handle low self-esteem and unhappiness related to love trauma, and represents a dangerous and pathological defense of self-esteem. People who are attracted to guns as a way of handling their problems typically have an intense desire for power and a perverse sense of how to obtain such power.

Turning to Cults

For some teenagers (as well as adults), the pain of Love Trauma Syndrome propels them to join various cults or pursue unusual religious experiences in their quest to find relief. These cults help the members dissociate from their previous sense of reality. With dissociation, there is a breakdown of the person's normal sense of who they are, and how they experience the world around them. Things that previously seemed real now seem "unreal," and things that were previously painful are no longer painful. Hence, their symptoms of Love Trauma Syndrome are attenuated.

In fact, the common denominator of dissociative experience is the disruption of the "usually integrated functioning of the mind and body." This paves the way for those who are dissociated to take on the new beliefs of the cult. Armed with these beliefs, they feel stronger and transcendent, and feel able to transcend the pain of Love Trauma Syndrome.

However, they lose their personalities. They lose their capacity to experience pain, which is a normal aspect of life. Cult members often lose their motivation to excel in other areas of their lives, and they can become closed and narrow minded.

Teenage Drug Use

Alcohol and illicit drug abuse by teenagers has garnered increased attention in the media. The alcohol- and drug-using culture is attractive to teenagers who are struggling to regulate their mood, including the distress of Love-Trauma-Syndrome. As described previously, Love-Trauma-Syndrome-afflicted teenagers are quick to assume an "I don't care" attitude and therefore are quick to dismiss the risks of alcohol and drug use.

The more teenagers experiment with addictive substances to anaesthetize their Love-Trauma-Syndrome-related pain, the more likely they will be trapped by addiction. As mentioned earlier, people become addicted to drugs in two stages. The first stage is a period of drug experimentation.

This first stage can be precipitated by a love trauma event. Additionally, adolescents with Love Trauma Syndrome are more vulnerable to engage in drug experimentation despite warnings of the dangers of addiction because of the syndrome's capacity to induce an "I don't care" attitude. They just want to be free from the pain. They hope that the drugs will be able to numb them from the pain of their Love Trauma Syndrome, in much the same way a shot of novocaine numbs up one's gums and teeth prior to dental work. In fact, some drugs of abuse and alcohol, do support an "emotional numbing" from psychic pain.

Unfortunately, after they have experimented with the drug, the unconscious emotional memory of the drug intoxication automatically begins to drive cycles of future drug use. While the person initially experiments with the drugs ability to diminish their love trauma-induced distress, the addictive drug gets its hooks into them. Teenagers then move into the second stage of drug use—addiction. The pain of their Love Trauma Syndrome is now compounded by the pain of their addiction. Once addicted, the teenager now feels driven to use the drug again and again, even if they do not want to. As described earlier, it is a trap that takes incredible effort to escape. Much important "developmental" time (e.g., in school learning developing academic and social skills) is lost while the teenager is intoxicated or searching for ways to access more drugs or alcohol.

One teenager I saw in a college infirmary had begun using hallucinogenic drugs about 3 months earlier. At that time he had broken up with his girlfriend of over a year. She had left him for another man. He spoke with friends about the incident, and got no relief from the pain that he felt. He even spoke with his mother and his father, and felt infantalized and ashamed during the interaction. He then spoke with an older cousin at a family wedding. This older cousin spoke of people of his generation who used drugs to "liberate" themselves from the bondage of conventional mores. He encouraged his brokenhearted younger cousin to try hallucinogenic drugs to "transcend himself." However, the patient experienced no such transcendence, only more pain, as his hallucinogenic experience was nightmarish for him. It was only after seeing a psychiatrist and being treated for a moderate depression that this brokenhearted college student started seeing hope for the future.

As discussed in an earlier chapter, Love Trauma Syndrome can profoundly lower a person's self-esteem. Adolescents are particularly sensitive to insults to their self-esteem. Love trauma can make adolescents think less of themselves, feel unworthy, and feel subordinate to others who are more successful in love. Studies of animals have shown that subordinate lower ranking animals—that is, those with lower RHP—have an increased drug and alcohol intake when these substances are made available to them compared to higher ranking animals (i.e., those with higher RHP).

After a love trauma event, I have seen adolescents who previously shied away from drugs and alcohol have a sudden change of heart. They approach friends who they know have access to such substances. These love-traumatized adolescents are looking for relief, and they have not been able to find it within themselves, friends, or family. It is the intensity and severity of the Love-Trauma-Syndrome-associated pain that drives many teenagers and young adults into drug use. Their self-esteem has been damaged by the love trauma, and the drug use often represents pathological defense of their remaining self-esteem.

Pathological Attractiveness Display Activity

Adolescents typically are preoccuppied with their outward physical appearance. They want to maintain a fashionable demeanor. This is because they understand that their ability to attract and hold onto desired love interests and allies during adolescence is largely based on their outward physical appearance and the "air" they have about them. Adolescents who have been rejected by girlfriends or boyfriends and suffer from Love Trauma Syndrome can become overly invested in their overall attractiveness in an effort to impress potential replacements. They are sometimes willing to go to extremes to service their appeal to others. For instance, they might become involved in illegal activities (robbery, drug dealing) in order to have the money to buy the most fashionable clothes.

The attention of potential mates is garnered through "attractiveness displays." Sometimes attempts to improve attractiveness represent healthy and nonpathological behavior. However, some of the displays can become problematic when people go to extremes to service their attractiveness. Some adolescents and adults feel compelled to spend an inordinate amount of time and energy in generating as perfect an attractiveness display as possible. This is to attract—or keep—the attentions of a love interest. Some adolescents expend so much effort servicing their attractiveness that they do not have the time or energy to attend to more important matters, such as schoolwork, family, friends, and community.

What Is an Attractiveness Display?

Attractiveness displays advertise your potential worth as a mate and ally. What is displayed are the resources and attributes that you will be able to bring to the relationship. During the attractiveness display, the displayer tries to give their potential mate a sense that they will get something substantial out of a relationship with them. During the early stages of a relationship, when attractiveness displays are first being responded to, there are changes in brain chemistry that support the formation of the relationship. It becomes pleasurable to be with the mate. It is via attractiveness displays that alliances are initiated.

There are many different kinds of attractiveness displays. They include exhibitions of physical strength, stamina, and athletic prowess; such attributes attract a variety of different allies, including mates. Physically attractive individuals usually have an easier time attracting allies, as allies automatically assign worth to such attractiveness. The billions of dollars spent each year in this country on cosmetic supplies to enhance our physical appeal are testimony to the importance we place on physical attractiveness. Less physically attractive people usually have to work harder to attract mates. Adolescents know this.

Displays of your good "character," that is, your trustworthiness, are also included as part of an attractiveness display. Such displays demonstrate your interest in helping others and in not just servicing your own selfish needs. Attractiveness displays also include demonstrations of your intellectual and emotional competencies. One emotional competency that makes others regard you as a worthy potential ally is demonstrating your capacity for empathy. Your demonstration of empathy signals your ability to detect distress in others, and shows that you know when you are needed. Empathic capacity is an important quality of a competent mate. Your attractiveness display can be further improved by your demonstrating an ability to make others feel better.

Showing off your "resource" supply (e.g., your physical attributes, wealth, access to a car, intellect, wit, emotional "sensitivity," ability to "play" and have fun), and demonstrating a willingness to share those resources (e.g., engage in sexual activity), are forms of attractiveness display. Resource sharing can be a powerful tool for forming an alliance with a potential mate. Potential mates are more likely to cooperate with someone who has greater access to desirable resources, and with someone who demonstrates a willingness to share those resources. People often mentally estimate the resource holdings of potential mates to determine how attractive a potential mate really is. It also helps decide whether entering into a relationship with this person will be worth the effort.

One of the most common sources of anxiety is the fear that your attractiveness display will not be maintained. You feel that your attractiveness display is in danger. The fear is that your mate and others will discover that you really are not as attractive as they initially thought you were, and as a consequence the relationships will suffer.

People invest a lot of time, energy, and resources in their often desperate attempts to maintain their attractiveness display so they do not lose the affection of the person they love. For some people, the anxiety related to maintaining their attractiveness display is so great that they avoid entering relationships—their hearts are broken even before they enter a relationship. Such avoidant individuals see themselves as inferior to others, unappealing, and socially inept. They are often quite shy and overly sensitive to the negative evaluations of others.

The Fear (and Ancient Dangers) of Being Snubbed

Attractiveness displays can either be accepted or rejected. People with successful displays are allowed entry into a relationship—people whose displays are not accepted are snubbed. After relationships form, they can fall apart, especially when you are unable to live up to expectations created by your attractiveness display. Snubbing can also signal an unwillingness to continue to engage in an alliance. Snubbing communicates that the snubber does not want to be your partner anymore.

There are few things teenagers and young adults fear more than being snubbed. This is because we have evolved as social animals, and we want to feel connected to others. People who are well regarded are given access to resources and to other forms of support. Our brain usually makes us unhappy if we do not have mates and allies. Most of us feel propelled to want to associate with other people and to be involved in romantic relationships at some time.

Our brains are "wired" to want to be attractive to others and to fear being snubbed. As described in an earlier chapter, in our ancient ancestral environment, being socially unsuccessful and not having allies meant that you would be given less "permission" to access the resources of the group. You would have had fewer allies to help you obtain food for you and for your offspring. And perhaps most important, having allies meant that you would be attractive as a mate, because your mate (or your mate's brain) "knew" that you had "what it takes" to get your genes propelled into the future. In part, that is why people are so attracted to others who appear connected to a social network. Adolescents' self-esteem is improved when they feel they belong to a social group.

Being a member of a group gives us the opportunity to share resources. We are also provided the extra protection and strength that group membership offers. There is no single activity more important for the perpetuity of your genes than finding and keeping mates, bearing and raising offspring to reproductive potential, and finding and keeping allies who will help you do so. When the brain's hidden agenda is threatened, the alarm switches in our brains are thrown. When we are being snubbed (or when we think we are being snubbed) by mates or other allies, the alarm mechanisms in the emotional part of our brains (the limbic system) are activated—because our brains know that our genes are under threat. Our offspring will be less likely to survive. We become distressed and unhappy. In aboriginal and primate environments, offspring of parents who are less well "socially connected" are more likely not to survive to a reproductive age.

Having mates and allies who do not snub us increases our overall level of happiness and life satisfaction. Having loving and devoted mates and allies also decreases our perceived levels of stress, and diminishes the physiological evidence of stress on our bodies. Our immune systems function better when we have mates and allies—and they are better able to resist infection and the growth of nascent tumor cells (e.g., Spiegel et al., 1998; Cohen et al., 1998; Glaser et al., 1998). Studies have shown that the more social supports we have, the better we are able to deal with infectious and neoplastic challenge and emotional stress. We'll also live longer in the face of other potentially life-threatening illnesses, such as serious heart disease.

Some teenagers and young adults experience distortions of their attractiveness display. After a love trauma, some people feel that it (i.e., rejection) must mean that they are not attractive enough to hold onto their love interests. Whereas most people try to improve upon their attractiveness in nonpathological ways, some teenagers begin to go to dangerous heights to improve upon their attractiveness displays. Dangerous, pathological attempts to improve attractiveness displays can have serious health, psychological, social, and legal repercussions for teens.

For instance, patients with anorexia nervosa and bulimia nervosa have a profound disturbance in the way in which they perceive their body weight and shape. They tend to see themselves as fatter and heavier than they really are. Patients with these eating disorders overvalue the importance of appearing thin as part of their attractiveness displays. They can inadvertently kill themselves in their compulsive efforts to service their attractiveness displays and not appear fat and unappealing.

Many teenagers regard their physical appearance as vital for attracting and holding on to romantic interests (i.e., mates). They are sometimes driven to desperate measures to achieve their desired appearance. For instance, some teenage bodybuilders use illicit substances such as steroids to increase their muscle bulk beyond that of others. Recent studies report that some children as young as 10 years old are using steroids to enhance their physical appearance and athletic performance. Teenagers and others who use steroids often have a compulsive need to'appear maximally attractive to others, despite having knowledge of the multiple risks associated with steroid use. I had one teenage patient who described to me his "need" to "look the best in the school." He resorted to using steroids. "Everyone else is," he rationalized. He told me that "in order to attract the type of girl I'm interested in, I have to look big." Importantly, this patient had a Love Trauma Syndrome related to a breakup with a girlfriend. This teenager was acutely aware of the size and the stature of the rival who successfully stole his girlfriend's heart. This rival was smaller in size than the patient but "better built . . . he has quite a big chest and big arms." When my patient looked in the mirror he was always comparing himself to this other boy. His desire to be better than him motivated his use of steroids. In psychotherapy he saw that he was even willing to do harmful things to himself to prevent a recurrence of losing a girlfriend. However, he was only able to 20% "endorse" the idea that looks were not all that a girl was seeking. When he looked at guys who did not have the muscular look for which he was striving but who did have girlfriends, he claimed that these were the girls in whom he was not interested. His Love Trauma Syndrome also caused some avoidance and withdrawal from other relationships in favor of his exercising all the time. "All I want to do in my spare time is lift weights," he said.

The energy and anger associated with Love Trauma Syndrome can fuel a lot of intense exercise and efforts at bodybuilding. Although this often is a healthy response to a love trauma, when the exercise becomes dangerous (e.g., involves the use of illicit or harmful substances such as steroids), and is so obsessive that it curtails other social and occupational activities, it can become problematic. However, the excess energy associated with Love

Trauma Syndrome has motivated many young men and women to build better bodies.

Red-Light Girls

Some teenage girls become involved in promiscuous sexual activity in order to attract the attention of boys. As soon as they lose a boyfriend, they can quickly try to capture a new one to blunt the pain of a love trauma. They might have unprotected or unsafe sex to attract boyfriends and maintain the relationships. They often experience some degree of dissociation while involved in the promiscuous sexual acts. Although offering sex can be a way of attracting and holding on to boyfriends, it carries the dangers of unwanted pregnancy and sexually transmitted diseases such as AIDS.

Chapter Seven

When Love Trauma Syndrome Turns Violent

T hankfully, serious Love-Trauma-Syndrome-related violence is rare. When it occurs, it represents the sufferer's attempt to regain control over the lost object of their affections. In the context of Love-Trauma-Syndrome-related violence, there has often already been a relationship history of violence and abuse. If the violence employed is unsuccessful in improving the sufferer's control over their love interests, the intensity of the violence can escalate, until—often to the horror of the sufferer—they murder the one whom they love the most. The murder occurs during a misguided attempt to regain control. As discussed in a previous chapter, there is a lot of energy locked up in the psychic storm created by a love trauma, and this energy can be directed into violent deeds.

Rivals for the affection of a love interest can also become violent with each other. In the ancient ancestral environment, your first instinct when presented with a competitive threat to your love interests would have included attempts to repel the rival. This often would have required physical stamina and strength in excess of that of your rival. Love-Trauma-Syndrome-associated hyperarousal and anger enhances your sense of physical power as your brain and body are prepared for a possible fight.

O.J.'s Tragedy

Although it is not known for certain, it was suspected that on June 12, 1994, O.J. Simpson, in a fit of jealous rage, brutally stabbed to death his estranged wife, Nicole Brown Simpson. Ronald Goldman, a 25-year-old restaurant waiter, was also there on that fateful night. Some suspect that Ronald Goldman was Nicole Brown Simpson's lover. The way that Nicole had the house lit with candles—even going down the steps to the walkway—suggests to some that Nicole was expecting to be involved in some romantic tryst that night. Others believe that Ronald Goldman was there by happenstance, and was simply returning a pair of glasses that Mrs. Simpson had left at the restaurant. Ron Goldman was also brutally murdered.

Some believe that O.J. Simpson was fixated on his wife's sexual involvement with other men. Although he was estranged from his wife, according to some sources he still appeared to have had a sexual relationship with her as recently as 3 weeks before the murder. It is suspected by some that O.J. was particularly upset by the arrangement of the candles in the Brentwood home on the evening of her murder.

On a tape made years before the murder, when Nicole Simpson called 911 while O.J. Simpson was beating her, Mr. Simpson can be heard in the background shrieking at her. He can be heard calling her a "whore." Even though Mr. Simpson clearly led an adulterous lifestyle, his affairs with other women were not able to cure him of his Love Trauma Syndrome related to his deep love of Nicole. He wanted it all—the other women—and his wife, his love, the mother of his two children. The brutality of the murders is perhaps consistent with someone in the throes of a severe Love Trauma Syndrome. Perhaps he could not remove from his mind his wife's sexual involvement (real or imagined) with other men.

I believe O.J. Simpson when he says that he loved his wife. In the opening statement of O.J. Simpson's suicide note written on June 15, 1994, he wrote, "I loved her, always have and always will. If we had a problem it's because I loved her so much." I believe it.

If O.J. Simpson killed his wife and her lover, Ron Goldman, O.J.'s Love Trauma Syndrome represents one of the most dangerous aspects of the syndrome—it can be accompanied by the desire to punish, maim, and even kill. Nicole Brown Simpson was brutally murdered, and experts testified that the person who stabbed her multiple times (almost severing her head) must have done so in a fury of crazed passion. Love Trauma Syndrome can do that. Sometimes Love Trauma Syndrome ends in homicide–suicide (called dyadic death in the medical literature). In fact, O.J. Simpson was on the verge of committing suicide in the week following Nicole's death. Studies have found that the most common motive for homicide–suicide is jealousy and the desire for revenge.

Usually the desire for revenge—or to punish—is not manifest as murder. Many suspect that O.J. did kill his wife (again there is no absolute proof), and they suspect that his motivation was jealously and the desire for revenge and for punishment. We will never really know if O.J. committed the murders. (Although O.J. Simpson was found guilty of the "wrongful death" of Nicole Simpson and Ronald Goldman in the civil suit, Mr. Simpson was found not guilty in the initial criminal trial.)

O.J. Simpson is being used here as a *possible* example of someone who commits violence in the context of a Love Trauma Syndrome. As I have never examined Mr. Simpson, there is no way I can know for certain that the scenario I have described is accurate. However, this scenario has been laid out before by others. I also do not know for sure that Mr. Simpson had a Love Trauma Syndrome. I would like to say that I was a fan of O.J. Simpson's, both on the football field and during his movie career. He was a football hero to me, and his movie performances made me laugh (he was in a number of movie comedies). I even enjoyed his commercials with his mother. He always struck me as a charming and likeable fellow. I also know that Love Trauma Syndrome can transform someone from the compassionate Dr. Jekyll into a violent Mr. Hyde. It seems to me that Nicole Brown Simpson was about as gorgeous and loveable a person as there is— and O.J. knew it, and so did his brain. She could cause a Love Trauma Syndrome in someone who loved her very much—especially someone who "loved her so much." However, murdering your wife, and her boyfriend, is about the worst way to deal with a Love Trauma Syndrome.

When Love Trauma Syndrome is accompanied by a desire to punish, for example, to beat or somehow physically harm someone, this is a reason to seek immediate psychological or psychiatric help. Luckily, most people with Love Trauma Syndrome suffer more quietly with their pain, and do not resort to physical violence.

As described earlier, sexual liberation has increased our freedom to perform sexually with others, but it has also increased the amount of love trauma as people feel hurt when their mates choose (or have chosen in the past) other sexual partners. In a sexually liberated culture, Love Trauma Syndrome comes with the turf. Not everyone in this culture will get the syndrome, but many will. Not everyone will be bothered by their mate's past sexual involvement, but some will.

Whereas some suffer quietly, others become violent in their attempts to maintain their self-esteem. When possessed by a desire to punish someone, some will be able to resist this desire. Others cannot. Only rarely will someone kill those whom they feel have wronged them. However, they can be driven to other violent expressions of punishment. They might intimidate, threaten, destroy property, or physically abuse the people they feel have wronged them. However, people must learn to resist their urges to violently punish those who have broken their hearts.

INFIDELITY AND THE DEFENSE AGAINST HUMILIATION

Humiliation is the emotional and physical *sickening* that occurs when one is reduced to a lower hierarchical position in the eyes of oneself and of others. The process of humiliation is both biological and psychological; brain mechanisms are reset to lower one's sense of rank and of self-esteem. The brain experiences feelings of shame and sets into motion more submissive behaviors designed to signal to others your loss of social standing. As described earlier, this has been described in the medical literature as the brain's ISS.

One powerful form of humiliation comes when you discover that your mate is having or has had an affair. Not only is the discovery a blow to your self-esteem, it lessens your status with others in your community, who now see you as less capable of holding on to your own (i.e., they see your RHP as being less). People want to defend against decreases in social standing and to continue to feel good about themselves. They invest tremendous amounts of time and energy trying to protect themselves from feeling humiliated and from experiencing a drop in self-esteem.

Not only does the discovery of an infidelity reduce the cuckold's self-esteem, a person's status in their community is jeopardized by a mate's infidelity. The mate's infidelity was a betrayal of your trust, and both privately (i.e., within yourself) and publicly demonstrates your decreased RHP. In fact, there is often a public fascination and preoccupation with the infidelities of others—the public seems fixated on learning all they can about the affair, who has been wronged, and how the wronged have responded. The tabloid media is partly supported by people's interest in the infidelities of others. We are naturally interested in the social status of others in our environment, as we want to continuously make adjustments to the social ranking estimations of others (and determine where we stand).

When you have been cuckolded, you have been unable to keep your mate faithful to you; you have been unable to keep him or her in love with just you. Some biological–social brain imperative might have evolved that motivates a more violent response to cuckolding in some people than in others. Such a response was designed to reestablish the cuckold's status in the group. A violent response to a love trauma might mitigate the person's fall in self-esteem and self-efficacy, diminish ensuing negative evaluations of themselves, and help them deal with their shame and humiliation (and block subsequent emotional and physical sickening). By destroying the love who has rejected you, you not only punish them, but remove them as a sickening influence on you. Their removal diminishes their sickening power. But such removal of a faithless love is a totally unacceptable solution to your feeling poorly because of their actions.

These potentially violent responses to a love trauma can occur in both men and women. A well-publicized and notorious case of a woman who committed murder in the throes of a Love Trauma Syndrome was Jean Harris, who murdered her lover of 14 years—Herman "Hi" Tarnower—the famous "Scarsdale Diet" doctor. Harris was the headmistress of the elite Madeira School for Girls in McLean, Virginia. She usually took the train up to New York on the weekends to be with Tarnower at his home there.

However, in Tarnower's home she began to find more and more of the personal belongings of Tarnower's office assistant, Lynne Tryforos, a woman some 20 years younger than Harris. It appears that Harris knew that Tryforos was sexually involved with Tarnower, and feared that she was being displaced by Tryforos. Harris became increasingly jealous and agitated. The day before Harris murdered Tarnower, Harris wrote an 11-page letter to Tarnower calling Tryforos "a vicious, adulterous psychotic," and saying, "I stay home alone while you make love to someone who has almost totally destroyed me."

It was argued that on the night when Harris killed the doctor, she drove up from Virginia with a loaded gun, and in a fit of jealous rage, shot Tarnower four times. He died as a result of his wounds. Harris claimed that Tarnower was accidently shot while trying to stop her from killing herself with the gun. While in jail serving time for the slaying, Harris reported that she received a lot of mail from other women who said they understood why she did what she did. Harris states that a common refrain in these letters was "There but for the grace of God go I." As illustrated by this case, by the letters to the jailed Harris from other women, and by my clinical experience, women are no strangers to the more violent expressions of a Love Trauma Syndrome.

There are other cases that have been described in the news media where women appear to have been driven to murder when in the throes of a Love Trauma Syndrome and were possessed with a desire for revenge. A recent notorious case illustrating a woman's involvement in the murder of a sexual rival is the case former U.S. Naval Academy midshipman, Diane

Zamora. Zamora's boyfriend, David Graham (a former Air Force Academy cadet) was unfaithful to Zamora and had a single sexual encounter with 16-year-old Adrianne Jones. When Zamora learned of Graham's infidelity with Jones, she apparently told him that the only way for him to "make it right" was to kill Jones. Together, it is suspected that Graham and Zamora shot and beat Jones to death. Love Trauma Syndrome can make murderers out of both men and women.

As discussed in an earlier chapter, there are basically two ways of dealing with a love trauma related to rejection or infidelity. We can accept the love trauma, and allow the subsequent sickening and emotional pain to occur, or we can defend ourselves from fully internalizing the defeat, thereby minimizing the extent of our sickening and suffering. The psychological mechanisms we use to protect ourselves from sickening are called *defenses*. They defend us from precipitous drops in our self-esteem.

Demonization and Devaluation

Two common defenses used in the context of a perceived rejection or infidelity are *demonization* and *devaluation*. During demonization, there is an automatic cognitive elaboration process by which you demonize people who you feel have wronged you; that is, you paint an evil face on them. Harris demonized Tryforos, her rival for Tarnower's affections, as "a vicious, adulterous, psychotic." This cognitive elaboration allows you to make your rival into an evil enemy worthy of destruction. The demonization process involves selective memory of only the person's misdeeds and offenses against you. It allows you to focus on the "bad" aspects of your rival's character, and to ignore any "good attributes."[1]

With the defense of devaluation, you are further able to minimize someone else's worth. Demonization and devaluation are linked—when someone is demonized they are also devalued. In both demonization and devaluation, there is often frank distortion of the reality of the rival's nature in service of envisioning them in as evil a way as possible.

Demonization and the Preparation to Punish

Demonizing is mental preparation for fighting. Demonization "psychs you up" for the fight, and makes you a more formidable adversary. By demonizing someone, you release powerful motivating and energizing forces that increase your willingness, vigor, and desire to fight. When you can view your enemy as evil, bad, and morally corrupt, you increase your morale and your boldness to fight. You become a person with a mission. Demonization of someone inculcates "righteous indignation" and gives you an edge over your adversary. This is because so-called "justified aggression" is the hardest type of aggression against which to defend.

The demonization process allows you to convert in your mind someone who has wronged you into someone who is evil and worthy of destruction. It often involves distortion of the person's true character, or distortion of past events in service of the demonization. False memories are manufactured to support the demonizing beliefs. People repeat and rehearse the memories over and over in their minds until they truly believe that their foes are demons. They forget how elaborated their "memories" are.

Love-Trauma-Syndrome-Induced Dissociation

As someone becomes angrier and prepares to fight, they can also unconsciously mobilize brain mechanisms that promote dissociation. Studies have found a link between hostile attitudes, aggressive feelings, and proneness to dissociative experiences. As described in an earlier chapter, dissociative conditions involve a disruption of the usually integrated functioning of the mind and body. With dissociative experiences, there is a breakdown of the person's normal sense of who they are and how they experience the world around them. Things that previously seemed real now seem unreal and they might describe feeling numb. They might further lose access to memories that counter their demonization and devaluation of the partner.

As alluded to in the second chapter, victims of Love Trauma Syndrome usually have some degree of dissociative symptoms as part of their condition. The syndrome itself often has a trancelike quality, and people with the syndrome are at an increased risk of further dissociation. Dissociation commonly is triggered by severe stress—and a love trauma can be a severe stress. I have had patients tell me that the stress of Love Trauma Syndrome was the most severe stress that they ever experienced—and some of these patients had experienced the stress of direct involvement in military combat! Hence, that which we cannot overcome we can dissociate from.

Dissociation under stress is quite common, even when you are not a direct victim of the stress. Simply watching something stressful can precipitate considerable dissociation, even if only for a short time. In one study, researchers examined journalists who were eyewitnesses to an execution in a gas chamber at the San Quentin Prison (Freinkel, Koopman, Spiegel, 1994). The man being executed was convicted of brutally murdering two San Diego adolescents. Through a glass window, the journalists had a clear view of the convicted murderer being asphyxiated by poison gas and dying in the gas chamber. Over half the journalists studied who witnessed the execution experienced dissociative symptoms. These symptoms included feeling "estranged from other people," feeling that things around them "seemed unreal or dreamlike," and having a sense of "timelessness." Over half of them reported feeling "distant" from their emotions. The intensity of the dissociative symptoms experienced by these journalists was similar in intensity to people who actually experienced a firestorm in the Oakland/Berkeley area of California.

We cannot say with certainty which parts of the brain or which neurotransmitters are involved in the phenomenon of dissociation. However, neuroscientists are looking to identify naturally occurring endogenous substances secreted during stress which increases our predisposition to experience dissociation. The secretion of such substances in our brains play a role in generating the dissociative phenomena seen in the context of Love Trauma Syndrome.

We know that dissociative experience involves some form of detachment from our memory stores. Our sense of reality, which is altered during a dissociative experience, is supported by our brains' memory systems. We *remember* what is real and what is not real. To disconnect from reality, we need to disconnect from our memory systems. Dissociation also involves an interruption of accurate perception of our external world, which also contributes to our disconnection from reality.

With numbing dissociation in the context of severe Love Trauma Syndrome complicated by severe anger, demonization, devaluation, and a desire to physically punish, the potential for violent and cruel acts against others increases. In our ancient evolutionary past, the ability to dissociate and desensitize ourselves to the feelings of others might have facilitated our ability to kill during hunting and battles with competitors. Dissociation made us more lethal killers. If we need to dissociate to be better fighters, our brains will help us dissociate. The neural machinery involved in generating dissociation will be recruited into action automatically beneath our conscious awareness.

An example of how dissociation in the context of a Love Trauma Syndrome can be associated with tragic violence is illustrated by the following example. I have already mentioned how in March, 1998, two young boys, Mitchell Johnson and Andrew Golden, opened fire with rifles and killed four people outside of an Arkansas middle school. The boys had activated a fire alarm in the school, and when the teachers and the children came out into the schoolyard, the boys started shooting at them. The precipitant for the shooting reportedly was the breakup of Mitchell Johnson and his girlfriend. Johnson was in the throes of a Love Trauma Syndrome, and he reportedly wanted to kill his girlfriend (as well as others who had "made him mad" in the past).

After the tragedy, Andrew Golden told his father that he did not remember shooting anyone during the incident. He was perhaps somewhat dissociated during the shooting, as evidenced by his lack of memory. Severe dissociation can wipe out the memory of an event. You can commit horrible acts, and not remember them, or think they occurred only in a dream. This way you can maintain your sense that you are a good person and not some evil, murderous monster.

Demonization and Dissociation Make Monsters

As alluded to previously, when we demonize those who have wronged us and work ourselves into a frenzy of excitement and anger, our aggressive instincts can be amplified still further by dissociation. Severely dissociated people can also display remarkable strength and insensitivity to physical pain, making them particularly lethal adversaries. For instance, while patients are high on the dissociation-inducing anaesthetic drug PCP—a drug capable of producing dramatic levels of dissociation—they commonly describe feeling physically powerful and insensitive to normal pain experience. One patient to whom I once spoke who had a lot of experience using the dissociative drug PCP described feeling that he could crush solid objects such as ashtrays (or my skull) with his hands while high on PCP. He also thought he could lift very heavy objects such as automobiles. Another patient told me that when he was high on PCP, he felt that he could lift his barbells "with all the heaviest weights put on it to max it out." Under the influence of these forces, formidable foes emerge. Someone who is seriously tranced out and dissociated can cause a lot of physical damage.

For an example of just how physically powerful someone can become during naturally occurring (i.e., non-drug-induced) dissociation, consider the case of the grandmother who saw her grandchild pinned under an automobile. The grandmother was suddenly transformed into someone able to lift the car off of the child with her bare hands. At the time she lifted the car, she was not thinking that she had superhuman strength—she just did what had to be done to save her grandchild. She was temporarily dissociated from her normal sense of strength. The shock of seeing her grandchild run over by the car triggered something profound in this woman's brain that allowed her to lift the weight of a car. It temporarily gave her extraordinary strength.

I have seen patients in the throes of a severe Love Trauma Syndrome engage in physical violence to which they seemed anaesthetized. One patient of mine who had just learned of his girlfriend's past affair punched his hand completely through a drywall wall. His hand emerged in the neighboring room. He had been experiencing considerable dissociative symptoms. He later told me that he felt that his hand had moved through the wall almost effortlessly, and he felt no pain.

Interestingly, O.J. Simpson reportedly told a friend that he thought maybe he might have killed his wife "in a dream," suggesting that O.J. was dissociated at the time of the murder. The power and strength of the man who killed Nicole Brown Simpson and Ronald Goldman, based on the nature of their knife wounds, was noted throughout Mr. Simpson's criminal trial. One wonders if Mr. Simpson was not dissociated, and made unusually powerful during this dissociated state, immediately prior to and during the murder. Mr. Simpson's football career was filled with instances where he was able to conjure up unusual strength and stamina. He unconsciously knew how to tap into these transcendent dissociative forces to find the power and strength he needed. No amount of degenerative arthritis would have slowed O.J. down in such a dissociated state.

Love Trauma Syndrome and Violent Responses to Infidelity in Aboriginal Cultures

Cuckolded men can become violent and murderous in their attempts to contain their humiliation. They are ready to seek revenge against unfaithful mates and their consorts. They primarily want to resist the profound sickening associated with humiliation and regain the upper hand.

Even in societies marked by egalitarianism and cooperation, such as the !Kung Bushman and the Central Eskimo, illicit sexuality is a cause of murderous and frenzied violence. In one such murder among the !Kung, a researcher counted over 60 arrows in the body of the murder victim (Knauft, 1987). In fact, the most common cause of homicide in the !Kung and Central Eskimo societies has been reported to be "sexual impropriety" such as adultery or wife stealing. This is what causes the usual nonviolent nature of these people to be ruptured by periodic outbursts of murderous violence. Indeed, the homicide rates in these groups are surprisingly high. The !Kung homicide rate is three times the homicide rate in the United States. Studies of the Central Eskimo found that 60% of the adult men had successfully committed at least one murder, and 13% had attempted murder without success.

In these aboriginal societies, the violent declarations of rage over perceived sexual violations can be so profound that the aggression is focused imperfectly and innocent bystanders are injured or killed. Even among the !Kung Bushmen or the Central Eskimo, bystander killings are common. In such cases spears or arrows hit accidental targets. Ronald Goldman might have been such a target.

The largest war of early recorded history, the Trojan War, was started by an infidelity. Paris, a Prince of Troy, successfully wooed the beautiful Helen away from her Greek husband, King Menelaus. This was the affair "that launched a thousand ships," a reference to the largest fighting force ancient Greece had ever seen that descended upon Troy to punish Paris. Not only was Paris killed, but so were most of the inhabitants of Troy. The women who were not killed were taken in slavery. The city was burned to the ground and reduced to rubble.

Lessons from the Gebusi

For over 99 percent of human evolution, we have lived as hunter-gatherers. The lifestyles and behaviors of the modern Gebusi of New Guinea are thought to represent this hunter-gatherer way of life that existed for the hundreds of thousands of years of our recent evolution. The Gebusi society is comprised of about 450 people who live in the New Guinea rain forest. Interestingly, the Gebusi murder rate is the highest ever reported—40 times greater than the U.S. murder rate. Most of the murders are between neighbors. In fact, many victims are *related* to the murderers.

The murder victim can usually be identified as being a rival of the murderer. Bruce Knauft, an anthropologist at Emory University in Atlanta, has closely studied the Gebusi society. He has hypothesized that the murders are really about "male disputes over women" (Knauft, 1987). Knauft thinks that the motive underlying most of these murders is "the control of marriageable women" and regulation of sexual relations in the tribe. In fact, other experts have noted that one of the most potent stimuli for homicide worldwide involves "male competition over female reproductive capacity." Over half of the murdered Gebusi were young men establishing themselves as sexual entities in the community.

Jealous Mates

People have made reference to O.J. Simpson's "jealous heart." Jealousy is a form of suspiciousness and paranoia where a person is concerned that rivals are trying to steal their mate. Jealousy is associated with hypervigilance for these rivals. One jealous patient of mine would go to a party and relate to me all of the people who looked at his wife. When people cast their gaze toward him he thought that the rivals were "sizing" him up, or others were trying to determine whether he was "good enough for her." He was not able to enjoy the relationship he had with his devoted wife because of jealousy and possessiveness. People who are overly possessive often destroy the love they want to protect. Although some do better with reassurance, some cannot be reassured, and might actually need antipsychotic medication to help them deal with their intense and unrealistic jealousy. O.J. Simpson was not able to tame his jealous heart on his own.

The Role of Envy and Jealousy

People are unconsciously (and often consciously) aware of who is doing a better job than themselves at acting in a way that will get his or her genetic material propagated into the future. This often induces the emotion of envy toward those who seem to be doing a better job. There is often an automatic *compulsive comparing* of the resource holdings and status of others, and a comparing of their behaviors, which are designed to get genetic material into future generations, to theirs.

We have evolved as social animals that try to maximize our hierarchical position within a social group—thereby maximizing our access to resources and to mates. Resources include food and other material supplies needed to feed and protect ourselves and our offspring, and to help assure that our genetic material has a better chance of making it into the future.

The greater your access to resources, the more appealing you are to potential mates. Having a higher group status is associated with greater resource access, and is also associated with having more offspring who survive into adulthood and who bear offspring of their own.

There is a range of envious feelings that result when others are perceived as doing better than you (to your brain, it means that they are going to have a better chance than you of getting their genetic material into the future). The envy is associated with an unpleasant emotional state and level of arousal. The envious brain is activating the body—arousing the body—for action (e.g., a possible attack on your successful rival). The brain does not want to feel that others are superior to you or have it better than you, and are likely to get more genetic material into the future than you (most of the later assessment is occurring beneath our level of awareness).

Envy and jealousy about a rival's better rank and resource access motivates challenge of the rival. The challenge is designed to diminish the rival's status, and to redistribute resources between the challenger and the rival.

Envy and jealousy inspire *leveling behaviors*. These behaviors try to reduce the rival's status and resource access. Leveling behaviors equilibrate the asymmetrical statuses of the two parties. The hidden agenda behind much envy- and jealousy-motivated fighting (often even hidden from the conscious awareness of the combatants) is the "automatic" desire to diminish the rival's heightened status. And by diminishing the attractiveness of rivals, leveling behaviors can also be a form of "mate guarding." After a rival has been effectively leveled, desired mates are made to feel that they have nothing to gain by switching their affections to the leveled rival.

Envy and jealousy over another person's access to better rank and resources are linked to reproductive and sexual competition. Better rank and resource access makes you a more attractive mate or ally. This was true in the ancient ancestral environment in which we evolved, and is still true today. In the ancestral environment, heightened rank and resource access generally resulted in more offspring and a greater chance of the person's genetic material being passed along into future generations. Our brains know this, and we are equipped with the ability to experience envy and jealousy to detect those who are doing better than ourselves, and to consider whether there is anything that we can do about the situation.

There are a variety of leveling behaviors, including fighting, threatening, vandalism, and other behaviors designed to lower the rival's status. Leveling behavior also includes people working hard to reach or exceed the social status of others. In all fields of endeavor, much excellence is propelled by people trying to raise their own rank and status in the hierarchy. However, some people are not beyond raising their social position by bringing others down in whatever way they can.

The Blame Game

People with Love Trauma Syndrome want someone to blame. By blaming someone else, you are able to assume less responsibility for the problems in the relationship, and you resist some of the internalization of defeat. This resistance is important for preventing the sickening and restraining brain changes that support and maintain a "defeated position."

As you further *elaborate* in your mind why the other person is to blame, there can be "expansion" in your thinking from simply blaming them for your misfortunes to assuming that they want you to do poorly. You might assume that the person you are blaming is in some way evil and *dangerous* (to you and others), and that they want you weakened or destroyed. In this way, blame can expand into paranoia. Interestingly, the person you blame usually is in some way your rival. The rival will eventually need to be dealt with anyway for you to secure future success—be it in love or in some other matter. Because of this, you might as well come up with even more reasons to confront them.

More Lessons from the Gebusi

One dramatic example of this "blame game" occurs among the Gebusi tribespeople described earlier. For over 25% of Gebusi who fall ill and die, someone in the tribe is blamed for practicing sorcery to bring on their death, and the accused sorcerer is later murdered (Knauft, 1987). In fact, most of the murders in Gebusi society are "sorcerer killings." The motivation for the sorcery is thought to be that the sorcerer is evil and spiteful. Bruce Knauft, who has studied the Gebusi, states that the murderer often feels that the sorcerer's motive is "he (or she) is just a bad person; he sent sickness and death just because." In fact, some prior tension between the murderer and victim can usually be identified. The conflict is usually about women.

Love Trauma Syndrome and the Desire to Punish in
Aboriginal Folklore

Stories about the need to contain Love-Trauma-Syndrome-associated
desires to violently punish or seek revenge can be found in aboriginal folklore. Such inclinations for revenge need to be inhibited lest one risk retal-
iatory punishment. One Yanomama myth describes the fate of someone
whose jealousy drove him to murder. In the story, two girls go to the home
of Opossum and his mother, the Mushroom woman. Opossum offers the
girls food, but the girls find the food offensive and reject it. He sends them
to his friend Honey to get some tobacco. The girls find Honey so handsome that they forget Opossum. Opossum is consumed with jealousy, and
that night Opossum shoots Honey with a magic dart that kills him. After
committing the murder, Opossum becomes very anxious about being
caught and punished. To escape punishment, he grows wings and feathers
and flies away. But the birds, lead by Toucan, search for Opossum and kill
him. The birds paint themselves with his blood. The Yanomama say that
some birds today have red coloration because they are still stained with
the blood of Opossum. Toucan gave each bird a rock to live in, and these
birds became the first spirits of the forest.

So, according to legend, avenging angels were the first spirits to pop-
ulate the rainforest of the Yanomama, and birds with red markings are a
continual reminder of what happens to people who cannot contain their
murderous rage. Unfortunately, Opossum was not able to experience sufficient anxiety *before* murdering Honey. Such anxiety might have served to
contain and inhibit the expression of violence and keep him from committing the murder.

In fact, the gods of many peoples are punishing gods—gods who retaliate against those who act on their jealousy-driven, murderous proclivities.
In general, threats of retaliation or of punishment for committing violent
acts provide powerful inhibition against engaging in such behaviors.

Unfortunately, the brains of certain individuals are not able to appropriately inhibit them before they commit heinous acts. Their violence
against others usually is in part designed to prevent sickening in an attempt to reassume their dominant status and view of themselves. Social
prohibitions are not sufficient to keep them from acting on these more aggressive impulses to destroy those who have humiliated them in the context of love.

Had O.J. been appropriately anxious about what he was about to do
to his wife on the night he allegedly murdered her, he might have never

carried out the alleged murder. However, just as Opossum was not able to get away with murder because of the avenging angels of the Yanomama, O.J. Simpson was not able to get away completely from the avenging angels of our culture.

Resisting the Desire to Punish

As described earlier, most people with Love Trauma Syndrome possessed by a desire to punish others do so in ways that fall far short of murder. Nevertheless, even lower grade desires to punish—often reflected by chronic arguments between partners—can have a corrosive effect on relationships. Just how corrosive to a relationship a partner's Love-Trauma-Syndrome-related desire to punish can be is illustrated by the following case example.

Sue and Elliot were a young college couple who came to me because they were "fighting all the time." Although they had lived together for over a year, the fighting began after they were married about 6 months. "We fight about everything," Sue said. "We fight about who will take out the trash, who will do the dishes, who will vacuum." They were fighting every night "for hours," and were no longer sleeping together.

During their fighting both of them had damaged furniture and dishes. They had physically struck each other. Sue said that she was sometimes scared by "the look in Elliot's eyes," and Elliot was quick to say that his ears were still ringing from all the times "she's hung up on me." "I don't know how the phone can still work after she slams it down so hard."

The fights had become "real personal." They often resorted to exchanging insults. For instance, Sue called Elliot "a dumb jerk," and made disparaging comments about his family, his friends, and the junior college he had attended. Elliot, on the other had, used words like "slut" and some that were worse. "We now fight about anything we can," Elliot said. "It's all out warfare." Both of them were spending time crying separately.

Sue had an expectation that each of them would contribute "equally" to what had to be done around the house. Before getting married, Sue said that she tolerated Elliot's "laziness." However, she would tolerate it no longer. They both worked (although her income was slightly more than his), and she had the thought that they would "both make the meals and clean the dishes." "I understand occasionally not doing your share, but not night after night," she said. "I've got to stand my ground." As a number of earlier relationships she had with men had not worked out, she wanted her relationship with Elliot to continue. "But not at the cost of my sanity," she said.

Elliot, on the other hand, had different concerns. In private, he told me "I think I could've done better." He was ashamed to admit that he thought Sue was "damaged merchandise." He thought she had exhibited certain "moral character defects" a few years earlier. Sue had been married right after high school to her high school boyfriend. "Why did she get married so quickly" he said, "and to such a loser?" "What does that make me, an even greater loser, getting sloppy seconds?" he asked. Her first marriage ended after she started an affair with an older married man. "How do I know that she won't have an affair on me?" he said. Elliot wanted a more perfect mate, and also wanted to punish her for her "flawed past." Sue wanted a more understanding companion who would strive to strengthen their relationship rather than·tearing it down. "There's nothing I can do to change my past," she once said to me through tears.

Elliot had a Love Trauma Syndrome associated with a desire to punish Sue for her past sexual involvement with other men. He was often provoking fights driven by his unconscious and his conscious desire to punish her. Sue responded by engaging in the fight, and wanting to punish Elliot "for being an idiot." Both Sue and Elliot were trying to sicken each other with their threatening gestures and self-esteem-toxic verbal insults. The relationship was being consumed in the flames of battle. Each of them was hardening their positions. What started out as small skirmishes was now all-out warfare.

Importantly, they both said that they still loved each other, and wanted to try to work out their problems. After almost a year of work, their battles stopped. The last I heard, they remain married and have two children.

The case of Sue and Elliot also illustrates how physical violence can become a feature of problematic relationships. It has been reported that over 10% (in fact, maybe over 25%) of both men and women have hit, slapped, or kicked their partners. Some studies have suggested that women initiate the violence just as often as men (McNeely and Robinson-Simpson 1987; O'Leary et al., 1989).

How often elements of a Love Trauma Syndrome are involved in these physically abusive relationships is not known at this time. However, it is known that when someone kills their mate (and sometimes themselves afterwards), the relationship is more likely to have been marked by past episodes of physical abuse and violence. Additionally, if one or both partners have another psychiatric condition, such as serious depression, or suffer from addictions to drugs or to alcohol, the likelihood of serious physical violence, murder, or suicide complicating a Love Trauma Syndrome increases.

In the context of a Love Trauma Syndrome, mental health clinicians should always ask their patients whether they have murderous or suicidal ideas. If they do, it is important to investigate how likely they are to act on them. Such ideation is rare, but should nevertheless always be thoroughly explored. Thankfully, murderously violent people make up a very small minority of people with Love Trauma Syndrome. Literally, they are only the tip of the iceberg. Most people with Love Trauma Syndrome suffer silently and do not bother others.

Chapter Eight

Self-Help Strategies for Overcoming Love Trauma Syndrome

The Goals of Self-Help Treatment of Love Trauma Syndrome

Most people with Love Trauma Syndrome want to rebuild their love relationships or start new, more rewarding romantic involvements. They want to break the chains that hold them back from one of the most wonderful feelings that life has to offer—the experience of being in love. These people want to realize their romantic dreams. They often tell me they "want to be able to be happy again."

The overall goal of both self-help and professional help strategies for someone with Love Trauma Syndrome is to try to *contain* the malignant spread of love-trauma-associated feelings, thoughts, memories, and distress, and to diminish the emotional pain, hyperarousal, and pathological behavioral responses (e.g., alcohol and drug abuse). People want to be able to *replace* their Love-Trauma-Syndrome-associated emotional pain and negative thoughts with more positive and pleasant emotions and ways of thinking. The concept of *replacement*—that is, the exchange of unhealthy, dysphoric and dysfunctional thinking and feeling with more healthy and positive attitudes and feelings—also forms the core of both self-help and professional techniques. Although self-help strategies are often effective in ameliorating some of the pain of Love Trauma Syndrome, severe cases are often best helped by professional counselors, psychologists, or psychiatrists.

Self-Help Your Way to Freedom

People often try to help themselves as much as possible without resorting to professional psychotherapy. There are a wide variety of self-help
techniques that can be employed. Some techniques will work better for
some people than for others. You should read through this chapter and
chose a few of the methods described and see which ones work best for
you (sometimes referred to as the "cafeteria approach" to self-help therapy). Interestingly, many patients in professional psychotherapy are also
often encouraged to try out different self-help techniques to see which
ones are most effective for them. There are a wide variety of self-help techniques, some of which will be reviewed here.

Bibliotherapy

One way to first find out about different self-help techniques to deal
with the stress and emotional pain of a condition such as Love Trauma
Syndrome is to go to the psychology or self-help section of any bookstore
or library. Much of the self-help literature found there is devoted to helping people escape from feelings of despondency brought on by a variety of
problems.

Some people feel too ashamed to talk to others about their Love
Trauma Syndrome, and want to first see if they can tackle the problem on
their own. They read self-help books and find techniques that they find
relevant to their problems and situation. Very often these self-help books
usefully prepare patients for psychotherapy.

Self-help books of all kinds, including inspirational books, describe all
manner of techniques for turning off the emotional pain and dysphoria of
conditions like Love Trauma Syndrome. Following is a partial laundry list
of many of these self-help techniques.

Exercising Your Way to Freedom

One very effective way for people to begin to recover from the physically sickening effects of Love Trauma Syndrome is to physically exercise. I routinely recommend to my patients that they get involved in a
regular schedule of physical activity. It helps patients to better cope with
the hyperarousal associated with the condition. Patients also report that
involvement in exercise helps distract them from their Love-Trauma-
Syndrome-related thoughts, feelings, and memories. Distraction is an

important curative element in the treatment of Love Trauma Syndrome. It facilitates convenient forgetting, and some degree of forgetting is important for recovery from Love Trauma Syndrome.

Love Trauma Syndrome is often associated with considerable sickening feelings such as fatigue, weakness, achiness, and fuzzy-headed feelings. Physical exercise helps to counteract these symptoms. Exercise physically and mentally "conditions" you to feel stronger and more energetic. The physical conditioning afforded by exercise can counteract many of the sickening effects triggered by Love Trauma Syndrome.

A lot of furious and intense exercise is fueled by the nervous system arousal, anger, and agitation of Love Trauma Syndrome. This is a good place to direct Love-Trauma-Syndrome-related hyperarousal. Indeed, this can be a healthy use of the agitation from the syndrome. Sometimes, after a person recovers from a Love Trauma Syndrome, they become upset because they have lost some of that motivation and energy they had for exercising. The arousal helped sustain them when they became exhausted. It is now harder for them to exercise as hard or as long as they did previously.

Some people will periodically consciously tap into their hyperarousal by voluntarily allowing themselves to get into touch with their old, more uncomfortable Love-Trauma-Syndrome-related feelings. It should be noted, however, that some people with Love Trauma Syndrome will excessively exercise to the point where they hurt themselves physically (e.g., they lose too much weight, or exercise to the point where they begin to do damage to their muscles and joints). People should avoid overexercising and hurting themselves in a desperate attempt to cope with love-trauma-related emotional pain.

The Power of Positive Thinking

Many self-help books urge you to assume a more positive and optimistic attitude about your problems. This is an important stance to take with Love Trauma Syndrome. The intensity of the emotional pain can be overwhelming, and people in the throes of the condition can become very pessimistic that they will ever feel better.

A part of thinking positively involves ignoring certain aspects of an unpleasant reality—something people with severe Love Trauma Syndrome need to be encouraged to do. In general, it is not good to simply wallow in the misery of Love Trauma Syndrome. Wallowing in the pain of

Love Trauma Syndrome involves becoming drowned in "thinking negatively." The person should try to engage in positive thinking.

Although victims of Love Trauma Syndrome should be encouraged to accept reality as it is, they also need to be encouraged to develop a *positive vision* of what they want for themselves now and in the future. Thinking positively increases our options and diminishes the sense of our limitations. Being positive is *emboldening* and *activating* and allows us to better develop and act on plans that will help us realize our visions. People should be persuaded to focus more on their positive vision of what they want to achieve rather than concentrating on the emotional consequences of their love trauma.

Self-serving distortions of reality can be allowed as long as they foster an optimistic attitude. Optimists argue that people with a positive and optimistic attitude are healthier and recover more quickly than those who are pessimistic. In "positive thinking mental health strategies," people are often asked to imagine what they *want to happen* as what is *going to happen*. Certain self-help books encourage you to adopt this ability to visualize what you want. These books have you make daily *affirmations* and focus on your desires coming to fruition.

Positive thinking strategies also advocate learning how to engage in "positive self-talk." This self-talk is in reference to the inner dialogue we all periodically have; that is, the private conversations we have with ourselves. The goal of positive self-talk strategies is to replace your negative self-talk with more positive self-talk. However, positive self-talk needs to be practiced so that it can become second nature.

When you engage in positive self-talk, you learn to think like an optimist. As an optimist you will be able to visualize more options and solutions to your problems. Your problem solving abilities will improve. As an optimist you will be less prone to giving into defeat, which will lessen your defeat stress (and the physiological effects of defeat stress). Optimists feel empowered to overcome adversity. They are less likely to give up.

I have patients who sometimes use certain cues in the environment to stop negative self-talk and to start positive self-talk. For instance, when patients see a "Stop" sign on the road, or a red light at a traffic stop, I ask them to use these as triggers to stop their negative self-talk and begin to engage in self-talk that is positive. If the self-talk slips into a more negative line of thinking, they are urged to resume their more positive self-talk. I also ask patients to use green traffic lights as a cue to engage in positive self-talk. The ability to talk to yourself more positively is a skill that must be practiced in order for one to become proficient.

Remember that people who are able to think on the bright side of things and remain hopeful and positive have fewer physical and emotional illnesses. And when they do become physically or emotionally ill they recover faster (e.g. Scheier et al., 1989; Segerstrom et al., 1998). People with an optimistic attitude recover more quickly from Love Trauma Syndrome.

The problem with positive thinking strategies is that for some people, try though they may, they are unable to shift from their negative self-talk to more positive self-talk. Even though the ability to think positively is a skill that must be practiced in order for one to become proficient, some people have a very difficult time acquiring the skill. Such people often cannot really believe their positive thoughts, and the roots of their negative thinking run quite deep. For these people, their positive thinking rests on shaky ground. They do not really believe their positive self-talk, and find the positive thinking exercises "artificial" and "phony." Such people often benefit from cognitive therapy, which addresses the underlying roots of their negative thoughts. Cognitive therapy is discussed in the following chapter.

You Have the Right to Be Happy

Some of the self-help methods designed to diminish the pain of conditions such as Love Trauma Syndrome involve telling yourself repeatedly (in as many different ways as possible) that you can be—and have the right to be—happy. Tell yourself that "I deserve to be happy." In fact, some religious doctrines (e.g., Judaism) dictate that it is your religious responsibility to be happy. In the self-help literature, authors often focus on the fact that if someone else can do it (i.e., be happy), so can you! There is so much pain and suffering in this world that if you wanted to be sad and down all of the time, you could be. These books encourage you to actively seek rewards in your environment. "Go out and have fun—and be happy."

Some people do not feel that they have the right to be happy and experience pleasure. One straight "A" college student whom I saw was depressed. When I asked him what he did to have fun, and what sort of pleasurable activities he was involved with, he could come up with none. "Oh," he said, "I haven't earned it yet."

Keeping Connected

We have evolved as social animals. We want to feel connected to others. We are unhappy if we do not have friends and allies. Most of us feel propelled to want to associate with other people. Being connected to others increases our overall level of happiness and life satisfaction. Being with good friends improves our mood. Having allies also decreases our perceived levels of stress, and diminishes the physiological evidence of stress on our bodies. Friends and allies are important sources of support for people with Love Trauma Syndrome. You should tell your friends and allies that you are suffering. Some of them might have to take an active stance to prevent you from becoming socially withdrawn and isolated, which is often the natural inclination for someone with Love Trauma Syndrome. People with Love Trauma Syndrome should resist the impulse to withdraw from others. I have even seen certain patients with Love Trauma Syndrome have plastic surgery to increase their overall physical attractiveness to others. The surgery allowed them to be more confident that they could attract and hold onto more allies and romantic interests.

People with Love Trauma Syndrome should never abandon the idea that they will be able to fall in love again. (This might even be with the person that caused their syndrome in the first place.) As described in an earlier chapter, most people with Love Trauma Syndrome instinctively know that a good way of recovering from a love trauma is to find someone else with whom they can fall in love. There is always the danger that people will accept replacements for their lost love without carefully considering their merits. However, many successful relationships have been forged on the rebound.

Unfortunately, for many people with Love Trauma Syndrome, they are unable to think of becoming involved with anyone else, as they remain fixated on the person who precipitated their Love Trauma Syndrome. Although some might contemplate seeking out new loves, they find it difficult to find the motivation to do so. They might even *avoid* getting involved with others for fear of getting another helping of Love Trauma Syndrome. However, in some patients with Love Trauma Syndrome, involvement with a carefully considered replacement can quickly restore them to their normal state of emotional and physical health.

Looking to the East

To reduce the pain of emotional distress, a variety of books advocate that you adopt more Eastern (i.e., Taoist, Zen, Buddhist) philosophical attitudes about life. Such attitudes emphasize achieving harmony with your surroundings and "going with the flow" rather than battling your environment. Eastern philosophies view emotional distress as resulting from a lack of congruence between your internal *desires* and external *reality*. In these philosophies, all distress is born of desire—the desire that your internal wishes match your external reality. In fact, an important part of Love Trauma Syndrome work is to define what aspects of the love trauma are incompatible with your view of yourself, and the world and to reconcile those incompatibilities without becoming overwhelmed.

Eastern philosophies encourage you to achieve a "desireless" and "egoless" state. You are urged to accept all and "go with the flow" to achieve harmony. You also need to learn to ignore your "value judgments." The Ninja warrior applies these principles in battle. If a Ninja is in a poor position when fighting an adversary, the Ninja does not say "Oh no, I'm in a bad way." The Ninja focuses on the position that they are in, not on the one that they want. This liberates them to see the strength of the position that they have and to capitalize on it. They have no regrets. They value full acceptance of external reality, regardless of how bad it is. In the case of Love Trauma Syndrome, this typically involves acceptance of the love trauma events and the blow to your self-esteem, as well as the blow to your view of how you would want things to be. Some writers and songwriters are able to "Mine" their Love Trauma Syndrome and produce successful works that earn them a living.

I have seen people with Love Trauma Syndrome use it as a way to improve themselves or their relationships. Some are able to let the void left by their "departed" partner be filled with others or other activities, resulting in a better outcome for them than remaining in the previous relationship.

One benefit of achieving the ideals of harmony with your surrounding and "going with the flow" is that you begin to experience life as being "effortless." You are able to deal with the challenges in your life without feeling strained. Traumas can be dealt with while maintaining a sense of inner peace.

Battling the Curse of our Entitlement

Many people expect, in fact, feel *entitled* to "perfect" (or near perfect) lives and relationships. They feel entitled to always having it their way, and having it the best. Some people were raised by doting parents who instilled this sense of entitlement into them. Years after leaving home, they still feel entitled, and expect their mates to be as indulgent to them as their parents were. They become upset and angry when their mates do not comply with these expectations (which are often hidden from their awareness). They cannot believe that their mates would inflict a love trauma upon them, or that something bad would happen to their love interest (e.g., death or disease).

Some have an *unconditional* sense of entitlement, where they feel they should have things their way even in the absence of working for it and thus "deserving it." Others have a more *conditional* sense of entitlement. This conditional entitlement is performance based, where they feel that if they are "good" (i.e., they are good workers, good students, good homemakers, etc.), they are entitled to having things their way, having it the best, and having it the way they want. They become depressed and angry when they do not get from their loved ones what they feel they deserve—that is, what they feel they have *earned*. But their partners very often do not see it that way. Their partners never saw the private contract.

For people with this "I've earned it and I should get it" type of entitlement, they are often plagued with trying to be perfect (they practice "perfectionism"). Their self-esteem suffers when they cannot be perfect. Their self-esteem is performance based, and many become workaholics. Their lives are made miserable because they have to work so hard. They might even feel that if they work harder still, then they will be able to get what they feel they have earned. However, they still do not get from others and life what they feel they deserve. Such performance-based operators work under the assumption that if you work hard enough, you will get what you want. Unfortunately, when it comes to love, it does not always work that way.

Part of growing up is realizing that we can't always get what we want. Our sense of feeling entitled to having our way becomes a source of our misery. In many of us there is a sense of "grandiosity"—that is, on some level we feel so superior that we feel entitled to having our desires and wishes fulfilled. When we cannot accomplish this, we feel ashamed. We reason that there must be something defective about us (something shameful) that prevents us from having our way. Many of us alternate between feelings of grandiosity and feelings of shame.

We need to learn that we cannot always get things our way, and that we will not fall apart when our childish expectations of perfection are not fulfilled. We need to learn to not allow the shame to overwhelm us.

Recognizing "Shadow" Elements

The great psychiatrist Carl Jung described the *shadow* as the part of the personality that contains its hidden, repressed, and unfavorable aspects. This often includes selfish, aggressive, and taboo sexual impulses that the mind tries to keep out of conscious awareness. It contains our darker inclinations—for example, our desire to control, to punish, to overwhelm, and to feel powerful. The shadow also includes uncomfortable, unpleasant, and unhappy elements of one's past that have not been resolved, and our desire to make others pay for our misery. Love-trauma-related memories and thoughts, and the desire to act viciously and violently in response to a love trauma, are part of our dark inner shadow. Jung thought that we are all drawn to our shadows, and that if we did not learn to recognize and deal with our shadows their power could overtake us.

Dark shadow elements can intrude into consciousness during the day while we are awake and thinking and also when we are asleep through our dreams. Jung saw it as a task in everyone's life to "become acquainted" with their personality's and life's shadow elements in a process he called "the realization of the shadow." The shadow elements need to be recognized and integrated into the personality. Otherwise, the person loses control over their shadow elements, and the shadow begins to unconsciously influence their life decisions. Again, people are drawn to their shadow elements, and they need to learn to understand their shadows before they are controlled by them. Some therapists refer to this process as "befriending the shadow" or "reclaiming the repressed."

Looking to God

Some of the literature designed to liberate people from emotional distress encourages readers to "rise above," or transcend, their problems. Very often the message is to "let God" into their lives so they can be helped. I have seen people who were able to place their lives and problems into the "Hands of God" blast their way out of considerable anxiety, depression, and pain in the context of a Love Trauma Syndrome. It is said that "in God's Hands we rest untroubled."

If you can, you should give your love-trauma-related problems to God. Jung thought that people over the age of 35 could not be helped with their emotional problems unless they discovered their Higher Power in God. It is important to remember that God is with you always, during the good times and the bad times.

Related literature invites people to see their concerns in the context of a religious life. Religion gives people guidance and strength to handle their problems, no matter how big or small these problems might be. Some of this literature mitigates feelings of alienation and failure by advocating that you see yourself "as one" with everyone and everything in the universe. Some writers advocate appreciating the miracles in your life—no matter how small—and thanking God for them. This allows you to focus on the more positive aspects of your life. Finally, some religions, such as Judaism, emphasize God's desire for you to be happy. In fact, it is a religious responsibility that you—despite all the bumps along the road that life has to offer—be joyful.

Prayer is an important link to God. There are different types of prayer, including petitionary prayer, thanksgiving prayer, colloquial prayer, meditative prayer, and ritualistic prayer. In *petitionary prayer,* you ask God for something, such as health, happiness, or relief from the pain of a love trauma. Prayers of *thanksgiving* involve being appreciative for God's gifts to you, however large or small they might be, and thanking God for those gifts.

In *colloquial prayer,* you talk with God in your own words. You might outline a problem that you have in your life, and ask for God's guidance or assistance. Colloquial prayers also include informal prayers of thanksgiving. In *meditative prayer,* the attempt here is to come into contact with God's presence, or to feel the presence of God. For instance, in Kabbalistic Judaism, there is an effort to "move beyond words" and become aware of God. Meditative prayer can be wordless.

During *ritualistic prayer,* a prayer is read from a prayer book or repeated from memory. A classic ritualistic prayer is the "Lord's Prayer." In the Christian religion, the basic elements of prayer as taught by Jesus are contained in the Lord's Prayer. The Lord's Prayer goes:

Our Father, who art in heaven,
Hallowed by they name,
Thy Kingdom come, thy will be done, on earth as it is in heaven,
And give us this day our daily bread,
and forgive us our sins,
as we forgive those who have sinned against us.
And bring us not into temptation,
and deliver us from evil.[1]

Some Christian teachers use the acronym "C-H-R-I-S-T" to convey these basic prayer elements. The first element ("C") is *concentration* on the Father, the Higher Power. Indeed, most prayer begins with a period of silence, inactivity, and an attempt to focus attention (i.e., concentrate, meditate) on God's presence. The second element ("H") is getting in touch with the *hallowedness* and *holiness* of God. This helps to activate transcendent potential. The "R" stands for *rule,* and your acceptance of submissiveness to God's higher power and law. Carl Jung, the famous psychiatrist who provided the intellectual foundation for the 12-Step movements such as Alcoholics Anonymous, thought that older people with emotional problems could only get better if they accepted a "Higher Power" greater than themselves. You need to understand that God might not always answer your prayers the way you want or expect, and sometimes we need to be patient before we get any response. We live in His kingdom and He is in control.

The "I" represents our more personal needs (as in the need I have), and our desire to have God help us fulfill these needs. It is all right for us to petition God for specific things, such as healing, health, victory, or even material things and wealth. The "S" stands for *sin,* and our request that God forgive us for our sins, and help us forgive those who have sinned against us. Christian doctrine emphasizes the need to forgive those who have wronged us. Even when Jesus Christ was dying on the cross, he asked God to forgive those who brought about his unjust murder.

The "T" stands for *temptation,* and the request that God help us not to fall prey to sinful temptations. This can also include temptations to engage in Love-Trauma-Syndrome-related negative and self-destructive thoughts, feelings, and behaviors that lead us, our families, and our friends into despair and unhappiness. All temptations are resistible—but sometimes we need a lot of help from a Higher Power to successfully resist these temptations. Sometimes, the temptations are to act on revenge fantasies and to commit destructive and violent acts—clearly evil deeds that we need to ask God to help us resist. We might feel aroused to fulfill certain temptations, but we can resist these temptations, and direct the arousal to support other activities.

The Importance of Forgiveness

As described previously, many religious teachings emphasize the need to learn to forgive those who we feel have wronged us. God wants us to forgive. However, this is quite difficult for some of us, and we often need to pray to God to help us find the strength to forgive. Many of us are not ready to give up our anger and resentment. However, some teachers believe that if you do not forgive those who have wronged you, it could make you mentally and physically ill. Once you have forgiven those who have hurt and offended you, they no longer have power over you. You have liberated yourself from the clutches of those who have wronged you.

There are eight steps that one can take to forgive someone who has hurt you:

1. Identify the offenses (Be specific.). What did the other person do to offend you? What rights or privileges were violated? Or what did you feel you were entitled to that you did not get?

2. What would a "jury of your peers" (i.e., people in your community and religious institutions, your friends, family, or colleagues) feel is appropriate punishment (if any)? This anchoring to the judgement of others is called *reality testing*. You might even ask trusted confidants what they think.

3. How satisfied would you feel if the person was punished by the community standard? Estimate your satisfaction rating as a percentage (e.g., "I would be about 50%, or about 95% satisfied").

4. What do you think the punishment should be? What forms of punishment would you really want delivered before you would feel satisfied that justice was done? How satisfied would you feel if the person was punished in the way you wanted? What is the gap between the punishment you feel the person deserves and what you think the community standard would be? Is the gap large or small?

5. How satisfied are you with the punishment the person received—or will receive—for committing the offense against you?

6. Can you relinquish your desire to further blame and more severely punish the person who wronged you? To forgive you need to be able to rebalance the scales of justice evenly and to feel that justice has been served or is already being served. When you have forgiven someone, you no longer feel that the person needs to be punished more than they have been or are being punished. About what percentage of you is willing to forgive your desire to further punish the person who offended you? With prayer and God's help, can you get this percentage closer to 90% or 100%? This might take time.

7. After you have forgiven (or at least partially forgiven) the other person, what feelings remain? Do you feel disappointed, angry, resentful, hopeless, sad, hurt, defeated, humble, vulnerable, exhausted, or weak? Do you feel relieved, or even happy? Do you feel like crying? You will often have many mixed emotions. Very often your anger, hatred, and desire for revenge and punishment has blocked your experience of these emotions. By removing the desire to punish, other emotions sometimes rush in.

8. Just because you have forgiven someone does not mean that you need to reengage in some relationship with them. In fact, it might be

good to keep your distance from someone who is deceitful, unreliable, or violent, or has done something so heinous that you could never forgive them completely for what they did to you.

Forgiveness is not easy, and requires God's help to transcend your inclination to punish and reset the scales of justice by getting "an eye for an eye, a tooth for a tooth." We often feel that the severity of the judgement and punishment for an offense should be based on the severity of the unhappiness and distress the offense caused in us. Granting forgiveness requires that we absorb (or release) some of this unhappiness without compensation or restitution. The image of Jesus Christ on the Cross is the ultimate symbol and representation of someone granting forgiveness. Jung saw the symbol of the cross as a symbol of "transcendence," (Jung et al., 1964) whereby we are instructed in how to transcend our more base human inclination for retribution when we have been wronged and how to replace it with forgiveness. God and his son forgave us for killing the physical Jesus on the cross. We reject God's presence and His ways, yet He still forgives us.

Prayers of Thanksgiving

One way of recovering from a Love Trauma Syndrome is to offer God prayers of thanksgiving. Some of us find it difficult to fully appreciate what we have. We want to remain preoccupied with what we do not have, or with what we have lost and want replaced. Sometimes we need to pray to God to help us be more appreciative of what we have left, and to not be so self-centered and to ask God for only what we want or think we need. God has given many of us wonderful gifts that we do not recognize. Thank God for what you have, whatever it might be (or might have been). I find myself often praying to God to help me be thankful—and to truly appreciate—what God has given me.

Taking Life Less Seriously

Still another simple method of dealing with the distress of Love Trauma Syndrome is to try not to take life so seriously, and to treat your problems as if they are minor. My grandfather was a student of this self-help method, and his motto was "nothing important, nothing serious."[2]

Smaller problems induce less stress and distress than larger ones. One of the problems for people who have Love Trauma Syndrome is that they see their problems as overwhelming. Their problems loom large over them. If you see the problem as "trivial" and consider your life to be "just a game," then adverse consequences "really don't matter."

One simple technique to help you trivialize your seemingly overwhelming problems that have taken control of your life is to think of the problem and respond with a "So," or "So what." To prepare yourself to use this technique, initially practice saying to yourself "So" or "So what" often, even if your obsessive thoughts are not problematic at the time. As soon as the obsessive thoughts, feelings, or fantasies begin to intrude, your brain is "loaded" with the "So" or "So what" response.

Developing a sense of humor about your failures in love can further decrease the seriousness of the situation. Finding the humor in your problems diminishes their sickening influence. Laughter evokes feelings of joy and cheer, which counteract bridling feelings of despair and immobility. People need to learn how to laugh not only in the context of the victories in their lives, but also in the settings of failure. There is a Latin saying, *"Hilaritas sapientiae et bonae vitae proles"*—"Hilarity is the child of wisdom and a good life."

Devaluing Bad Memories

A number of self-help disciplines encourage you to devalue past events as representing "old moments" unworthy of too much attention. In this way past events associated with toxic and sickening memories and thoughts are devalued and discounted. This can be an important self-help intervention for people with Love Trauma Syndrome. In fact, the aim of treatment for people with Love Trauma Syndrome is to get them to live in the present, and to remove their preoccupation with trauma-related past events.

One benefit of remaining in the present is that you can decrease contact with painful love-trauma-related memories. Many patients with Love Trauma Syndrome do better when they are able to stay in the present moment. You should try to love in the moment.

Alternately, you can selectively choose to connect with positive recollections. Indeed, some self-help techniques advocate contact with old moments associated with *good* feelings to counter bad feelings. If past memories are toxic to your feeling good about yourself and your life, try to forget them.

For many people, negative remembrances activate considerable Love-Trauma-Syndrome-related misery that lasts anywhere from minutes to years. Patients often need to disconnect from these memories and be pulled out of the abyss of the past and anchored to the present. I sometimes have patients visualize themselves as somehow severing the ties that bind them to their past painful memories and thoughts. This is the process of "changing focus" and "letting go." You need to rip yourself away from a negative focus on the past. This can only be detrimental to your health. If you cannot do this on your own, seek professional help through a psychiatrist, psychologist, or other trained mental health worker.

Living in the Present

An important corollary to devaluing old moments is the important concept of needing to "live in the present," or to "live in the now." The people who are happiest are those who are most able to live in the present. The more you live in the present, the happier you will be. The "House of Pain" is usually built on old memories.

You need to live in the present moment and try to derive as much fulfillment from the current moment as possible. Live fully each and every moment. By doing this, you will actually be able to change your past. You will be creating new moments that are more fulfilling than those in your past. You will also change your remembered history.

One trick to help you live in the moment is to become involved in some recreational sport activity, such as biking, skating, or skiing, which requires your full attention while participating in the sport activity. I have had patients tell me that during such activities they were finally able to distract themselves from their love trauma. However, I offer one word of warning. People with Love Trauma Syndrome are accident prone. When you are suffering from Love Trauma Syndrome, your body and your mind have been under significant stress. Your reflexes are slowed, and you need to be extra careful while engaging in sport activities. Take it slow and do not push yourself.

One patient tried to remain in the present and distract himself from his love-trauma-related thoughts by placing a plastic container full of beads in his pants pocket. When he walked, the beads would rattle and make an annoying sound. He had to hold the plastic container still to keep the beads from rattling and making noise. When his intrusive love-trauma-related thoughts returned, it was usually associated with his loosening his grip on the plastic bottle, and the noise of the rattling beads would return. When he shifted his attention to holding the bottle with the beads still, he was distracted enough to stop engaging in his love-trauma-related thoughts. He was then better able to focus on being in the present. The only problem was that he had to keep a hand in his pants pocket.

On a related note, it is important to realize that you cannot change what happened in the past. It does you no good to wallow in the misery of past love trauma events. Wallowing represents your brain being stuck and unable to make the thoughts, feelings, and memories of the love trauma go away. It is like a skipping phonograph record that is caught in a groove. Your brain is locked into continually processing the event to help it figure out some way to resolve the problem. It wants the problem fixed and it cannot give it up because it thinks/feels that the stakes are too high if you do.

However, wallowing in your Love Trauma Syndrome misery is the path to unhappiness. Often it is useful to speak to a trained therapist (e.g., psychiatrist, psychologist, counselor) to help you understand and put into some perspective, some framework, the particular meaning the love trauma event has for you (e.g., feeling unlovable, feeling that you have failed once again, feeling that you are "no good"). There is a whole litany of toxic meanings that people attach to their love trauma events—and through psychotherapy these toxic brain influences can be neutralized. These psychotherapeutic "talking therapies" are discussed more fully in the next chapter.

Trancing Out to a Better Feeling State

Some people are able to remember how they thought and felt prior to a love trauma, or prior to feeling the symptoms of a Love Trauma Syndrome. They become wistful for the way things were. However, they can imagine thinking and feeling that way again. This way the more pleasant feeling state of the past is able to replace the negative love trauma-related feelings. To accomplish this trance state, you need to try to hold on to the memory of the better feelings from the past and experience it.

Actually, Love Trauma Syndrome itself has trancelike aspects. However, it is a "bad trance"—almost like an evil spell. It is not a state in which you want to remain. You need to try to replace the bad trance state with a more pleasant one, one that can be borrowed from the past. Your memory of these better feelings are stored in your memory banks. You simply need to access them. Professional hypnotists can sometimes assist in this endeavor.

People can also use self-hypnosis techniques to help them "trance out" to a better feeling state. Hypnosis is a state of focused attention in the awake state. Contrary to a popular belief, you cannot "get stuck" in a hypnotic trance. During the trance state you can program your mind with positive states, such as "I am healing," "I can cope," or "I am immune to the pain from my past."

To achieve a self-hypnotic state, simply sit in a comfortable chair, or lie down in a comfortable place (e.g., bed, sofa). The first step to achieving a self-hypnotic state is to become comfortable. If you are sitting in a chair, you should try to use a chair with armrests so you can put most of the weight from your arms on them. Try to put both feet on the floor if you can, again to support as much of the weight in your legs on the floor. Become comfortable.

After you have become comfortable, look at a spot on the ceiling. Direct your eyes to the ceiling, although you will often have to move your head as well to visualize your spot. The spot might also be high up on a wall.

After looking at the spot for about 10 seconds, count backwards from 100 to 90. "100, 99, 98, 97, 96, 95, 94, 93, 92, 91, 90." You can count farther backward if you would like to deepen your trance state. When you feel ready to go into your hypnotic state (either at the count of 90, or 80, or lower), say to yourself "I am now hypnotized." At the time you say this, you should close your eyes. You can also put in the time frame that you wish to remain hypnotized, such as saying to yourself "I am now hypnotized for 5 minutes (or 1 minute, or even some time in seconds [e.g., 30 seconds]). You should not constantly look at a clock or watch to time yourself during your self-hypnotic session. Simply estimate in your mind about how much time has passed. An occasional peek at a timepiece is permissible.

Breathe slowly and feel your body become heavier. Your jaw should open just slightly, without even parting your lips. Breathe evenly. Now give yourself a positive suggestion, such as "I am healed," "I am loveable," "I will find a soul-mate," "I am immune to the pain of my past," "I can cope," "I live in the present moment," "I am focused on my vision," or "I can function." Try not to let any negative statements enter into your suggestion—try to make the statements as positive and as simple as possible. Keep repeating the statements to yourself over and over. If you have negative thoughts, feelings, or memories, try to stay focused on your positive self-statements.

At the end of your hypnotic session, simply say to yourself, "Hypnosis ended, I am now awake and invigorated." Open your eyes, and take a moment or so to become fully aware of your surroundings. You can even repeat your suggestions to yourself in the awake, nonhypnotized state.

Don't Spread Yourself Out too Thinly

People with Love Trauma Syndrome are often under a great deal of stress. They need to be good to themselves and to not add too many other stressors to their already overfilled plate. People with Love Trauma Syndrome are prone to look for things to distract them from their pain, and they sometimes take on too much and find themselves stressed and depleted. During this time one should avoid unnecessary battles that will be draining.

Finding Acceptance

The wise person knows when they cannot change reality, and when the battle to change reality is lost. Such battles are simply not worth continuing. Surrender and acceptance is sometimes the best option. You simply cannot win every battle that you fight, and expecting that will only make you sick and miserable. We all lose from time to time.

Many people begin to learn the art of acceptance by learning the Serenity Prayer of Alcoholics Anonymous, a large self-help organization for people suffering from addiction to alcohol. One version of the prayer is as follows:

> God give me the serenity to accept things which cannot be changed;
> Give me the courage to change things which must be changed; And the
> wisdom to distinguish one from the other.[3]

Many people try to battle things that cannot be changed. They are destined not only to lose the battle, but to weaken themselves unnecessarily in the effort. They diminish their stamina to fight battles that can be won.

Some of us are only able to see ourselves as victorious fighters. The pain of surrendering is unbearable. Western tradition tends to foster an attitude of never surrendering and not giving up. Eastern and Buddhist traditions tend to emphasize acceptance, surrender, and going with the flow. Some people will not even accept partial victory, as they view such victory as equivalent to total loss (a mistaken view). Such people would rather sustain the physical and emotional pain resulting from continued fighting than sustain the sickening effects of surrender. They are unable to contemplate defeat as a tolerable option—the idea of surrendering is toxic to their self-esteem. Without their pride and dominant status entirely intact they feel destroyed.

However, people need to be able to save themselves before it is too late. Surrender is often the best way to hold on to some pride, resources, and quality of life. Sometimes the surrender represents a complete loss, and sometimes it represents only a partial loss. Paradoxically, sometimes you can win only by surrendering. For instance, John, the veteran described in chapter 2 who discovered that his wife had an affair while he was in Vietnam, told me that only when he was able to "surrender to his Love Trauma Syndrome" because he was too tired to fight it anymore did he begin to notice himself starting to feel better. People often just want their Love Trauma Syndrome to "go away," or do not recognize that the healing is a process that takes time. Although it is understandable that people would want it to disappear quickly, this is not what happens. Accepting—really trying to accept—that you are heartsick with Love Trauma Syndrome is the first step to getting over the condition.

Many chronic and futile battles are related to nonacceptance of defeat in a relationship. This nonacceptance of defeat is related to the person's refusing to accept some diminution of their self-esteem, with its subsequent weakening and sickening effects.

There is an "art" to surrendering. Surrendering involves the acceptance of defeat. The art of surrendering includes attention to both certain internal and external activities. Regarding the internal elements of surrender, you need to surrender in such a way that you can privately contain some of the sickening effects activated by the failure (or partial failure). You must swallow your pride without eliminating it completely. You must be careful not to exaggerate the loss to yourself, and not to blame yourself entirely for the failure. You must be able to accept the defeat without accepting unnecessarily harsh negative self-evaluations of yourself, and without allowing these negative self-evaluations to contaminate other areas of your confidence and your sense of self-esteem and of self-efficacy.

Regarding both the internal and external elements of surrender, it is useful to formally and respectfully acknowledge both to yourself and to others that you have surrendered, and that the battle is over. Such formal surrender provides private and public closure to the battle, and permits the period of readjustment to your new life to begin. After a relationship has ended (or the idealized "image" of the relationship has died after the discovery of infidelity), some people benefit from a private symbolic funeral service. There the they can "bury" the ended relationship (or old valued image of the relationship), which furthers their grieving process and the adjustments to their new life.

An important aspect of mental health is the ability to surrender successfully and gracefully to the inevitable defeats that life has in store for all of us. For the renowned psychiatrist Carl Jung, the goal of psychotherapy was to start the patient on a life of "normal disillusionment." Sometimes people get just what they don't want (e.g., cancer, AIDS, heart attacks). The acceptance of failure needs to be accomplished without inducing excessive despair in the patient.

Full acceptance of the situation is usually necessary before you can start to feel better. Some forms of psychotherapy require a full acceptance of the situation before a change for the better can occur. Acceptance of the situation might feel uncomfortable, but it will not kill you. As the philosopher Nietzsche said, "That which does not kill me makes me stronger." Sometimes, in people with Love Trauma Syndrome, attempts at acceptance are "pulsed," that is, they are only intermittently attempted at first, and are gradually increased. The acceptance of the defeat should never be accompanied by an excessive reduction in self-esteem. However, some humility is allowed.

The Taoist symbol of the "yin–yang" is often useful in helping people understand how to master the art of surrender. The yin–yang symbol contains two intermixing teardrop shapes (see Figure 8.1).

One of the teardrops is dark, whereas the other is light. The yin and yang represent the balance between pairs of opposites. Defeat and victory are examples of such opposites. Within the dark teardrop is a small light area, and within the light teardrop is a small dark area. Applying the principles of the yin–yang to the defeat of love trauma—within defeat there is

Figure 8.1 *The yin-yang symbol.*

some victory, and within victory there is some defeat. For the person who surrenders, they must find the victory that has been won. They must seek "victory through surrender."

This victory is often hidden, and the nature of victory can surface unexpectedly. For instance, one patient of mine whose husband had recently had an affair could see no possible victory in this loss. She told me that she thought the exercise was ridiculous. However, just 2 weeks after she discovered her husband's infidelity, her sister called and described a similar situation with her husband. The patient noticed how much more sensitive she was to her sister's pain, and they grew much closer together. "Yes, Dr. Rosse," she later said to me. "There was some good that came out of it. I felt much more empathic with my sister, much more human and humble."

One victory that can always be gleaned from defeat is what you can learn from the defeat. Defeats should always be viewed as learning experiences. This is the gift of defeat and trauma. If you cannot see what can be learned from a defeat or trauma and how you can be made stronger, you should seek counseling to help you with this task.

Part of the art of surrender involves using the sickening associated with the defeat and trauma to help you readjust to your new role. During this readjustment, you need to be able to halt any dramatic descent into an unnecessarily low mood or an overly sickened state. The art of surrendering involves not allowing yourself to be too sickened by defeats, and to accept defeats as a normal part of life. Attempting to defend against all defeat and failure is a position that cannot be held forever. Trying to do so will exhaust and deplete you. Some defeat is inevitable. We will all be wounded from time to time.

After a love trauma I will sometimes guide patients through accepting their love trauma wound. It is often useful to allow the patient to cry about the love trauma event, as some might have never done so, even though it has profoundly affected their emotional lives. I might even have them visualize the site of their love trauma on their body to make the trauma more tangible, to create a place where they can hold onto it, cradle it, and soothe it. Some choose the wound to be on their belly, some choose their heart, some choose their genitals, and others choose a location in their head. Some choose multiple sites. I have them think of accepting their wound. I have had patients fall out of the chair and onto their hands and knees, sobbing in pain. Some will cry for a few minutes. Others cannot cry, although I might encourage them to moan to help them fully conjure up the pain.

However, as a therapist I do not allow the wound to completely over-whelm patients—that is, to paralyze them. If I have to help them to get up from the floor after a few minutes I will. The wound cannot be overly indulged. People must be made to focus on their vision for a happy and healthy future, and to act to realize the vision.

In chronic love-trauma-related pain, some of us remain focused and preoccupied by our wounds and remain crippled by their effects. Others are more accepting of their wounded fates and try to adapt. Some wounds heal more easily than others. The lucky ones among us are able to disregard their wounds and carry on undisturbed by their defeats. However, the wounds from love trauma usually can heal, and should be encouraged to do so.

I Can't Stand It

Some people in the midst of a Love Trauma Syndrome find their distress unbearable. They want the pain to go away, and they worry that the pain might destroy them. They do not want to have to stand it. They want it to "just go away"—but it won't.

People often benefit from accepting that they have Love Trauma Syndrome, and accept the fact that they are temporarily injured. Many do not want to accept the idea that they are so vulnerable. People can sometimes advance their recovery by simply accepting and fully experiencing their Love Trauma Syndrome—without being so focused on changing the situation or "making it all go away."

People do not have to accept their love trauma and subsequent Love Trauma Syndrome all at once. They can do it incrementally. For instance, you can ask yourself how much—as a percentage of the love trauma and of the syndrome—could you accept at this point. If you can accept 0%, then you have a long way to go in terms of coming to some acceptance. But as you become willing to accept small portions at a time, even if it is 1%, or 10%, you are moving in the right direction. You do not have to accept it 100%. What is most important is seeing that you can survive the syndrome, even when you imagine the worst.

It is understandable that many of us do not want to accept having been struck with a Love Trauma Syndrome, and simply want it to go away as soon as possible. It is permissible to have this "I can't stand it" style of thinking. But everyone has their cross to bear, and at this time, if you have Love Trauma Syndrome, this is your cross. We all don't want to have to bear our crosses, but we have to just the same. We might as well accept it. You can learn to run with it, and even be happy with it. With time it will become lighter and lighter, to the point that you won't even notice it.

Relax!

As already discussed in previous chapters, Love Trauma Syndrome can be associated with considerable dysphoric arousal, anxiety, and agitation. In order to target the symptoms of hyperarousal and anxiety associated with Love Trauma Syndrome, another focus of the self-help literature designed to help people handle their emotional overstimulation advocates periods of escape through rest and relaxation.

There are a wide variety of techniques for "de-stressing," reducing hyperarousal, and achieving relaxation. These techniques range from breathing exercises, to muscle relaxation strategies, various forms of meditation, and Yoga. Any strategy that reduces the stress experience will help you break free of some of the pain associated with Love Trauma Syndrome. The reduction of anxiety helps the syndrome victim be less distressed.

It is wise to retreat from the stress and hyperarousal of Love Trauma Syndrome for short periods to allow your mind and your body time to recuperate. You owe it to yourself to periodically disengage from your daily love-trauma-related distress. Retreat also allows you to reassess your strategies for handling your condition. Religious people will remind you that God is described in the Bible as having worked 6 days and having rested on the 7th day. Even God retreated and rested. He also commanded us to rest and be with Him on the Sabbath.

Indeed, relaxation is a helpful form of retreat. You can try a simple relaxation/meditation exercise and see what effect such retreat has on your Love Trauma Syndrome. Sit in a comfortable chair, ideally one with armrests on which you can rest your arms and hands. Attain a comfortable position in the chair, close your eyes, and place both of your feet flat on the floor. By placing both of your feet flat on the floor, this will permit you to maximally relax the muscles of your legs and feet. Relax the muscles of your jaw by unclenching your teeth so that your upper and lower teeth are separated slightly.

You should also relax the muscles of your shoulders by letting your shoulders drop. You should not hold your shoulders up at all; they should be relaxed and lowered. Breathe in slowly by expanding the muscles of your abdomen to let the breath in, and then breathe out slowly by letting the muscles of your abdomen relax. Some people find it useful to gently massage the muscles of their abdomen to help release some tension there and to permit easier deep breathing. You should inhale slowly from your abdomen for a relaxed count of six (i.e., "1,2,3,4,5,6"), and breathe out also for a slow count of six. Allow yourself to yawn periodically if you can. Just focus on how relaxed you feel.

You should try to do this relaxation/meditation exercise for about 10 to 20 minutes. After you finish meditating, you should give yourself a few moments before becoming fully active again. If you have less than 10 minutes to do this relaxation/meditation exercise, that will be sufficient, as some retreat is better than none. You should not do this full exercise while you are driving or doing anything else that requires you to be attentive. By practicing relaxation exercises, you allow yourself to experience the feeling of retreat (or attempts at retreat) from your Love-Trauma-Syndrome-associated pain.

Being in the Now

Additionally, it is useful while doing the relaxation meditation to "stay in the present moment." To accomplish this, some people like to use any of the following mantras (or similar mantras), such as "I am in the present," or "I remain in the present," or "this moment." Again, the mantra is repeated over and over silently to oneself. Others simply practice "breathing observation," whereby they listen to the sound of their breathing, or feel their breath moving in and out of their nostrils, or feel the breath moving in and out of their abdomen with the movements of their diaphragms.

Staying in the present moment is often hard for someone with Love Trauma Syndrome, as they have a tendency to want to view their life through events of the past—sometimes the distant past (years or decades ago). Understand that it takes practice to learn to live life in the present, and meditation is a good place to start to learn this important aspect of good mental (and physical) health. People with Love Trauma Syndrome often resist attempts to have them live in the present, and they easily slip back into experiencing their whole lives through their painful past. You should not be too discouraged if you cannot achieve this state of mind quickly—it sometimes takes a lot of practice. Interestingly, some people report acquiring the ability to "be in the present" suddenly after a life transforming revelation or insight.

One meditation exercise useful for getting you to be in the present involves your taking notice of things in your meditation environment. Try to focus on the sounds and smells around you, and on the feeling of your buttocks and back against the chair. Try to experience "the now" as fully as possible. See the world through the present, not the past.

The Use of Mantras

Relaxation and retreat meditation usually emphasizes the use of certain words or phrases (i.e., mantras) repeated to yourself silently while meditating. The use of these words or phrases provides some cognitive focus that helps prevent shifting your attention from relaxation to distressing problems. Aside from the mantras described previously, another useful mantra that can be used is "retreat from pain."

During your meditation, when a love-trauma-related thought or feeling or other stressor breaks into your awareness, you can counter the stress by silently uttering the phrase "retreat from pain." This allows you to mentally pull back from the stressor that has intruded into your consciousness. The retreat mantra helps you to less fully engage the stressor with your mind and your body. Of course, there are many other mantras that can be used, including such statements to yourself as "let go," "into the hands of God," or combined as "let go into the hands of God." Other mantras include any of the statements described earlier in this chapter that are used to neutralize the sickening effects of your love trauma. You can also develop your own mantra that best fits your situation. Other meditation concentration aids include focusing on visual stimuli (e.g., a burning candle), somatic sensations (e.g., your breathing or the feeling of your buttocks against the chair), or imagined images (as described in the following section, "There's a place for us").

It is important to realize that as you meditate, you cannot always expect total disengagement from your love-trauma-related problems. Early relaxation therapy involves evaluation of just how much disengagement you can achieve. You take what you can get, and slowly work your way up to achieve a fuller disengagement. Do not expect perfection immediately—accept progress, no matter how little. If you find that there are some memories, thoughts, or feelings from which your mind or your body will not let you escape, you might want to seek psychotherapy to help evaluate and treat the problem.

There's a Place for Us

There are people who augment their relaxation by imagining that they have retreated to a place where they have felt particularly safe and relaxed in the past. This could be a prized garden, a place by the seashore, or some mountain retreat. Ideally it would be someplace not tainted by love-trauma-related associations. If people cannot remember such a place, I have them try to invent such a place in their imagination. By imagining themselves in these special environments, they can activate memories that support a mental state of calmness, peace, and transcendence.

The Mind and the Body Rebel

Some patients who try to temporarily withdraw from their Love-Trauma-Syndrome-associated pain by practicing relaxation exercises find it difficult to disengage from love-trauma-related ideas, thoughts, fantasies, and memories while they relax and meditate. When they close their eyes and try to relax, thoughts, feelings, and images related to their love trauma keep coming into their mind.

"When I try to relax, Dr. Rosse," one patient recently told me, "my problem keeps coming back at me. I think about my wife and I get butterflies in my stomach and all nervous." Another patient told me that it was as if his "brain was protesting" during attempts at relaxation. He thought that his brain wanted him to think continuously and to try to work out his relationship problem. "It's as if my mind is trying to figure everything out, and it doesn't want to lose any time doing it."

Anxiety associated with attempts at relaxation is called *relaxation-induced anxiety* (RIA). In fact, such initial flooding of thoughts, feelings, and images related to your problems is not uncommon when relaxation exercises are first started. Some patients have to tolerate their initial RIA, and need to continue to try to relax while they "cook off" their RIA. Some patients will even experience some desensitization to their love trauma by doing this. They are usually able to reach a point where their anxiety dissipates and they can relax. This can take from a few minutes to weeks or months to be fully successful. Withdrawal from love trauma can be difficult, and it can almost seem as if your brain is "stuck in the mud," as one patient described it to me. Your brain does not want to let down its guard. Obviously, patients with Love Trauma Syndrome who find relaxation intolerable should not be compelled to do it.

The Key to Relaxing

Aside from physical pain and discomfort, the root causes of your distress are your desires for dominance, control, and defense of your self-esteem. Once you relax your need for dominance and for control, and decrease your need to compulsively defend your self-esteem, you help release your stress. Too many people want to dominate and control all of the aspects of their lives. They also want to control the people in their lives—the people whom they love. However, it cannot be done. Life is too complex for all of its aspects to be controlled. People who overcontrol their lives end up not really living life—they end up just trying to control it. You have to release your grasp somewhat in order to live.

We have a compulsive need to set up the environment so that things go our way. We want to control the environment so it makes us feel dominant and important. Most of us accept failure and subordinance only under duress. Some people refer to the need for feeling important, dominant, and in control as "egotism." Those who try to escape from the gravity of this egotism often find themselves being pulled back into its orbit. The person becomes trapped by an ancient brain programming not of their choosing, a programming that fosters a need for dominance and control over potential rewards and punishments in the environment.

Feeling Safe Again

One of the aims of treating people with Love Trauma Syndrome is to help them to feel "safe" again. In Love Trauma Syndrome, the brain alarm systems located in the limbic system are stuck in the "on" position. Your brain detects some danger to your love interest and activates the alarms, even though there is nothing there, or there is nothing you can do about it anymore. Relaxation exercises might be able to help diminish your hyperarousal from the activation of these brain alarms. Interestingly, the alarm systems can be turned down (and often off) by certain psychotropic medications, such as antianxiety medications (e.g., buspirone [Buspar]) and antidepressants (e.g., fluoxetine [Prozac], sertraline [Zoloft], or paroxetine [Paxil]). However, it usually takes weeks for antianxiety medications such as buspirone or antidepressants to have a clearly demonstrable subjective effects on these alarms. Some of these medications are discussed more fully in the next chapter.

Getting Away from it All

Some people search for a geographical escape from the environment with which they associate the love trauma. They want to find a new environment with fewer love-trauma-associated cues. Some people might want to escape only briefly (e.g., by taking a vacation). However, others look for more long-term solutions to reduce their exposure to these cues.

Improving Yourself

Anything which will improve your skills and competencies and heightens your self-esteem should help reduce some of the pain of Love Trauma Syndrome. Some classic strategies for improving self-esteem and competencies are going to school or taking training classes. The involvement in these activities will help distract you from your love-trauma-related thoughts and will also improve your mastery and skills and raise your sense of resource holding potential (RHP).

For instance, you might take computer classes so that you will feel more confident when you are working with computers. If you are an auto mechanic, you might go to school to learn to improve your skills at repairing cars. If you want to be a better tennis player, you might take tennis lessons. Good training with a good and nonsadistic teacher can be a tremendous confidence and self-esteem builder. If the teacher appears cruel or potentially sadistic, get out of the class if you have a significant Love Trauma Syndrome. You do not need to be knocked down any more than you have been.

Learning and developing skills "reprograms" your memory so you can replace memories of "I can't do that" with "Yes, I can do that." It also helps counter the malignant spread of Love-Trauma-Syndrome-related decreased self-esteem and negative self-evaluation to other arenas of your life (e.g., work, academics, hobbies). Learning new skills and improving the skills you already have helps bolster your self-esteem, and the increased confidence can also spill over into other areas of your life. One important overall theme for treating Love Trauma Syndrome is to improve your self-esteem in as many ways as possible. and acquiring new skills, and making yourself feel more confident is a good way to start.

Tapping into "Universal Themes"

The entertainment media is filled with songs and movies about almost every nuance of love trauma. Just turn on any radio station where popular songs are played, and you will hear lyrics filled with descriptions of the pain of love. In fact, I have had patients who feel that they "cured" themselves of their Love Trauma Syndrome by carefully listening to popular music lyrics. I asked one patient who felt alone with his Love Trauma Syndrome to listen more carefully to the lyrics of the songs on the radio while he worked out in the gym. "Gosh, I didn't realize that so many of these songs are about what I'm going through. I guess lots of us are in the same boat." I called it his "music therapy."

Other art forms can have a curative effect on Love Trauma Syndrome. For instance, many stories, be they in books, in movies, or in television shows, are tales of how people experienced a love trauma and rose to overcome it. They were able to transcend their Love Trauma Syndromes and ultimately achieved greater happiness. By your involvement with the story, you vicariously undergo the release from the oppression of love trauma experienced by the characters.

In Search of Magic Potions

People are drawn to use a variety of substances to enhance their sense of well-being when they feel distressed or down. Caffeine-containing products (e.g., coffee, soft drinks, chocolate) and cigarettes are the predominant legal substances used. These substances can be employed in an effort to break free from the fatigue and ennui associated with Love Trauma Syndrome. However, cigarettes should be avoided because of their well-known and documented deleterious effects on your health. Caffeine-containing products should be used only in moderation—if at all. Although the stimulant effects of nicotine and caffeine will take you up for a short period of time, in the long run they will take you further down.

It is my recommendation that people with Love Trauma Syndrome avoid all use of addictive substances. Alcohol and illicit drugs of abuse such as cocaine or opiates should be absolutely shunned. There is much medical literature to support the notion that people who are in emotional distress are more prone to becoming addicted to substances of abuse. In fact, I have seen people fall into the trap of drug and alcohol addiction while suffering from a Love Trauma Syndrome.

The craving for addictive drugs is often best predicted by the intensity of the emotional distress that the addict is experiencing. For instance, the more stressed and anxious the addict is, the greater the craving. The greater the feelings of hopelessness that the addict reports, the greater the craving (and Love Trauma Syndrome can be associated with profound feelings of hopelessness).

This drug craving perpetuates future cycles of drug use. When the addict uses their drug of choice, they often crave relief from their emotional distress. The hope of many people who use addictive substances such as alcohol, cocaine, or heroin is that they will be able to overcome feelings such as fatigue, depression, hopelessness, anxiety, and emotional paralysis.

People often use food as a way of diminishing their emotional distress. For some people, certain foods (e.g., high-carbohydrate sweets, cookies, cakes) can improve their mood and decrease their anxiety. In the context of a Love Trauma Syndrome, their appetite and cravings for such foods increase. Consequently, they can begin to lose control of their weight, and might even develop eating disorders such as bulimia. People with a Love Trauma Syndrome should carefully monitor their appetite and watch their eating habits to ensure that they do not eat too much (and gain excessive amounts of weight) or eat too little (and lose weight). Some patients with a Love Trauma Syndrome might benefit from joining a formal diet program, where their food intake and weight can be carefully monitored. Such programs usually include monitoring of the emotional triggers for excessive food intake.

There is a growing interest in the use of various vitamin and herbal preparations to improve people's mood and to help them better deal with stress. I have had patients tell me that using some of these preparations while suffering from the effects of a Love Trauma Syndrome has helped them to feel better. They are convinced that these vitamins and natural herbal supplements have helped them to overcome some of the sickening effects of Love Trauma Syndrome. "You need to be as good to yourself as you can," one patient told me. In fact, the use of vitamins and herbs should help to maximize your body's ability to ward off some stress-induced physiological changes.

Practice Good Sleep Hygiene

Many people with Love Trauma Syndrome have difficulty sleeping. They might have difficulty initiating sleep, where it can take hours to fall asleep. Conversely, they might have difficulty remaining asleep—what doctors call middle insomnia or early morning awakening (EMA). Middle insomniacs wake up in the early morning hours (e.g., one or two o'clock in the morning) after sleeping only a few hours, and it might take them an hour or two to fall back asleep. The person with EMA might fall asleep at 11:00 p.m. or midnight, but awaken an hour or two later (i.e., in the early morning hours), unable to fall back asleep at all. People with EMA have difficulty resuming sleep even though they have slept for only a few hours and still feel tired. Whatever sleep insomniacs do get, they often describe it as "fitful" and "not enough." When they get up in the morning, they feel tired. Sleep researchers describe the sleep of these individuals as "nonrestorative."

After a love trauma event, or with the exacerbation of a Love Trauma Syndrome, people need to be attentive to their sleep hygiene. One important aspect of proper sleep hygiene in the context of a love trauma stress is to not allow yourself to lie awake in bed for more than 20 to 30 minutes without falling asleep. If you toss and turn for more than 30 minutes, your brain begins to learn that the bed is not a place where you can sleep well. You develop what is called *conditioned insomnia,* or *chronic psychophysiologic insomnia.* Your brain becomes conditioned to not being able to sleep in your bed.

After 20 to 30 minutes of tossing and turning in your bed and being unable to reinitiate sleep, you should get up out of bed and engage in some other quiet activity (e.g., reading a relaxing, inspirational book, watching a relaxing television show, listening to gentle music on the radio, or having a small nighttime snack). Exercise typically is not recommended as it is too invigorating. You should engage in these gentle activities until you feel tired again. When you feel tired again and think that you might be able to fall asleep, you can then return to your bed. If you still have difficulty falling asleep after 20 to 30 minutes, you should again get up out of bed, engage in your quiet activities, and wait again until you feel tired enough that you stand a good chance of falling asleep in bed. This way your brain learns to associate the bed with sleeping, rather than with being aroused, awake, and unhappy.

Another important aspect of sleep hygiene is to only allow yourself a definite "window" during which you can sleep (e.g., between 10:00 p.m.

and 7:00 p.m.). Naps during the day are prohibited, as each nap will make it more difficult to achieve restful sleep during the night. Patients who are unable to sleep well during the night will often complain that they need to take naps—but they do so at the cost of a restful night's sleep.

Other important sleep hygiene tips are to not drink any caffeinated beverages after about four in the afternoon—or even earlier for some individuals. It is often best to cut out all caffeinated drinks until the insomnia is resolved. Smoking cigarettes around the time of sleep can also disrupt nighttime sleep patterns. Cigarette smokers who experience Love Trauma Syndrome often increase their cigarette consumption, resulting in higher blood nicotine levels and an increased need to consume more cigarettes. The higher amounts of nicotine in the blood result in a disrupted sleep pattern.

Whereas some people with Love Trauma Syndrome are unable to sleep for an adequate period (called *hyposomnia*), for others Love Trauma Syndrome is accompanied by people wanting to sleep too much (called *hypersomnia*). Some hypersomniacs sleep over 12 hours a day. Such people can find that their sleep patterns change dramatically—they might end up sleeping 12 hours during the day, and staying up much of the night. People with hypersomnia who experience shifts in the sleep–wake cycle need to establish for themselves a clear sleep window (e.g., between 10:00 p.m. and 7:00 a.m.), and to not allow themselves to sleep before or after their window. They should be encouraged to get up and become active after 8 to 9 hours of sleep.

Love Trauma Syndrome can also be associated with a greater frequency of upsetting dreams and nightmares related to the love trauma event. The dreams are often frightening and upsetting, and also can be described as "odd" and leaving the dreamer with a "funny, uneasy" feeling. Many people are unable to fall back asleep easily after such dreams. The person should get up out of bed, engage in some gentle activity, and return to the bed after he or she feels tired again and perhaps feels ready to fall back asleep.

For some people with Love Trauma Syndrome, their sleep becomes seriously disrupted for long periods of time. They develop a chronic insomnia associated with a dysphoric arousal that is difficult for them to control on their own. Such people need to see a physician (preferably a psychiatrist) who could help them with their insomnia and restore some of the quality into these patients' lives. Sometimes the insomnia is related to a depression that has become superimposed on the Love Trauma Syndrome, and appropriate antidepressant medications are needed to restore a normative sleep pattern.

The Search for Rebirth and Renewal

Some people find it difficult to recover from a love trauma. An example of how rebirth and renewal is possible after a love trauma is illustrated by the case of a 77-year-old man. This patient had a dream that provided him with a transcendent and transforming experience. His love trauma had cast a spell on him for decades—his dream and reconnection with his faith in God helped liberate him from the pain of compound love traumas.

In his dream, he saw a robed man with long hair. The man appeared before him, and the patient said, "I could just feel his tremendous kindness and compassion." The patient kneeled before the man, wondering if the man was Jesus. The man touched the patient's head, and the patient described feeling calm and at peace. "My bitterness vanished. I felt like I had been healed," he said. He found himself invigorated and wanting to go to church—something he had not done in years. He became interested in reading the Bible.

The patient had a transcendent experience associated with a dream that transformed him. When I asked him what happened to him, he said, "I don't know what happened. I just know something happened." The experience had an ineffable quality, which is a common feature of transcendent phenomena. The dream allowed him to no longer look at his life through his sad past, but to face life in the present.

In fact, dreams can be a source of transcendent experience over misery and sadness. During my years as a psychiatrist, I have had several patients relate dreams to me that gave them the strength to handle severe disappointments, losses, and other difficult health and life situations. Sometimes the renewal and rebirth that can be offered by a dream can best be unleashed when working with someone experienced in dream interpretation. In this case, the patient needed no such assistance.

Finally, there are many other ways to achieve renewal and rebirth. You do not need to have a profound and transforming dream. Just applying many of the principles set forth in this chapter are sufficient to start you on the road to renewal and rebirth into happiness.

Vision Work: Replacing Love Trauma Syndrome Pain with a
Positive Vision

One of the most important interventions for overcoming Love
Trauma Syndrome is to develop a vision of what you want for yourself
now and in the future. Vision work allows you to focus on the present and
the future, rather than only on the past. It allows you to turn your back on
a painful past, and to move forward toward new possibilities for yourself
and for your family. The vision you choose must be based on reasonable
available choices.

Vision work is based on the concept that life must go on. Even if you
have to move toward your vision on your hands and knees because you're
in so much pain, that is what you need to do. This vision work includes accepting the reality of the love trauma as much as you can for now, putting
your love trauma "baggage" in the trunk for now, and becoming active in
realizing your vision.

Although people should be encouraged to accept reality as it is, this is
sometimes difficult because of the sickening feelings that often accompany
attempts at accepting the love trauma. However, most people can "bite the
bullet" and achieve some degree of acceptance. It is sometimes useful to
set some time aside to grieve the loss of love and the love trauma event.
People often find it useful to cry about the loss. However, fully accepting
and experiencing the pain will not always make it go away. Catharsis does
not always release all of the pain. It can persist despite your best efforts at
acceptance.

One of the greatest problems with vision work in the context of Love
Trauma Syndrome is the tendency for the vision work to be overcome by
thoughts, images, feelings, and fantasies related to past events. These phenomena related to the past are toxic to vision work and to the execution of
the vision work plan. When engaged in vision work, it is best to "remain
in the moment," or remain centered in the present. Nothing can be done
about the past.

Many patients complain that they "feel too badly" to engage in any
vision work. Additionally, often as a consequence of a love trauma, self-
esteem has taken a hit, and the energy and the will to change things dissipates. However, you do not need to wait until you feel completely better
to move on with your life, as you might wait a lifetime before moving on.

Some of the sickening and upsetting feelings you have with Love
Trauma Syndrome are deeply embedded, automatic reactions in the more

primitive part of your emotional brain (i.e., the limbic system). It might take some time for this primitive reflexive emotional reaction to settle down. You need to accept the fact that you will not necessarily be feeling your best for a while, but you still can perform either academically, at your job, or with your family despite your Love Trauma Syndrome. People often have the expectation of "emotional perfectionism," that is, the expectation that they should feel good all of the time. In fact, we are often possessed by unpleasant emotions, especially in the context of a Love Trauma Syndrome. You can usually function anyway. You need to develop and grab on to your vision and move on, adjusting your vision periodically if necessary. It is often useful to write down just what your vision is, and watch it develop as time goes on.

People should not allow themselves to wallow in their Love Trauma Syndrome misery. When people find themselves trapped in distressing love-trauma-related thoughts or memories, they should shout to themselves, "Vision!" They should try to displace the distressing thoughts with the vision as much as possible. They should not expect that they will be able to displace all of their love-trauma-related thoughts—this will take time, and they will be able to handle an occasional minor flare-up here and there. The key concept here is to replace the love trauma pain with a vision for the future, and to develop a plan to actively realize that vision.

You should first try to develop a simple *vision statement* for yourself. For instance, your vision might be "I want to have a warm and loving relationship with my spouse," "I want to be able to be friends with my spouse (or ex-spouse)," "I want to continue to have a loving relationship with my husband and children," or "I want to be able to love, and be happy and healthy." A simple vision is one that can be easily grabbed when you are being inundated with upsetting love-trauma-related thoughts and fantasies (see Table 8.1). Some patients include in their vision work statements regarding their wanting to refresh or change their appearance by having plastic surgery (e.g., face-lifts, tummy-tucks, breast augmentation) as they follow their vision to feel better about themselves. They treat themselves to makeovers, expensive hair salons, massages, and expensive cosmetics.

Part of vision work is "following your bliss." You need to define your bliss. What do you want to emphasize in your life: is it love, family, friends, work, helping others, or spirituality? Or do you have a number of goals? You do not need to be restricted to one vision for yourself.

Table 8.1 Other Sample Vision Statements

I want to live and love untainted by traumas of the past.
I want to remain healthy and alive and capable of loving others.
I want to remain friendly with my previous mate, who is a parent to my children.
I want to enjoy life, music, art, and love. I want to dance.
I want to help other people.
I want to be loving and supportive to my family and my children.
I want to be able to love and enjoy my family and all of the wonderful little things that they do.
I want to be able to appreciate all of the miracles in my life (no matter how small).
I want to return to a loving and sexually satisfying relationship with my partner.
I want to have a fuller religious and spiritual life.
I want to be able to keep up with my work and my career.
I want to keep up with my classes.
I want to be able to balance my love life and my work life.
I want to be able to balance my academic life with my social life.
I want my love relationships to be romantic.
I want to feel healthy.
I want to grow emotionally and spiritually.

However, you need to follow your bliss (or blisses), rather than your agony (or agonies).

As alluded to previously, the vision does not have to be simple, or involve just a single element. In fact, many of my patients develop elaborate visions for themselves, which include their exercising, stopping their smoking or drinking, losing weight, feeling physically and emotionally better, or becoming rich! Some people say that it was the love trauma that became their catalyst for change. They were able to grab victory out of the jaws of defeat.

Love trauma victims should be persuaded over and over again to focus more on their vision of what they want to achieve than to concentrate on the emotional consequences of their love trauma. In this way, people are encouraged to overcome their tendencies toward Love-Trauma-Syndrome-induced passivity. Hold on to your vision and embrace love.

Throwing Out the Brain Trash

Much of the pain we feel after a love trauma (and sometimes long after a love trauma) is automatically offered to us by our brains because some ancient (i.e., millions of years old) brain program has been triggered. It is triggered because our brain is concerned that our genetic material's chances of making it into future generations is somehow in danger.

When the brain alarms are triggered:

1. Your brain wants you back in control of your love life. And sometimes it does not care how you get the control back, as long as you get it back. It might have you mount frightening intimidation displays to regain control. It might even have you injure or even kill your love in order to get back control over your mate. For some reason the brain just wants control back at any cost. It's brain trash! (Some call it "stinkin' thinking.") The brain trash might have served an important function in our ancient ancestral past—i.e., to get our genes propagated into future generations. But it does not need to apply to the current situation.

2. Your brain tries to convince you that the past love trauma event is somehow still relevant to your current life situation—even when it clearly is not. Your brain registers a threat—now probably largely imagined.

3. Your brain thrusts in your face all sorts of painful thoughts, memories, fantasies, and images that are no longer relevant to your life. It is forced to process old painful memories and images over and over in an attempt to figure out what happened—so it won't happen again. Remember, your brain wants you to keep that genetic material "trucking" into perpetuity. You are being kept on guard.

This happens because your brain takes no chances when it comes to trying to pass on your genes into the future. In chapter 2, I described emotions as highly evolved brain and body mechanisms that motivate the execution of certain behaviors that serve to promote the survival of our genes into future generations. We have evolved with brain mechanisms that assess dangers to our genetic material automatically, beneath our conscious awareness. The triggering of the alarms in your brain is often quite illogical, and old traumas can trigger the alarms and make you feel that your love interest is threatened when it really is not.

Again, your brain is more interested in trying to guarantee your being able to pass your genes into posterity than in your being happy. It will often stir up quite a bit of unhappiness to guarantee the safe passage of your genetic material. It often has little interest in holding onto love (and happiness)—it is willing to drown the love with pain and unhappiness. The brain trash is heaped upon us even long after the love trauma event and even after the situation that produced the trauma is resolved. Brain trash poisons love and happiness.

However, we have an interest in holding onto love. We also have a right to be happy. We have a greater interest in holding onto love than in holding onto some ancient brain program solely concerned with the safe passage of our genes. Unfortunately, this brain program keeps heaping the pain and unhappiness upon us. I sometimes refer to this pain as brain trash. Brain trash raises your arousal level, and it makes you agitated and feel that something is wrong when it really is not. Included in this brain trash are the love-trauma-related intrusive painful feelings, thoughts, memories, fantasies, and other elaborations. The brain trash also includes love-trauma-related anger and the desire to punish and subjugate.

If O.J. Simpson killed his wife and Ronald Goldman, it was brain trash that caused him to do it. If he did commit the murders, then it can be said that his life was ruined by his brain trash—his desire to control Nicole at any cost. His brain wanted to control her, and it came up with the ridiculous—and tragic—solution of killing her to regain control. Just as it possibly ruined O.J.'s life and love—and the lives and loves of countless others—it can also ruin yours. You need to rebel against the brain trash.

All of the temptations to indulge in self-destructive behaviors in the context of a Love Trauma Syndrome are resistible. Although you might be inclined to "act out" some of these impulses, you are not predetermined to do so. You can curse your brain trash aloud and silently to yourself. People tend to overvalue their brain trash (because it feels so important). It needs to devalued—it's trash! Throw it out. Throw it out now! You have to fight the brain trash, as it's only going to pull you down.

Try cursing at your brain trash for a few minutes and see how it makes you feel (but don't get carried away and hurt yourself). Throw away the brain trash, and hold on to your desire to love again. Some patients like to "scream" silently to themselves "brain trash!" when their minds begin to engage thoughts, feelings, memories, or fantasies that make them feel unhappy.

Again, your brain is less interested in your being happy—and more interested in your genes (and not someone else's) making it into the future. In Love Trauma Syndrome, the brain does not want you to "give up" these people with whom you are in love—even though they treated you badly. In such cases, your brain liked something about these people—they were for some reason viewed by your brain as good for the propagation of your genes. You have to stop the brain trash, which almost always represents an exaggerated response to what is in reality a trivial provocation that is no longer worthy of brain processing. It is certainly not worth your being made miserable by it.

One patient whose wife had been unfaithful to him decided to stay with her because he loved her. She had recommitted to him and asked his forgiveness. His wife said she had made a mistake, and that it would not happen again. Although he did lose some trust in her, he was able to forgive her for her betrayal. "I just realized that it didn't make sense to continue to be so upset about her affair. She has told me that it would not happen again, and I believe her. I wasn't going to let the feelings ruin my marriage. I still love her, and I'm not going to give her up because of some brain trash. I'm not going to let my brain push me around. I fought the war [against her rival] and I won her back. Now I'm going to enjoy it."

This patient was also able to laugh at his brain trash. "Whenever I just see that old brain trash coming at me I just have to laugh," he told me. "The other day we [my patient and his wife] drove by a Wendy's. I knew that's where they would sometimes meet [his wife and her lover], and I started getting all upset. I felt myself getting all tense, irritable, and ready to pounce on her. She put her hand on my shoulder, and I was ready to throw it off of me, and tell her to 'Get off bitch!' But then I just shook my head and laughed. My wife asked me what I was laughing about. I told her what you [I, his therapist] had said to me, that I was just 'a caveman driving a pickup truck.' She laughed too. And I told her not to go off and play any of those cavegirl tricks on me, and she said 'Oh, don't worry about that.' And I believe her."

Thought-Stopping Techniques

The intrusive thoughts, feelings, and memories often represent a "replaying" of the love trauma. This replaying is an attempt by the brain to figure out what happened, and how not to let it happen again. Sometimes, however, the brain will not quiet after long periods of replaying, and it is necessary to try to stop them using various thought-stopping techniques.

These are also a useful way to stop the brain trash from ruining your relationships. These thought-stopping techniques keep the brain trash from falling all over you. One popular thought-stopping technique is as follows: When you have an uncomfortable thought or fantasy related to the love trauma (e.g., the thought of your lover with someone else in bed), you simply snap a rubber band that you wear on your wrist. (If you let the rubber band strike the bottom of your hand rather than your wrist, it will hurt less.) You can also shout to yourself (or out loud) the word "Stop!" This is an especially good technique when you are in social situations and where using the rubber band technique would be awkward (i.e., shouting "stop: to yourself silently, not aloud).

Remember that indulging in love-trauma-related fantasies expands the love trauma and exacerbates the Love Trauma Syndrome. Some Love Trauma Syndromes are actually the result of an imagined love trauma. Many cases of Love Trauma Syndrome are exacerbated by these fantasies. The fantasies fuel the syndrome. The simple behavioral techniques described previously, when used consistently, can be remarkably effective for stopping unpleasant thoughts, recollections, and intrusive fantasies about the love trauma.

Do not expect these techniques to completely stop all your intrusive love-trauma-related thoughts. Accept partial success. Thought stopping is a skill not unlike learning to ride a bike—give yourself time to learn how to better stop unwanted thoughts. You should not be discouraged if your initial thought-stopping attempts seem to be no match for your preoccupations with your love trauma. Just steel yourself even more and do battle against the thoughts, memories, and fantasies.

In fact, I often recommend that you declare war against your upsetting love-trauma-related thoughts! I sometimes have patients imagine that they have an army of helpers dedicated to defeating and "sealing off" upsetting intrusive contemplation. This army is always ready at your command—and you should not forget to use them.

One patient told me that his imagined military army was transformed into an army of angels who swooped in to stop his negative love-trauma-related thoughts and reveries from getting out of hand. "Originally I had to summon them, my army," he said. He had a number of summoning cries, such as "My angels come forth," "God and my angels protect me," "My angels help," or "My angels attack." In his mind he envisioned the angels coming from all directions and containing his painful thinking and quieting his mind. "Eventually," he told me, "these angels often came into mind automatically at the onset of negative thoughts, and they even seemed to be able to anticipate my going into these negative reveries before they happened." The arrival of his "angels," and his use of their power, eventually was associated with a dramatic improvement in his quality of life and his Love Trauma Syndrome.

Following are the estimate of the percent penetration into consciousness graphs (see Figure 8.2); one showing the percentage before the introduction

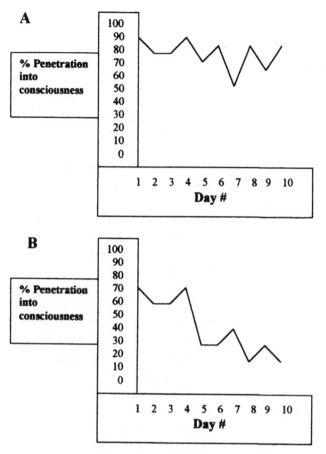

Figure 8.2   Introduction of thought-stopping techniques. A) Before the introduction of thought-stopping techniques B) After the introduction of thought-stopping techniques.

of thought-stopping techniques, the other showing it after their introduction. (Alternately, some patients like to graph the severity of their distress associated with their love-trauma-related thoughts on a 0–10 scale, with 10 being the worst distress, and 0 being an absence of distress.) As can be seen in the following graphs, after the use of thought-stopping techniques, the percent penetration into consciousness of love-trauma-related thoughts and fantasies dropped. Again, don't expect it to drop to 0% immediately. Finally, sometimes thought-stopping techniques become more effective when combined with "antiobsessional" medications such as sertraline (Zoloft) or fluoxetine (Prozac). This is discussed more extensively in the next chapter.

Switching Focus

Another important group of thought-stopping techniques includes active attempts to switch your mental focus from the upsetting love-trauma-related thoughts to something else. This can include thoughts about your vision, or simply exercising, taking a walk, listening to music, washing the dishes, doing laundry, or engaging in a hobby.

It is also useful to be able to switch to your vision and to try to act on elements in it. For instance, if part of your vision is your becoming healthier and more active, you can shift your focus from upsetting intrusive and obsessional thoughts to exercising or taking a walk.

As described earlier, you should not indulge your love-trauma-related obsessional fantasies and thoughts. Although they represent an attempt to "figure things out" and solve the problem, they usually make things worse. Patients often experience an almost primal-like pain (as in Primal Scream therapy) when engaged in these fantasies and thoughts. Some patients experience some release from their pain after screaming and crying during the process.

Some people describe a bewitching quality to love-trauma-related obsessional fantasies and thoughts that makes it hard for them to resist the temptation to indulge in these ruminations. The temptation to indulge these thoughts and fantasies is not unlike the temptations of the Sirens of ancient Greek myth. The Sirens lined the shores of certain ocean passages, and the sweetness of their voices bewitched passing sailors, compelling them to land and meet their deaths. In fact, skeletons lay thickly strewn on these shores. Ulysses was able to pass the Sirens by stopping up the ears of his crew so they could not hear them. Ulysses had himself firmly bound to the mast of his ship, so when he heard the music of the Sirens he would not be able to act on following it. Similarly, must you bind yourself to the mast and not allow yourself to be tempted to engage and indulge the love-trauma-related thoughts and fantasies, which are toxic to your happiness and well-being.

Over time, with repeated and often compulsive (i.e., difficult to control) self-exposure to love-trauma-related thoughts, feelings, and fantasies (typically difficult to control), the intensity of the negative emotional response to the love-trauma-associated stimuli diminishes. This is called *desensitization*. Some people desensitize more quickly than others. However, in most individuals the impact of the love trauma begins to attenuate. This is often accompanied by a sense of "rebirth" and renewal (as long as significant depression has not also set in).

You might also want to figure out how the love trauma fits into the overall pattern and themes in your life by working with a trained psychotherapist. Very often the intensity of someone's Love Trauma Syndrome is related to how the love trauma resonates with other issues in their lives (e.g., low self-esteem, lack of confidence, mourning lost youth) that amplify the pain of the trauma. Love Trauma Syndrome strikes at core self-esteem and self-image issues that are often best addressed during professional psychotherapy. These other life issues that resonate (i.e., are connected) with the love trauma often benefit from the fuller exploration of issues that only psychotherapy (individual and/or group) can provide. Such psychotherapy can also help prevent the Love Trauma Syndrome from becoming complicated (e.g., by depression or substance or alcohol abuse).

Remember that your brain has as its overriding concern the survival of your genes into the future. Any imagined threat to this concern can jam up your brain's processing capabilities. It is as if your computer became infected by a virus and will no longer let any other programs run (or run properly). You need to try to think about what else you would be doing if you were not ruminating about the love trauma, and do it. Obsessing about your romantic failure is the "prepotent"—or most natural and powerful—brain activity. You need to try to resist or override the prepotent brain response. But it is often easier said than done.

Sometimes, when a person is depressed, the other things that they would be doing seem very unexciting and unappealing. As miserable as the person is while ruminating about their love-trauma, they are almost as miserable thinking about the other things that they would be doing. The person is unable to snap out of their profound "funk" on their own. They are down and negative about everything. In this situation, the person needs to seek professional help, and often needs to be put on some antidepressant medication.

"Let it Rain"

With everything I've said about not wallowing in your pain, some people still like to let themselves feel overrun by the pain of their love trauma, and they find it therapeutic. "Sometimes I like to let it rain," one patient who had recently discovered that his wife was having an affair told me. "And I know it won't rain forever," he said. "I used to try to hold it back, but it was no use. Sometimes it makes me feel more alive."

Other patients have described the phenomena of facing their pain head on as "confronting the dragon." When directly facing the dreaded painful memories, thoughts, feelings, fantasies, and images, the person is practicing what is called *response prevention*. During response prevention, the typically instinctive response of wanting to withdraw from the painful intrusions is blocked, and they allow themselves to face the pain head on. By doing so, they begin to desensitize themselves to the pain. It is often the beginning of healing for a person with Love Trauma Syndrome. As they face their pain head on, some people like to clutch tightly something soft, like a pillow or a cushion. They let the memories come on like a hard rain. Their tears often contribute to the wetness of the situation. Such experiences should not be allowed to go on forever—they should be time limited (e.g., an hour or two).

People who "let it rain" on themselves believe that they are better able to move toward acceptance of the love trauma by weathering the storm with the rain and the wind in their face. One of the tricks of preventing the process from going on and on is to release your anger toward those who have wronged you. Such release has a liberating effect. Simply accept the trauma—the wound—and experience the associated grief. Allow the natural grieving process to occur, which should diminish in intensity over time. Grief is a healing process. However, if the grieving becomes complicated by excessive symptoms of depression and anxiety, a professional therapist often needs to be involved in assessment and in treatment.

Counting Painful Intrusions

Some people find it useful to count the number of times painful love-trauma-related thoughts, feelings, memories, or images intrude into their consciousness. For some people I have suggested that they use a wrist golf counter to count their love-trauma-associated painful intrusions. They can record the number of thoughts that they have on a daily log sheet, and track the progression of their Love Trauma Syndrome. I tell people to not worry if they occasionally miss, or overcount, the number of painful intrusions that they have. The daily number does not have to be exact. It is not worth becoming overly obsessional. If they are in a situation where intrusions occur but they cannot push the counter (e.g., they are talking to someone), they can simply estimate the number of intrusions they experienced and push the counter multiple times when they can more comfortably input the intrusions.

One woman whose boyfriend of 3 years left her for another woman developed Love Trauma Syndrome. She had painful intrusive visions of her ex-boyfriend having sex with his current lover. She felt a mixture of different emotions, including sadness, jealousy, anger, vengeance and hurt. During the first few days when she used the counter for the intrusive sexual fantasy images, she had daily counts in the high 500 range. She was amazed at how much time she was putting into thinking about her ex-boyfriend. She wanted the intrusive thoughts to stop. Within 2 weeks, the number had dropped below 100.

The Utility of Exhaustion

As implied previously, most Love Trauma Syndromes (and exacerbations of the syndrome) resolve over time. There is a reason for the old saying, "Time heals all wounds." Often what happens is that the intrusive love-trauma-related replaying and reworking of memories begins to physically and emotionally exhaust the person. As described in an earlier chapter, there is a lot of energy locked up in a Love Trauma Syndrome, a "psychic storm" if you will. The energy of all storms eventually becomes depleted.

However, the person with a severe Love Trauma Syndrome need not fear exhaustion. It is often a passage—a temporary way station—on the way to recovery, rebirth, and renewal. After such a period of exhaustion, people report beginning to be able to "snap out of it" ("it" referring to their Love Trauma Syndrome). Again, if someone's exhaustion is persistent and interferes with their daily functioning over a prolonged period of time, the person should seek professional help (which might include the use of antidepressant medication).

However, the exhausted person should beware. The period of exhaustion can be dangerous, as they will be less attentive during physical activity and while operating mechanical devices such as a motor vehicle. The exhausted period is a time of accident proneness. While in this state, it is important to be extra good to yourself. Take more vacations, relax, and rejuvenate. Drive more slowly and carefully. Don't drive if you feel so exhausted that you won't be able to fully concentrate on your driving. Be on the lookout for driving situations that require extra attention, such as congested rush hour roads and highways. It is during Love Trauma Syndrome's period of exhaustion that people can get themselves accidently killed if they are not careful.[4]

Confusing Preferences With Needs

Many people confuse their preferences with their needs. For instance, instead of feeling that they would *prefer* to have a certain type of relationship, they feel that they need, should have, or must have it. Once people make this error in thinking—that is, thinking that they must have something—it reaches a level of importance in the brain that is very activating and arousing. If you experience the preference as a need as important as food, water, or air, then you begin to think if your preferences are not met, you will perish. However, you could survive without having your preferences satisfied.

For instance, while it might be your preference to not have an adulterous wife, it is not a need (although your brain might want to fool you into thinking it is a need for the sake of your genes). You can survive having had an adulterous wife (although you might choose to leave the relationship to find a more loyal mate who makes you feel better about yourself and your life). Needs that must be met for you to survive are inflexible; preferences can be modified and changed.

The Importance of Laughter and Smiling

Many people in the throes of a Love Trauma Syndrome stop laughing and smiling. However, this contributes to a wallowing response to a love trauma, and you should try to keep a sense of humor, and practice smiling. You should practice smiling as a self-help technique, maybe as often as every half-hour. Look in the mirror and try to smile. There are actually more muscles in the face involved in your frowning than there are in smiling. You need to overcome the more numerous muscles involved in frowning by forcing yourself to smile. One mood theory that has been discussed in respectable scientific publications (but is still somewhat difficult for me to accept) postulates that your facial expression controls blood flow to certain areas of your brain (Zajonc R.B., 1985). The theory further speculates that when you smile, you increase blood flow to the part of your brain involved in generating "happier" emotions. On the other hand, frowning reinforces the blood supply to brain areas that support unhappier feelings.

Regardless of the accuracy of this theory of emotional regulation, people often report that forcing themselves to smile helps them to feel better. Smiley faces as reminders to smile might be corny, but they help some individuals feel better. Finally, look for jokes that will make you laugh. The Internet has become a good place to find jokes. You can also try to make yourself laugh by watching comedies on television, or go to a comedy club and listen to a few good comedians try to make you laugh. Take it from me, a doctor—laughing is good medicine.

A Summary of Some Self-Help Methods for Breaking Free From the Pain of Love Trauma Syndrome

I provide this 30-point summary to emphasize some of the important self-help ideas described previously. Additionally, this might be a useful starting point for some people with Love Trauma Syndrome who are so upset and distracted that their ability to concentrate and read a book such as this one is compromised. They also might find it difficult to remember what they read, or to organize it in their minds so they can begin to use it. This summary is provided to help such people quickly get a sense of some of things they can do to help themselves recover.

1. *Commit to an active stance toward your Love Trauma Syndrome.* Resist the temptation to submit to the love-trauma-induced sickening and passively accept a "victim" status. Be active. Do things that are good for you—such as exercise, being with friends and family, going to museums or the movies—rather than sinking into the abyss of misery. Wallowing represents your brain being stuck. Do not wallow in your love-trauma-related miserable thoughts, feelings, memories, and fantasies. Post signs for yourself to remind yourself not to wallow. Get active. Some people put up signs in their office, using the abbreviation DNW for Do Not Wallow.

Of course, if the love trauma event was recent (e.g., you just discovered your lover had an affair, or died, or you are recently separated or divorced) there is a period of painful grieving through which you need to go. Even so, you cannot allow yourself to continue to be completely overcome with grief and pain after a few months following the event. Do not allow yourself to remain so grief stricken that you are not able to attend to your social, familial, and occupational obligations. If you wallow, it should only be for a short time following the event. I prefer a minimum of wallow time.

One of the problems with wallowing is that when people with Love Trauma Syndrome wallow, they tend to think frequently about the love trauma event. Remember that Love Trauma Syndrome is a disorder of remembering too much—and the more you think about the trauma, the more you reinforce the memory.

2. *Commit to a vision for the present and future, and work toward that vision.* You can change and modify your vision as time goes on.

3. *Move toward that vision no matter how badly you feel.* As they say in Alcoholics Anonymous, "Fake it till you make it."

4. *Let go of the pain of the past.* Live in the present. The love trauma becomes the central event of your past, present, and future life. The trauma must be put in its place—the past.

5. *You have the right to be happy.* Don't let the brain trash ruin it for you. Reject the brain trash. Brain trash is emotions, thoughts, feelings, and memories that have no real relevance to your current situation. It is simply your brain's ancient evolutionary programs overreacting to perceived threats—past, current, or future—to your ability to project your genetic material into the future. Who cares?! These ancient brain programs have little relevance to your present situation. You might not even want to propagate your genes! Remember that your brain is not interested in keeping you happy, but is more interested in keeping you distressed so you remain vigilant to potential threats to your genes.

6. *Embrace the gap between what you wanted in your love relationship and what you got.* You felt entitled to your partner fulfilling your needs, and your partner let you down. In reality, we really are entitled to nothing. Life is often unfair. Let your anger be replaced by disappointment in your partner, and begin to grieve the loss.

7. *Accept the fact that your love relationships are vulnerable to being violated or destroyed.* Destroy your myths of invulnerability! You can't be all things to people, even those whom you love the most. Myths of invulnerability often lie at the core of Love Trauma Syndrome. How can this happen to you? This should not happen to you! But why not? Do not expect perfection from yourself or from your loved ones.

8. *Accept the wound—it will not kill you.* You must not let it kill you! Grief over what you have lost (i.e., the wound) will not kill you—it will liberate you. You can stand it. Do not allow the wound to become infected and spread throughout your body, mind, and spirit, and overtake and destroy you. You can accept the wound, the defeat, without being harsh on yourself, and without negative self-evaluation. And try to stop being so upset about being so upset—it's OK that you are upset.

9. *Discover—search for—the benefits that you have gained from suffering the love trauma.* You must do this. For instance, if you had never experienced

a love trauma, you would not have learned all that you did by reading this book!

10. *Relax (or at least try).*   Meditate. Use self-hypnosis. People stricken with Love Trauma Syndrome often benefit from using the phrase "Do not wallow" as their mantra which they repeat to themselves as they meditate.

11. *If your Love Trauma Syndrome has you lying in bed trying to sleep for more than 20 minutes without being able to fall asleep, get up out of bed in order to not become conditioned to associate the bed with not sleep.*   Such insomnia is called conditioned insomnia, or psychophysiologic insomnia. Such insomnias can become chronic if the sufferer of Love Trauma Syndrome does not use proper sleep hygiene. Proper sleep hygiene also includes using the bed only for sleeping or love making, not exercising recently (hours) before bedtime, not using caffeinated beverages before bedtime, and cutting down on nicotine use before bedtime.

12. *Resist the urge to punish and to seek revenge.*   Resist the notion that you have the right to punish someone who has hurt you. You might feel that they deserve punishment—but you cannot be the vehicle of that punishment. Releasing your anger is liberating, but the expression must be controlled and not in a way that is destructive or hurtful to you or to others. You can describe how hurt you feel without desiring vengeance.

You must also relinquish your desire to control the person whom you love. Releasing your desire to control is an act of "unselfish love." Unfortunately, the "psychological gravity" of our brains pulls us in the direction of "selfish love"—love that caters only to our needs, and our needs alone. Resist this gravity (and religion often helps us do so).

13. *Realize your romantic dreams.*   Remind yourself that you are lovable. You just need to be active and seek a soul mate. Think about a replacement. But remember—love isn't easy. Romantic love between two people is never perfectly timed or tuned. There are always bumps in the road, and some of these bumps are big enough to knock you out of the car. Use good judgement before you decide to get back in.

14. *See a doctor for a medical checkup.*   Tell your doctor that you want to get involved in a regular schedule of physical activity. Exercise regularly. Physical conditioning counteracts many of the sickening effects triggered by Love Trauma Syndrome. As Love Trauma Syndrome generates a lot of emotional and physiological arousal, exercise is an ideal avenue for you to direct the excess energy created by the syndrome. Remain active.

15. *You must try to be happy, no matter what the hardship.*   Do not waste your life being miserable because of things you cannot change. Reject

negative and toxic thoughts. Toxic thoughts are poisonous to your happiness, and should not be engaged. Psych yourself up to have only positive thoughts. As Peter McWilliams says, "You cannot afford the luxury of a negative thought."[5]

16. *Do not withdraw from others.* Maintain your contacts with friends, relatives, and acquaintances. Remain socially involved. Let them know you are suffering.

17. *Put your love-trauma-related problems in the Hands of God.* See what He or She does with them. Join a church, synagogue, mosque, or other religious institution where you can get your spiritual needs fulfilled. Remember that God is with you—both when you are in pain and when you are not in pain. God is always with you.

18. *Your love trauma is not such a big deal that you should remain upset about it for years and years.*

19. *Have more fun!* Remember that some religions tell you that it is your religious responsibility to be joyful. Live in the present. Teach yourself to smile more.

20. *Contain the defeat.* Do not allow the defeat to result in negative self-evaluations of yourself. If serious depression, anxiety, or sleepiness accompanies your Love Trauma Syndrome, see a professional mental health worker. Don't put it off. Get help.

21. *You can find love.* You are lovable. Don't allow your Love Trauma Syndrome to beat you up and make your feel otherwise.

22. *Avoid the lure of drugs, alcohol, and promiscuous sex in dealing with your Love Trauma Syndrome.*

23. *Do not even consider dealing with your Love Trauma Syndrome by using a gun or other such weapon.* It is not worth it! If you are even tempted to use a weapon to hurt somebody, get help immediately!

24. *Listen to music on the radio.* Come to the understanding that love is both joy and pain. When you can feel both the joy and the pain of love, you are alive.

25. *If you are currently experiencing a love trauma, you needn't be in constant pain.* Transcend it. Seek transcendence, beauty, and love in other areas. Try to take a break from the pain.

26. *If you feel that your self-esteem, your sense of yourself, has been severely damaged by the love trauma event, you should seek counseling with either a psychiatrist, psychologist, or other trained mental health care practitioner.* Love Trauma Syndrome can diminish—sometimes permanently—a person's sense of potency to fulfill their dreams and their life. It can stifle and retard

emotional, spiritual, and professional development. Maintaining your self-esteem is an active process, a process that requires that you "turn off" the more critical parts of yourself, and to learn to accept yourself and your wounds.

Sometimes only work with a trained counselor can help you discover why your brain has interpreted the love trauma event to be so devastating. Your life is too valuable, and often the love trauma is too trivial, to have such a long-lasting influence on your feelings and your behavior. Begin to focus on your strengths and your good attributes.

27. *Couples work is often vital for diagnosing the problems with the relationship and for fixing these problems.* Relationships work best when each of the partners makes the other feel good about themselves. When this does not happen, the relationship begins to break down. Some partners are more invested in working on improving the relationship than others. You try to work with what you have. Avoid the blame game. Force yourself to take some responsibility for the problems you have with your partner.

28. *Commit yourself to transforming the love trauma experience into a growth experience.* Make it become an experience from which you will become a better, healthier person.

29. *Make the love trauma a victory experience for you.* Surrender to the loss, and try to achieve "victory through surrender." Search for what you have learned or gained from the experience. Learn to forgive and to "let go." Obtain psychotherapy to help you in your quest if necessary. Search for rebirth and renewal.

30. *Give yourself time to heal.* Love Trauma Syndrome is rarely cured overnight. Don't give up hope. The chains that bind you to your pain can be broken, even if you have to get professional help. Using the Love Trauma Inventory (LTI) presented in chapter 2, if your scores remain high week after week, please consider seeing a professional mental health worker. They will have a lot to offer you. Sometimes people feel so anguished and ashamed because of their reactions to a love trauma that they avoid getting help from a professional. The thought of discussing their pain with a professional is too much to bear. But it will be worth it.

Chapter Nine

Professional Antidotes to the Pain of
Love Trauma Syndrome

T here are some patients, who, try though they may, simply cannot find adequate relief from their Love-Trauma-Syndrome-associated pain on their own. These people need professional help for their condition. There are also some patients, who because of their prominent avoidance of anything that reminds them of the love trauma event, do not even realize how their love trauma has altered their lives for the worse. Their Love-Trauma-Syndrome-associated avoidance, combined with their dissociative symptoms and sometimes impaired memory, contribute to certain patients being able to conceal just how distressed they actually are. These people do not communicate their distress to others (e.g., mental health workers). In fact, their intense desire to avoid love-trauma-related reminders results in their not desiring any contact with mental health professionals. These persons try hard to avoid any form of self-help or professional therapy. Paradoxically, people who might superficially seem to be doing quite well after a love trauma may be coping the worst, and it is only a matter of time before the pathologic defenses they are employing (e.g., alcohol or substance abuse, severe overwork syndromes, antisocial behavior or revenge fantasies) catch up and start to destroy them. The "self-help" strategies some people develop for themselves are actually programs for self-destruction. Indeed, the cost of not treating, or of under-treating a Love Trauma Syndrome can be high. As already discussed, the syndrome is not a trivial condition. It can become complicated with other potentially serious psychiatric disorders, such as depression, anxiety, and substance or alcohol abuse. In the worst case scenario revenge-motivated violence against others is involved. When severe, Love Trauma Syndrome also markedly diminishes the sufferer's quality of life.

There are numerous treatment options for people who go to a professional when seeking help for their Love Trauma Syndrome. There are two basic categories of treatments available—psychotherapy and psychotherapeutic medications (e.g., antidepressants). Certain patients will be able to recover from their Love Trauma Syndrome with psychotherapy alone, whereas others might also need psychotherapeutic medications (e.g., antidepressants) when their Love Trauma Syndrome is accompanied by serious depressive or anxiety symptoms.

Mental health workers who are not psychiatrists are able to provide psychotherapy, but as they are not physicians, they cannot prescribe medications. Psychiatrists are medical doctors and are able to prescribe appropriate medications if necessary. Often, nonphysician mental health workers, such as psychologists, social workers, or nurses, provide psychotherapy and refer the patient to a psychiatrist if they feel that a medication (such as an antidepressant) might be necessary. The nonphysician mental health worker continues to see the patient for psychotherapy, and the psychiatrist periodically sees the patient to assess the patient's medication response. The nonphysician worker and the psychiatrist remain in contact with each other and share impressions of the effectiveness of the combined therapy, and make corrections (e.g., change medications) in order to optimize the patient's response. Most psychiatrists are able to provide both psychotherapy and medications without delegating the psychotherapy to one clinician and the medication treatment to another.[1]

Regardless of the therapist you choose, it is important to find someone whom you feel really cares about you and is empathic. Having a relationship with a therapist whom you feel cares about you and about your situation is therapeutic in itself. Studies have demonstrated that if you feel that your therapist cares and is sufficiently empathetic, you will do better in the therapy. Of course, it is best if you can find a therapist who is caring, empathic, and skilled at the same time (e.g., Burns and Nolen-Hoeksema, 1992).

Whatever type of therapy is used, and with whomever you choose to do it, the overall goals of any treatment for Love Trauma Syndrome include:

1. remission of Love-Trauma-Syndrome-associated symptoms;
2. remission of associated depression, anxiety, and other complications (e.g., substance or alcohol use);

3. restoration of social, occupational, and academic functioning;
4. restoration of quality of life; and
5. identification and repair of vulnerability factors (e.g., chronic low self-esteem, high physiological arousal, narcissistic tendencies).

Some of the different psychotherapy and medication options for treating Love Trauma Syndrome are outlined in this chapter.

Therapeutic Conversations (i.e., Psychotherapy)

There are many different forms of psychotherapy. Some professionals are quite adept with certain forms of therapy, such as Cognitive Behavioral Therapy (CBT), or Interpersonal Psychotherapy (IPT), to name just a few. Many psychotherapists combine different forms of therapy as they see fit to best address the patient's problem and style of interacting with their environment.

Patients with Love Trauma Syndrome who present themselves to professionals have been unable to replace their Love-Trauma-Syndrome-associated negative thoughts and feelings with more positive ways of thinking and feeling. The goal of successful psychotherapy of Love Trauma Syndrome is to substitute these dysphoric thoughts and feelings with more positive and helpful attitudes and emotions, so the patient can go on with his or her life and achieve greater happiness.

The Need to Go Slow in the Psychotherapy of Love Trauma Syndrome

As discussed earlier in the book, a trauma is a stressful event that overwhelms a person's capacity to mentally process what happened. Because the trauma is experienced as overwhelming, patients are unable to neutralize the distress, anxiety, and other forms of dysphoria caused by the trauma. Defective processing of the events results in the persistence of love-trauma-associated memories and symptoms of hyperarousal.

Because of the intense pain associated with the love trauma event, people try to avoid any remembrances or thoughts related to the trauma, and hence never completely work things out or desensitize to the event. There appears to be a relationship between the severity of the pain and dysphoria experienced when first experiencing the love trauma event and the persistence of the subsequent Love Trauma Syndrome (should the syndrome develop). When love-trauma-related cues trigger the painful thoughts and memories, or when trauma-related thoughts simply intrude into consciousness without clear provocation, the person's psychological avoidance prevents them from fully desensitizing to the trauma. It is almost as if the trauma is occurring again for the first time.

The goal of many forms of psychotherapy for Love Trauma Syndrome is to help the person more fully process the trauma event and rob it of its ability to cause hyperarousal, dysphoria, and behavioral dysfunction. This can involve slow and careful exploration of the trauma event(s), gradually increasing the patient to greater degrees of exposure to the memories of the events without activating too much avoidance. This allows the patient to gradually desensitize to the trauma, and as a result the memories and thoughts of the trauma no longer function as powerful cues for dysphoria. The interaction of love-trauma-associated memories, emotional arousal, and avoidance is illustrated in Figure 9.1. Unfortunately, during the initial phases of treatment, as patients reconnect with their love-trauma-related memories, their symptoms can get worse before they get better. There is an increase in their symptoms of hyperarousal, including anxiety, insomnia, agitation, irritability, anger, and the intrusiveness of their love-trauma-related memories. Medications such as antidepressants can be useful in lessening symptoms of Love-Trauma-Syndrome-related hyperarousal. Eventually, the symptoms will lessen as avoidance of the traumatic memories are replaced

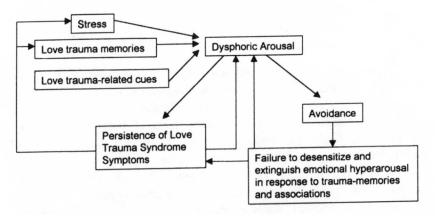

Figure 9.1 *The vicious cycle of Love Trauma Syndrome. Avoidance of love-trauma-related memories, associations, and "cues" (i.e., reminders) prevents desensitization and maintains dysphoric arousal in the context of future exposure to reminders.*

with some desensitization to the event, as well as a "reframing" of the meaning of the event in their lives.

People vary in the degree that they are initially able to directly *engage* and discuss their love trauma events. For some people, direct engagement of the event is too overwhelming and hyperarousal-associated for them to tolerate. It sometimes takes a professional mental health worker to determine when, how much, and in what manner the trauma should be engaged in an attempt to bring about some resolution of the Love Trauma Syndrome. Direct engagement and discussion of the love trauma event sometimes requires a professional with experience to help the patient tolerate the pain. Premature engagement can result in the patient fleeing from therapy. Direct engagement of the memories can be gradually increased over time.

One patient once told me how, years earlier, she had gone to a psychiatrist to discuss her husband's affair that occurred 2 decades earlier. She described learning of the affair as one of the most painful experiences of her life. However, the psychiatrist was too quick to engage the patient in the details of love trauma event, and she fled from therapy. Because she was never fully able to process the event on her own, she said that she became increasingly distant from her husband, who actually tried hard to win her back. Unfortunately, she remained "angry and hurt" over the affair, and the couple eventually divorced.

You as a patient need to feel comfortable telling your therapist when discussion of the love trauma has become too painful, and your therapist needs to give you permission to do so. It is not unlike a patient at the dentist who is having their dental caries drilled. When the pain from the drilling becomes too intense, the dentist asks you to put your hand up as a signal to her or to him that you need a break from the pain. Similarly, you need to be able to communicate to your therapist when the pain of the love trauma exploration is too much to bear at that time. The therapist does not want you to prematurely terminate therapy because the sessions have become too painful for you to bear.

One of the goals of therapy is to help the patient put their love trauma memories back into proper perspective—back into the context of their whole life story. One of the problems people with Love Trauma Syndrome have is that they lose the sense of their whole life story, and become increasingly preoccupied with their love trauma. For someone in the throes of a Love Trauma Syndrome, the love trauma memory becomes their whole life memory, and everything else becomes linked to it. In the ancient

Roman Empire it was said that "all roads lead to Rome." For someone with Love Trauma Syndrome, all memories become associated with their love trauma.

Patients in the midst of a Love Trauma Syndrome are often unable to attend to other life stresses, such as familial, social, financial, occupational, academic, or health demands. Someone who is already under a lot of stress—and then experiences a love trauma—can be a very unhappy person indeed. Love Trauma Syndrome is sometimes a significant contributor to burnout that people experience at work or in school. A love trauma can be "the straw that breaks the camel's back," leading to profound burnout. Hence, therapists must be attentive to the other stressors in a patient's life other than the love trauma, and make sure that the patient is attending to these other demands as well. Patients can become so fixated on the love trauma and on their symptoms of Love Trauma Syndrome that they neglect other important matters. They can find themselves evicted from their apartments, without their telephones and electricity being connected, flunked out of school, or their children not adequately attended.

If the Love Trauma Syndrome is complicated by depression, the psychotherapy also focuses on feelings of loss and defeat. Depression is caused by feelings of loss and of defeat. What does the patient feel that they have lost? Have they lost not only their love, but also their self-esteem? In the context of Love Trauma Syndrome, some self-esteem is almost always lost. The aim of the psychotherapy is to contain love-trauma-induced negative thoughts and feelings of loss and of depression. Antidepressant medications are also quite helpful in reducing the symptoms of depression.

If the Love Trauma Syndrome is complicated by anxiety, the psychotherapy focuses on the patient's fears. Anxiety is caused by a sense of danger—a fear of some dreaded outcome. What do they fear? Do they fear the loss of love, being unlovable, or never finding someone else who can love them? Where is the danger? When the anxiety is severe, and it interferes with the patient's social and occupational functioning during the day, and interferes with their sleep at night, antianxiety and sleep medications can be prescribed for short periods of time (e.g., a few weeks to a few months).

The Initial Phases of Psychotherapy

During the initial phase of therapy, the therapist gets to know the patient. This involves a full review of the patient's current problems and symptoms and their psychological history. For the history, it is important to understand the expectations that the patient had for the love relationship. What expectations were not met, and what was unsatisfying? On the other hand, what were the satisfying aspects of relationship? The therapist begins to assess whether the patient's emotional response represents an appropriate, healthy response to the loss of love, or is an inappropriate, exaggerated, unhealthy response. There is also an attempt to discover what might have made the patient more vulnerable to developing a Love Trauma Syndrome. For instance, people with greater degrees of psychological distress before a love trauma event, such as those persons already suffering from anxiety, depression, and rejection sensitive dysphoria, seem more prone to developing a Love Trauma Syndrome. Finally, some Love Trauma Syndrome patients benefit when they are permitted to assume the "sick" role. Accepting that you are sick is the beginning of the road to recovery.

The Education Phase

During this phase of the treatment, patients need to be educated about the syndrome. They are taught about the symptoms of the condition (*see* chapter 2) and its close relationship with Acute Stress Disorder and Post-traumatic Stress Disorder.[2] Patients are also instructed about the different course of the syndrome as can be found in chapter 2 (Figures 2.1 through 2.4). This illustrates to the patient that the condition almost always gets better over time. If the symptoms are severe, they will remain severe for only so long before they begin to taper off in severity, if not disappearing.

Patients are also educated about what constitutes "healthy" versus "unhealthy" responses to a love trauma. Not uncommonly, the psychological reaction to love trauma is intense, and it can involve a lowering of self-esteem, as well as the onset of grief, depression, fear, and anger. Some of these responses might be appropriate reactions to the loss of love. However, when the emotions foster unhealthy behaviors, such as alcohol or drug use, risk-taking behaviors such as promiscuous sexual activity, becoming sedentary and inactive, becoming stuck in a "negative focus," withdrawing from others, or having tantrums, these emotions need to be carefully explored and challenged.

Elucidating Triggers

For some people, it is useful to be in psychotherapy to help them better understand what triggers their Love Trauma Syndrome symptoms. In fact, one major goal of psychotherapy—or "talking therapy"—in Love

Trauma Syndrome is to identify and to try to neutralize these triggers (also referred to as *cues*).

The psychotherapist does this by trying to facilitate the patient's being able to attach "thoughts" to the uncomfortable (i.e., dysphoric) emotions. This typically is done by simply asking the patient what they think their distress is related to, that is, what does the patient think triggered the distress? Why is it distressing? Cognitive therapists search for the thoughts associated with a patient's unhappiness.

Sometimes, while the patient is talking, the therapist can detect subtle changes in the way the patient is behaving that suggest certain triggers. For instance, the patient's voice might begin to fall, or they might seem to lose vitality or to appear anxious. Some forms of psychotherapy use biofeedback equipment to enable the therapist to monitor closely the patient's physiological state (*psychophysiological psychotherapy*). Over the course of a psychotherapy session, different physiological parameters such as blood pressure, pulse rate, or forehead muscle tone are measured. The activation of triggers can be signaled by increases in heart rate or by sudden changes in blood pressure. At this point the therapist might try to tap into the patient's "stream of consciousness" to get at the underpinnings of the triggers. The patient is asked what they were thinking about or feeling at the time of the change in blood pressure or in heart rate.

An illustration of how this might work is illustrated by a patient named Jeremy. He was a 45–year-old man who had gone to a local emergency room on a number of occasions (usually on weekends), complaining of cardiaclike chest pain. He would become flushed and short of breath, and would develop chest pain that sometimes radiated down his arms. On all previous visits to the emergency room, a cardiac cause of his symptoms could not be found, although his blood pressure was noted to fluctuate into elevated levels. Twice he was admitted to the coronary care unit for observation.

Finally, someone recommended that he see a psychiatrist, which he reluctantly did. During his psychotherapy, his blood pressure and heart rate were continually monitored by an electronic blood pressure device capable of measuring his blood pressure every few moments. His blood pressure and pulse were noted to increase dramatically when he started talking about his wife. He initially could not see a connection between his blood pressure elevations and his wife. When he was asked directly if he were angry with her, his blood pressure increased, and he complained of feeling sick. He said that he felt "weak and tired," evidence that some sickening process was being activated. He later admitted that he was angry with her for an affair she had early in their marriage, but he said that they "had worked things out." He began to cry, and discussed feelings related to the incident that he had never discussed with anyone. "Everyone thinks that we're a perfect couple, but they don't understand the pain I'm in, and I'm ashamed to talk to anyone about it." The reason for his emergency room visits on the weekends became clearer. It was on the weekends that he was spending the most time with his wife. It was on the weekends that his anger was being most dramatically triggered.

After discussing his thoughts and feelings about his wife for a few weeks in therapy, his blood pressure responses when talking about his wife became less dramatic. He could retreat from the battle being waged inside him. He was finally making peace. He was able to focus on the good and reliable ally she had become.

Modern talk therapies also participate in the vision work described earlier. Again, patients are not allowed to wallow in their misery. They are actively encouraged to develop their vision and move forward from there. Modern talk therapies have the patient envision what they want, and promote activity designed to achieve their vision. Patients are persuaded to focus more on their vision of what they want to achieve than to concentrate on the emotional pain.

COGNITIVE BEHAVIOR THERAPY OF LOVE TRAUMA SYNDROME

Cognitive therapists agree with Shakespeare, who said that "nothing's bad but thinking makes it so." Stated somewhat differently, cognitive therapists and Shakespeare believe that your thoughts underlie your feelings. An outcome is "bad" only if you think it is bad, and if you think it is bad, then the emotion that will be generated by the thought will be dysphoric. The dogma of cognitive therapy goes like this: If you can identify the thoughts that make you miserable, you can change these thoughts. Many of these thoughts are wrong and distort reality and unnecessarily make you feel miserable. When you correct the thoughts, the miserable feelings will dissipate.

Obviously, this is an overly simplistic idea, and bad things (e.g., accidents, natural disasters, death, disease, war, starving children, divorce) do happen and it is appropriate to feel unhappy when such things occur. The goal of cognitive therapy is not to make you devoid of any emotional responses, sort of like the Vulcan Mr. Spock on *Star Trek*, but to get your emotional responses to be more rational and appropriate to the adverse event. For a case of Love Trauma Syndrome, the attempt is to "crank down" the often unnecessarily exaggerated dysphoric emotional effect of a love trauma. Cognitive therapists also struggle to free you of paralyzing depression and anxiety that prevent you from taking active steps to overcome your misery and live your life to the fullest.

The **"ABC's"** of cognitive therapy (sometimes referred to as rational emotive therapy [RET], rational emotive behavioral therapy [REBT], or cognitive behavioral therapy [CBT]) are illustrated in Figure 9.2.

The "A" stands for activating events, aggravating events, activating triggers, adverse events, or simply adversity. It can also represent a love trauma. You choose which of these you want the "A" to represent. In cognitive therapy, much of the focus involves identifying the triggers (the "A's") and the exaggerated, irrational "beliefs" (the "B's") the patient has about their emotional unhappiness (i.e., the "C's"—or emotional consequences to the activating events and subsequent beliefs). These emotional consequences are the dysphoric feelings caused by the irrational beliefs. These dysphoric feelings include despair, depression, and anxiety.

Linking the activating events and the beliefs are *cognitive distortions.* Table 9.1 identifies a list of cognitive distortions and beliefs that one can have after the activating event of a love trauma.

Some of these cognitive distortions (e.g., catastrophizing, awfulizing) support beliefs that promote a sense of inadequacy, depression, and helplessness. These distortions tend to poison hope, optimism, and action.

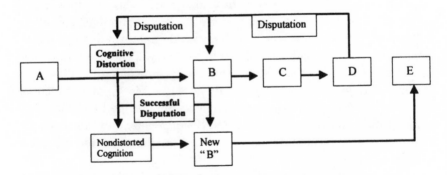

Legend Key. A = Activating Love Trauma Event, or Adversity; B = Beliefs; C = Consequence (i.e., emotional consequence); D = Disputation of cognitive distortion and belief (as occurs in cognitive therapy, where "disputation" is the equivalent of "putting the lie to" the cognitive distortion and belief); and E = new Emotional Effect (ideally healthier and more adaptive).

Figure 9.2   The "ABC's" of cognitive therapy (see figure legend above).

Table 9.1   Sample Cognitive Distortions

A. Cognitive distortions supporting pathological defense of self-esteem. These distortions foster a sense of superiority and confidence. They can fuel anger and increase morale for someone getting ready to challenge an opponent.

Cognitive distortion	Explanation	Examples of beliefs based on distorted thoughts
Grandiose thinking	Viewing your skills, talents, abilities, strengths as far superior to others	"I'm the best." "I'm better than they are." "I'm invulnerable." "I can't be beat."
Devaluing	Viewing the skills, talents, abilities, strengths of another as inferior to yours. Minimizing or reducing the value of that which has been lost (softens the blow to self-esteem of losing something previously valued).	"He's worthless." "She's weak and powerless." "He's no threat to me." "He was a loser." "I can do better." "Who cares that she's gone?"
Revenge thinking	Someone deserves punishment to "right a wrong."	"She *deserves* to be punished."
Demonization	Your adversary is evil.	"He's a bad and evil person."
Dissociative thinking	You recognize something is happening, but to some degree you cannot or will not accept it.	"This is unreal." "I can't believe this is happening." "I am numb to your pain." "I am numb to my pain."
Blaming	Someone else is responsible for your (or another's) distress.	"You're to blame for my problem."
Righteous thinking	Only you have access to the truth and what is right and good.	"I'm good and you're not." "I'm nice and you're not."

B. Cognitive distortions that foster diminished self-esteem. They support a desire to surrender and promote pessimistic, hopeless, and helpless attitudes. They encourage feeling anxious and depressed.

Awfulizing, catastrophizing	Assuming only the worst possible outcomes	"This can't be more terrible." (it actually can always be more terrible)
All-or-none thinking; black-and-white thinking; categorical, or dichotomous thinking	No appreciation of "gray areas" (i.e., the continuum of possibilities) in between extremes	"There's no one out there as good as him." "My life will never be the same!" "I'll never be happy again!"

(*continued*)

Table 9.1 Sample Cognitive Distortions (*continued*)

Mental filter	Only seeing the negative side and "discounting the positive"	"I've never been successful at anything."
Overgeneralization	Viewing a single negative outcome as a harbinger of all-to-come (or all-that's-been)	"I'll never be successful at love."
Emotional reasoning	If you feel bad, then the situation really must be as bad as you feel.	"I feel awful—it must really be awful!"
Labeling	Branding yourself with a negative label, assuming everything you do will be consistent with the label	"I'm a loser."
Personalization	Assuming full responsibility for a negative outcome, discounting other factors	"It's all my fault."
Magnification	"Making a mountain out of a molehill." Exaggerating the impact of adverse events	"My marriage failed, and my whole life has been a farce."

They are designed to make people feel worse about themselves, lower their self-esteem, and support submissive behaviors, withdrawal, and emotional and physical sickening responses.

Other distortions (e.g., demonization or blaming thinking) promote angry positions, and attempt to protect and bolster self-esteem. These later distortions can promote intimidation postures and fighting behaviors. At their worst they support violent responses against others. These distortions are self-serving patterns of thinking designed to defend against decreases in self-esteem and to support a sense of dominance. Such thinking tends to embolden people to be active and fight.

"D" is for disputing the belief and the cognitive distortion underlying the belief. This is done with the help of the cognitive therapist. "E" is for the new emotional effect (ideally less dysphoric) now that the therapist and the patient have successfully disputed the cognitive distortion and belief, and have installed acceptable and believable new thoughts and beliefs. The new emotional effect is decreased sadness, unhappiness, and despair, now replaced by more appropriate feelings (e.g., disappointment and decreased emotional and physical sickening).

Cognitive therapists believe in giving patients homework between therapy sessions. These therapists believe that being able to think more rationally is a skill that requires practice for it to permeate your daily thinking and promote full recovery. For instance, cognitive therapists might have you keep logs of your negative emotions, thoughts, and beliefs. They want you to be able to identify which cognitive distortions underlie different beliefs and emotions.

For homework, therapists might have you fill in blank forms for the "A" (i.e., activating events) and the "B" (i.e., your irrational beliefs). You write out the main cognitive distortions underlying the belief, and your emotional consequence (the "C"). Some therapists have you rate your conviction in the reality of the cognitive distortion and belief (e.g., as a percentage conviction, such as a 50% conviction that the belief is accurate). They will have you write in your disputations ("D") for both the cognitive distortions and beliefs, and ask you to rate (again as a percentage) how much you believe your disputation reflects reality. If you rate your original cognitive distortions and irrational beliefs higher than your new interpretations (the new thoughts and new beliefs), then you need to continue to work to find more effective disputations. Finally, if you are able to effectively dispute your cognitive distortions and irrational beliefs, has it led to a different emotional consequence ("E")? How much (as a percentage) has the distress been reduced by your disputations?

Learning to identify irrational thoughts is a skill that the patient needs to work on both in therapy and between therapy sessions (e.g., by completing cognitive therapy homework). To identify the irrational and toxic thoughts, you need to think of a specific instance where you felt bad. When you identify the event, you need to try to identify what thoughts you were having when you started to feel bad. The cognitive therapist will try to dispute (i.e., challenge) some of these thoughts using a variety of techniques. They will ask you to find the *data* supporting your irrational thoughts, find *alternative* explanations for the thoughts, and realistically assess the *impact* that the event will have on your life (and how you can alter any catastrophic outcome you envision).

If your boyfriend or girlfriend breaks up with you, and you think that you will never be able to attract or keep someone quite as good as him because something about you is unattractive, you need to ask yourself the following questions: What data supports my notion that I will never be able to attract or keep someone quite as good as him? In fact, you attracted him, didn't you? You simply have not tried to attract others for a long enough period of time to have enough data to support your notion that you will not be able to attract others "as good as him." The next question is "What alternative explanations are there for the breakup besides your belief that you are unattractive?" In fact, it might simply be that the two of you were not right for each other (e.g., have different interests, tastes, values), or that he thought he was not attractive enough or good enough to hold onto you! What is the long-term impact of the breakup anyway? Do you think it is realistic to say that you will never be able to be happy again? Sure you feel sad now, but how will you feel a year from now? Have you magnified the impact of the breakup in your mind?

Replacing "Irrational" With More "Rational" Responses

The goal of cognitive behavioral therapy is to replace irrational emotional and thought responses with emotions and thoughts that are more appropriate—that is, more rational. Once the specific dysphoria-inducing events and negative thoughts and self-evaluations have been identified, attempts are made to contain and to neutralize them. Similar to a contagious disease, these negative thoughts and self-evaluations related to the love trauma can generalize to other areas and become toxic to the person's overall sense of self-efficacy. Patients see one negative event as a pattern of never-ending defeats, and one failure as meaning that they are a complete failure. Efforts are made to contain the spread of negative thoughts to the area where a defeat was experienced, and to see if the negative thoughts can be replaced with interpretations of the defeat event that is more benign to the patient's self-esteem.

For example, a patient who feels depressed because her husband had an affair needs to learn that failure in one sphere (i.e., her marriage) does not translate into lack of success in all spheres (so-called overgeneralization). For a person to assume that they are bad at everything because of something their spouse did is erroneous. When you understand the faulty logic behind your distressing thoughts and feelings, you can devalue them and be released from their influence.

One of the aims of psychotherapy is *positive reframing* of distressing experiences. This switch from a negative to a positive point of view helps neutralize the thought trigger. Cognitive therapy does this by targeting the false assumptions on which the distressing emotions are based. A recent conversation with a college freshman with Love Trauma Syndrome illustrates how this works. She had just discovered that her boyfriend was having an affair with her best friend. She was crying. "Why are you crying?" I inquired. "It's all so depressing," she wailed. "Why?" I asked. "Because I just lost my boyfriend and best friend at the same time," she said.

Now here is where the cognitive therapist swings into action. Cognitive therapists search for *dichotomous* thinking—that is, "categorical," "all-or-none," or "black-and-white" thinking. Unhappy patients tend to lose sight of all the "shades of gray" between the black and white. Although it is understandable—and appropriate—that she feels some sadness about the loss of her boyfriend and her best friend, she probably also has an unstated false assumption that she will never find another—or as good—a boyfriend or best friend. Cognitive therapists tend to be quite active during therapy, and they pursue their hunches. I began to challenge the hypothesized hidden assumption that was causing her to feel miserable. "Do you think you will be able to find another boyfriend?" I asked. She shook her head. "Not as good as him," she cried.

She was demonstrating classic dichotomous *all-or-none thinking*. He was the only "good" boyfriend she could find. She thought she had just lost the best man on the planet for her. I countered this by asking her, "Are you sure there aren't some other good men out there who you might like? Have you looked?" "I guess not, at least not recently," she replied. She also thought that it was going to be difficult to replace her best friend. "Do you have other girlfriends?" I inquired. "Yes," she answered.

Her assumption that she would not be able to replace her boyfriend or girlfriend with others who are as good is also an example of what is called *catastrophic thinking*. Catastrophic thinking is a preoccupation with unlikely disastrous outcomes. It is also an example of the cognitive distortion of *jumping to conclusions*, where she assumes that she will never be able to find another boyfriend or girlfriend like the ones who just betrayed her.

She looked out the window, and began to tell me about some other friends she had, whom she had known for a long time but had neglected because of involvement with her new "best friend," who had just betrayed her. "I guess I don't need best friends like that," she said. Her "all-or-none thinking" was being successfully disputed, as evidenced by her reduction in tears. She had experienced a tremendous loss, but had also gained important knowledge about some of her friends and about herself. Her experience was being "positively reframed." At a later point she began to cry again. "But why does it feel so bad?" she asked. "There must be something very, very bad about it, or I wouldn't feel so bad!"

This is an example of what cognitive therapists call *emotional reasoning*. She assumed that because she felt very bad, there must be something very wrong. Cognitive therapists take aim at such emotional reasoning. They help the patient understand that just because you feel something is wrong does not mean that something is wrong. The "bad feeling" serves to direct your attention to a possible problem, but it does not automatically mean that the problem is as bad as it feels. "I thought you just concluded that there are other men out there, and that you probably have some better friends that you are not spending much time with," I said. "Yeah," she mused. "I guess you're right. I guess when you look at it that way I'm not so bad off. I just wasted a lot of time with those two creeps." She appeared surprised. "That's weird," she replied. "Feelings can be wrong."

Of course she needed more work to help her deal with the love trauma she experienced. She was hardly out of the woods. In fact, the need for ongoing and continued work in psychotherapy for people with Love Trauma Syndrome is often crucial for their recovery. It is rare that you can effect a significant long lasting change quickly. Usually you have to go over and over different aspects of the patient's thinking and address different nuances of their thoughts. The therapist actively searches for ways to preserve the patient's self-esteem, and to protect the patient from acting on potentially destructive ways of dealing with their Love Trauma Syndrome (e.g., alcohol or drug abuse). Patients often have to determine how the love trauma affected their self-concept(s), and how their sense of themselves and of their goals and purpose can be re-defined and reframed in a way that the person feels whole and good about themselves.

Other common cognitive distortions found in people afflicted with Love Trauma Syndrome include:

1. *magnification,* where the importance of an event is *exaggerated;*
2. *blame,* where you hold yourself (or someone else) completely responsible for events;
3. *the tyranny of the shoulds,* where you are overly hard on yourself, and you are filled with "should statements" such as "I should be able to keep my husband from having an affair";
4. *labeling,* where you hang labels on yourself—for example, you insist to yourself that a mistake or unhappy event labels you a "loser" through and through, or you label yourself a "moron," "schmuck," or "jerk"; and
5. *mental filter,* where you focus on only the negative aspects of a situation, and disregard potential good.

When a patient is depressed, there is almost always some degree of mental filter, labeling, "shoulding," and magnification. When a patient is anxious, there is almost always some catastrophic thinking.

One of the best outcomes in psychotherapy with a Love-Trauma-Syndrome-stricken patient is being able to have the patient appreciate some good that came out of the experience. For instance, with some affairs, the relationship can actually be strengthened after the original partners get back together and recommit to each other. I have had patients who had affairs tell me that the affair made them appreciate their spouses, boyfriends, or girlfriends more. Love Trauma Syndrome can serve to motivate certain patients to do things that they have been putting off for some time, such as losing weight, starting an exercise program, quitting smoking, or getting a medical checkup.

In the case example given previously, the patient was able to recognize that her boyfriend and her best friend were not good for her (e.g., they had taken her away from other more loyal friends and had encouraged partying instead of studying, which caused her grades to drop). Eventually, her Love-Trauma-Syndrome-related distress dissipated, and she found herself a more committed boyfriend and loyal best friend.

Why Do We Have Cognitive Distortions? (Or Why Have Our Brains Evolved With The Ability To Make Brain Trash?)

In the ancient ancestral past, cognitive distortions served to promote certain behaviors that were important for our survival. As outlined in Table 9.1, some cognitive distortions provide defense of our self-esteem, and promote anger and attack behaviors. These cognitive distortions exaggerate our sense of power, importance, and entitlement. Another set of distortions promote a lowering of self-esteem and of personal effectiveness (i.e., self-efficacy), and support acceptance of the defeat. These latter distortions exaggerate the negative impact of events on our lives. Both types of responses were important in our ancient evolutionary past.

As described in previous chapters, the brain has evolved with mechanism to defend against drops in self-esteem (i.e., if the brain thinks that you can get away with doing so). In service of defending self-esteem, the brain has evolved with the tendency to self-servingly exaggerate and distort certain aspects of a problem. This serves to maximize the emotional response used to counter and neutralize the threat to self-esteem. This maximized emotional response optimizes your resolve for a single behavioral response in defense of your self-esteem—such as physically attacking the person threatening your self-esteem. Such resolve would have been important in the ancient ancestral environment where maximal physical effort to counter a threat was often the difference between retained or lost self-esteem. Singlemindness born of distortion of reality tends to promote action, whereas mixed emotions tend to inhibit action.

Hence, in the ancient ancestral environment, cognitive distortions increased our power when fighting adversaries. For instance, by magnifying a rival's "evilness," you made them a better enemy, who now was a more worthy recipient of your vigorous attack. This process is called demonization, and was described more thoroughly in an earlier chapter. With demonization, there is often frank distortion of the reality of the rival's nature in the service of envisioning them in as evil a way as possible. The demonization process often allows you to convert in your mind someone who was simply a competitor for resources to someone who is evil and worthy of destruction.

These cognitive distortions can make people formidable adversaries, and can give them a physiological advantage over their opponents. When you are emotionally aroused, your brain sends out signals to the rest of your body to adjust it to meet the physiological demands necessary to be a victorious fighter. Your heart beats faster, and your blood pressure rises. Your breathing rate increases, and the flow of blood in your body changes to service the increasing metabolism in your brain and muscles. You begin to sweat as your body prepares itself for an increased metabolic rate needed to be successful in a physical fight. Thus, in the ancient ancestral environment, distortion of an adversary's character, and magnification of or even frank distortion of their evilness served a purpose. It made you better prepared to overcome them.

Such magnifying and demonizing distortions are often seen when couples quarrel. Before an argument, spouses demonize each other in preparation for the fight. The demonizing process involves some degree of distortion of reality in the service of the demonization. The ferocity of fights that seem out of proportion to the provocation are often fueled by magnifying and demonizing thinking. When you understand the demonizing thoughts, you better understand the reason for the intensity of the fighting between the combatants.

If your brain regards an intense behavioral response to a threat to self-esteem as futile and likely not to meet with success, then pathological defense of your self-esteem is not achieved. The person experiences a drop in feelings of self-esteem and of potency (i.e., self-efficacy). As discussed in earlier chapters, the brain attempts to defend against such drops. This is because in the ancient ancestral environment, drops in self-esteem would have diminished our sense of power and of potency, which would have resulted in our feeling less able to access resources from the environment in the face of competition from others. This ultimately would have translated into diminished survival potential for us and for our offspring. Hence, drops in self-esteem would impair our ability to project our genes into posterity.

As discussed in earlier parts of this book, being defeated in love by a successful rival causes a subsequent drop in self-esteem, which further inhibits attack against them (remember, some people call this the brain's ISS). In the ancient ancestral environment in which we evolved, the inhibition of further attack and activation of more submissive behaviors played an important protective role for both individuals and social groups. The inhibition of aggressive instincts in the context of defeat or of inevitable loss served to help the person act out the defeated role. Weaker rivals who were unable to be restrained by defeat and cease their intimidation display and fighting would have had reduced reproductive success. This is because they would have been annihilated by their betters. The ability to become depressed and surrender when appropriate gave you at least some chance of surviving and ultimately having offspring. Depression kept our ancestors out of fights that they could not win, and it helped the probable loser surrender before it was too late. Depression also enhanced the harmony and strength of the social group by diminishing the conflict between group members. Hence, cognitive distortions that fostered depression in the context of defeat—for example, labeling yourself as a "loser"—would have had some survival value in our ancient ancestral past. These cognitive distortions were part of the ISS.

Cognitive distortions could also help us to be better prepared emotionally and physiologically in a threatening environment. For instance, the emotion of anxiety almost always involves some element of catastrophic thinking. You experience anxiety because you fear the worst. This is often a distortion of reality. But how could such a catastrophizing distortion have helped us in the ancient ancestral environment? By assuming the worst, we would have been prepared for the worst. By contemplating and believing the catastrophic, you would have been able to increase your awareness of the dangers in your environment, and increase your guard and preparedness. Your brain does not want to lose too much response time should you be in imminent danger—for example, when a predator or a competitor is about to sneak up and attack you. Even the loss of a few hundred milliseconds could make the difference between escape and death. Predators and competitors typically try to overcome you as rapidly as possible—before you have an opportunity to mount a defense. Catastrophizing might be brain trash today—but it was a gem in the ancient ancestral past when such thinking saved our lives (and the lives of our loved ones).

During your rapid response to a possible threat, your brain makes an initial interpretation regarding the presence of danger. If its catastrophic way of thinking helps you to assume the worst, you will be better prepared for the worst, and will be more likely to survive should the worst materialize. Hence, catastrophic thinking is not always bad.

The Unraveling Technique

Being able to find and identify irrational thoughts that need to be replaced by more rational responses is a skill that someone with Love Trauma Syndrome needs to develop. One way of identifying irrational thoughts is by employing the "unraveling technique." This technique is used to identify some of the cognitive thoughts, distortions, and beliefs underlying unhealthy and dysfunctional emotions.

When someone uses the unraveling technique, it is like drilling for oil. However, with the unraveling technique, they are drilling for the conscious or unconscious thoughts and beliefs that underlie their unhappy feelings. Unraveling helps to make conscious the thought and belief structure underneath someone's dysphoric emotions. Thoughts and beliefs do not necessarily need to be conscious for them to have an influence on emotions. The unraveling technique reflects the potential flow and direction of a person's conscious and preconscious thought and belief processes.

The unraveling technique has the patient describe what they think will happen because of an upsetting event (e.g., a love trauma). They try to imagine an entire cascade of consequences, until they can arrive at the ultimate consequence.

An example of how the unraveling technique can be used is as follows. A patient of mine—a 58-year-old man who was recently remarried—went to Thanksgiving dinner at his stepdaughter's house. He complained to me of being "traumatized" during the after-dinner conversation. He and his 59-year-old wife had been quite happy for the year and a half they had been together. My patient had been married once before but had no children. My patient's new wife had three grown children from a prior marriage. Her marriage had ended in divorce some 15 years earlier.

After the Thanksgiving dinner, the patient's wife, children, and the children's spouses began to discuss his wife's ex-husband. During the discussion the ex-husband was described as "lots of fun and laughs," "a blast to have at parties," and "knowledgeable about everything." They related several jokes that the man had recently told them, and my patient had to admit that some of them were pretty good. My patient had also known that the ex-husband had a college degree and was a professor at a college. My patient had never finished college, and he had felt himself to be intellectually inferior to his wife's ex-husband. As the evening's conversation progressed, he felt his self-esteem slowly drop. He also began to feel angry with his wife and his family for their insensitivity.

My patient also began looking around the living room, and saw pictures of his wife and ex-husband before they got divorced. The ex-husband was quite handsome, and my patient knew that prior to his wife's divorce she had traveled extensively with her ex-husband to a number of exotic destinations. My patient remembered a conversation that he once had with one of his wife's girlfriends, who had characterized his wife's sexual relationship with her ex-husband as "wild." He also told me how on several occasions his new wife had told him to "lighten up" and "try to have more fun" (and he took this to mean "try to be more fun.") He began to imagine that not only was he intellectually subordinate to her ex-husband, but that his wife had a better sexual relationship with him as well. He felt he was "second best" in her eyes.

Although he did not let anyone know how he really felt, he felt himself becoming more and more upset and depressed as the evening wore on. He could not wait to leave his stepdaughter's house. "I kept smiling," the patient told me, "but I was dying on the inside." The patient kept imagining his wife having sex with her ex-husband when she was younger. He knew this was ridiculous, but he could not stop himself.

When he came in for the session and described how he felt, I asked him to outline for me the chain of thoughts that he had connected to the disturbing image of his wife having sex with her ex-husband. "I guess I think the sex they had was better than the sex we have now. You know, when you're younger the sex is wilder, hotter, more passionate." "And what if their sex was hotter, wilder, and more passionate?" I asked him. He thought for a moment. "Then I guess I'll always be second rate in her mind." "And what if you're second rate in her mind?" I queried. "I guess I'll be second rate in my mind" he said. "And what if you're second rate in your mind?" I asked, continuing with the unraveling of his thoughts and feelings related to the "traumatic" incident. He thought for a moment and shrugged his shoulder. "I guess I'll become depressed." I pressed on. "And then what?" "Then she'll leave me and want to go back to her husband who is better than me," he said. "And then what?" "Then I'll fall into a pit of depression and kill myself," he sighed.

After elucidating and studying the string of associations he had to the events of that Thanksgiving Day, we can see why he experienced the discussion as traumatic. His associations ended in his perishing in "a pit of depression!" The unraveling technique revealed his frightening thoughts and visions related to his experiencing himself as inadequate compared to his wife's ex-husband. His brain's "natural flow of thoughts" as revealed by the unraveling technique made it clear why he was so devastated by the discussion that evening. The discussion had triggered a Love Trauma Syndrome.

After a careful examination of the evidence supporting each thought, the patient was able to see the faulty reasoning behind each of his unraveled thoughts and associations. He was able to eventually see the different cognitive distortions underneath each thought. He prominently employed catastrophizing (e.g., he would end up dying), jumping to conclusions (e.g., assuming her ex-husband was better than him), all-or-none thinking (e.g., assuming that because the ex-husband had a college degree, and the patient did not, that the ex-husband was better), and labeling (e.g., seeing himself as "second rate," and the ex-husband as "better").

We have evolved with the need to feel good about ourselves. The favored behavioral response will be the one most protective of our self-esteem, and this behavioral response can be intense and irrational. For instance, I have seen many couples break up because something about the relationship was threatening to one of the partner's self-esteem. The threat was so great that they were not even willing to face it in therapy, even when they had invested decades of their lives in the relationship.

Interpersonal Psychotherapy (IPT) for Love Trauma Syndrome

The underlying premise of IPT is that interpersonal problems are the root of most personal distress and unhappiness. IPT often focuses on both feelings and thoughts people have related to a particular issue, and encourages appropriate "release of affect" (i.e., emotion), such as sadness, anger, surprise, and fear. During IPT for Love Trauma Syndrome, the initial assessment would include a thorough evaluation of the threatened or broken relationship, including exploration of the expectations that the patient had of the love relationship. Which expectations were fulfilled, and which were not?

IPT of Love Trauma Syndrome would focus on the following four themes as they were appropriate for an individual patient: grief, interpersonal disputes, role transitions, and interpersonal deficits.

Grief. This would be an especially important issue if the relationship is now over. Questions that would be addressed in the therapy include:

1. How is the patient grieving the loss of the relationship? To do this, there would be a historical "reconstruction" of the relationship, and discussions of how the relationship was satisfying, and of how was it not satisfying. What is being grieved? What has been lost?
2. What was going on in the patient's life before, during, and after the breakup?
3. What are the patient's feelings, both negative and positive; about the relationship?
4. What are the barriers to becoming involved in new romantic relationships?

Interpersonal Disputes. This would be an important issue if the relationship was still ongoing and attempts were being made to repair it. Some of the questions that would need to be addressed include:

1. What is the nature of the dispute(s)?
2. What are the "nonreciprocal" expectations of the partners?
3. What are the acceptable alternatives?
4. Are there hidden agendas that one or both of the partners are not addressing? (e.g., are one of the partners having an affair and looking for an excuse to leave?)
5. Is calm and productive negotiation possible?

Role Transitions. This element would be important if the relationship breakup will also involve a major change in one's role in life (e.g., the breakup will result in a change in their social or economic status). The focus is on how the patient will adjust to their new role in life now that their romantic relationship is over. Questions that would be addressed in the therapy include:

1. Can you mourn the loss of the old role?
2. Can you accept the new role?
3. What were the positive and negative aspects of the old role?
4. What are the positive and negative aspects of the new role?
5. What supports do you have to help your transition to your new role?
6. What new skills do you need to acquire in order for you to best adapt to your new role?

Interpersonal Deficits. This would be an especially important focus for a person with Love Trauma Syndrome who has been isolated, socially withdrawn, or has a limited or constricted social support system. Such individuals might be particularly vulnerable to complications from their Love Trauma Syndrome. Their broken relationship that caused the Love Trauma Syndrome might have been their only real relationship. The aim would be to encourage the formation of other relationships. This might not only be replacements for romantic relationships, but the formation of other (nonromantic) close relationships and allegiances. Some of the questions that would be addressed in the therapy include:

1. What have been the positive and negative aspects of relationships in the past?
2. What have been the problems that the person has had in relationships in the past?
3. Does the patient tend to experience the same problems in relationships? What are the repetitive problems?
4. How does the patient feel about the therapist? Does the patient experience similar problems with the therapist that they experience with others in both intimate and nonintimate relationships? What are the problems?
5. What can the patient do to expand and to maintain their support system?

Eye Movement Desensitization and Reprocessing (EMDR)

EMDR is a new technique that could be tried to help people recover from a love trauma. During EMDR therapy, as upsetting love-trauma-related thoughts race through the patient's mind, the patient is directed to follow with their eyes the trained movements of the therapist's finger. As the patient moves their eyes from side to side (i.e., they generate *saccades,* which are back-and-forth eye movements), the dysphoric and negative feelings associated with the trauma diminish or even disappear. Neural connections that are thought to reinforce the memory—and the pain associated with the memory—are hypothesized to be disrupted during the rapid back-and-forth saccadic eye movements.

During EMDR, the patient selects the target thoughts and memories to be "reprocessed." A specific scene from memory is selected that best represents the trauma. The patient then has to choose a statement that best expresses a negative self-belief associated with the event. Negative self-beliefs commonly associated with Love Trauma Syndrome are "I'm not good enough," "I am unlovable," "I'm a loser," "I am an inadequate lover," "I can't hold onto anything," or "I'm no good." To counter the negative self-belief, the patient needs to come up with a positive self-statement, such as "I am good enough," or "I am adequate." Just because you lost at love does not make you a loser.

EMDR then proceeds using the specific eye movements directed by the therapist. The patient focuses on the therapist's index finger. The therapist moves his or her finger up and down in a diagonal manner, and the patients are instructed to move their eyes (not their head) back and forth to follow the therapist's finger. The patients are instructed to think about their trauma while moving their eyes under the direction of the therapist.

If the positive self-beliefs are not adequately "installed" during EMDR, or if residual physical distress is experienced when the love trauma is recalled, the event is resubmitted for further processing. EMDR treatment is not considered to be complete until the patient can recall the event without feeling physical or emotional distress.

The Visual Trauma

Whereas many therapies for Love Trauma Syndrome emphasize the thoughts and feelings associated with a love trauma, EMDR highlights the prominence of *visual memory or imaging* of the love trauma event (and events surrounding the trauma). People can have vivid visual recollections and visions of the love trauma. Patients work hard to avoid contact with these images, although certain therapies emphasize the potential therapeutic benefit of being "flooded" and then desensitized to the dreaded love-trauma-related memories, visions, and fantasies (so-called "flooding" behavioral therapies).

Some therapists will ask the patient to bring in pictures of their lost love to desensitize them to their distress. If confronting the picture is too traumatic, they might be asked to confront portions of the picture, and gradually enlarge the area of the picture they are able to see until they experience no physical or emotional distress from viewing the picture. Some patients have "cut-out picture syndrome," where they cut out the part of the photo that shows their lost love. Many patients destroy or throw away pictures that have the object of their love trauma in them. Patients without photos can be asked to simply visualize in their minds the image of their lost love, and use this conjured image for the purpose of desensitization. Other items that remind the patient of their lost love, such as items of clothing, sports equipment, or shoes, can also be used to help desensitize the patient to their loss.

Group Therapy for Love Trauma Syndrome

Group therapy is often useful for people with Love Trauma Syndrome. Such therapies can use combinations of the different treatment options described previously. Instead of performing these activities alone, they are done in a group setting, and group members can benefit from the work in which others are engaged while trying to overcome their Love Trauma Syndromes. Patients feel less alienated and alone in the group setting, and are likely to feel better when they see that others "are in the same boat" as they are. By virtue of people wanting to share similar experiences and gain closeness with other group members, people become more willing to tell their stories in spite of their shame. Shame begins to lose some of its inhibiting power. Group therapy can also help to counter the social withdrawal from others that is so common for people with Love Trauma Syndrome.

A problem with group therapy of Love Trauma Syndrome relates to patients' reluctance to discuss their love trauma. Men particularly are often initially resistant to discussing their trauma, as it is associated with considerable shame and embarrassment. People often described feeling "humiliated" when talking about their love traumas, and feel that others will regard their concerns as trivial and as reflecting on their "defectiveness" (the latter because they were unable to hold on to their love object). People can be encouraged to discuss more neutral topics initially, such as their occupational, academic, or other less-anxiety-provoking concerns. They then might be encouraged to discuss other aspects of their relationship with their love trauma object before discussing the love trauma itself. Patients should be encouraged to first discuss events in their lives temporally surrounding the love trauma event (e.g., work, school, other family issues), and then later work up to discussing the event itself. This way you can gradually have patients work up to discussing and confronting the love trauma event in the group.

One type of group therapy that is sometimes useful for countering the pessimism and negativism of people with Love Trauma Syndrome is the "Positive Group." In such a group session, people are only allowed to discuss positive thoughts, feelings, and memories. If anything negative is brought up, there is an attempt to see what positive benefit can be gleaned from the otherwise negative material. Patients are forced to begin to think positively, and are able to carry this skill into their lives outside the group setting. Optimism replaces pessimism.

Our Two Memory Systems

Treatments for Love Trauma Syndrome need to emphasize work on the two different memory systems our brains possess—the *procedural learning system*, and the *declarative memory system*. The procedural learning system is involved in the acquisition of *new* skills and habits. When you learn to ride a bicycle, or to drive a car, you are utilizing your procedural learning system. Similarly, when you learn new cognitive skills, such as learning to think more positively in a Positive Group, you are using and exercising your procedural learning and memory system. If you read a book that describes "positive thinking," you are storing the information in the declarative memory system. But unless you practice positive thinking, you will not be able to use the positive thinking paradigm very well because it has not been stored in the procedural learning system (also sometimes called the "habit" learning system). For something to be stored in the habit learning system, you actually have to do it—that is, perform the task.

The declarative memory system is involved in your learning and remembering information. For instance, when you remember the title of this book that you are reading, you have used your declarative memory. Your name is stored in the declarative memory circuits in your brain. When you remember the details of a love trauma event, you are pulling these memories out of your declarative memory stores. In the treatment of Love Trauma Syndrome, your declarative memory is also used when you are educated about the symptoms and the course of Love Trauma Syndrome.

This sort of educational approach to treating Love Trauma Syndrome also often takes place in the context of group therapy. Your being educated by reading this book also involves using your declarative memory circuits.

"ROAR"

ROAR stands for *reality-oriented anger response*. ROAR therapy helps you determine whether your anger is reality based. Indeed, there are times when anger is an appropriate response to a love trauma. In some situations it is appropriate for you to remain angry, and in the future you might choose to not remain associated with the person with whom you are angry, as they have proved themselves an untrustworthy and unreliable ally. However, it is sometimes difficult to determine whether the anger is appropriate, and how much anger fits the perceived offense. Sometimes our anger is out of proportion to the specific offense that precipitated the angry response.

The eight steps of ROAR therapy for anger are as follows:

1. *Get in touch with your anger and crystalize in your mind about what you are angry.* Define with whom you are angry and about what you are angry. Be as specific as possible—provide specific examples of the interactions that caused the anger. Did the person specifically do something, or say something that was responsible for the anger, or is the anger related to something else (e.g., something that the person did or said in the past)? Is the anger specific to the incident, but also secondary to *residual* anger; that is, related to past events or to perceived offenses? What does your being angry about now remind you about from the past? Does the current offense that caused the anger most recently somehow resonate thematically with some past offenses, which exaggerates your anger response to the current offense and makes it seem out of proportion to the provocation? What is the current offense, what are the past offenses, and how do they resonate thematically? What is the theme? Does the current offense resonate thematically with something that someone else did; that is, is the current object of your anger paying for someone else's sins? What percentage of your anger is specific to the current offense, and what percentage is related to past offenses? What percentage of your anger is related to the person who precipitated the most recent bout of feeling angry, and what percentage is related to the deeds of others? Love-Trauma-Syndrome-related issues have the capacity to dramatically amplify the anger response to seemingly trivial provocations. However, the provocation was only the tip of the iceberg.

Note that there does not have to be only one issue about which you are angry. Usually you are angry about a number of issues, and each of these issues can resonate thematically with different issues in your past. You need to specifically identify all of the current and the past issues, and their thematic meaning to you. Always demand specific examples that precipitated the anger—do not allow the therapy to involve primarily vague issues. The vague issues are usually related to themes, and patients need to be able to separate anger appropriate to a specific offense from when the anger is "specific plus"; that is, related to a specific offense plus other past unresolved offenses (e.g., love-trauma-connected) as well. It is this resonant anger that often makes a seemingly trivial and unimportant issue precipitate a major flare-up of anger. Note that there can be a number of different offenses, and a number of different themes, some related to the person with whom the patient is angry, and some unrelated.

2. *Anger is ignited when there is a gap between what you want (expect) someone to do, and what they have done (or plan to do).* What is it that you think or feel that the party you are angry with *should* be doing, and what is it that they *are* doing? Clearly define the gap between what you believe they should do, and what you believe they are doing. Be as specific as possible.

3. *You feel angry because you feel entitled to having that gap filled.* You feel entitled to have someone do something for you, and have someone give you something. You feel that someone should have provided you with what you feel entitled. When you are angry, Karen Horney's "tyranny of the shoulds" is always in operation. (Although, again, there are times when your anger is appropriate—but you need to determine if this is one of those times. Again, this is not always easy to do.)

When you do not get what you want, you become angry. The more entitled you feel, the more you feel you should have something that you are not getting, and the angrier you become. Define what you feel entitled to. Be as specific as possible. What is it that you feel you should have? And who is responsible for giving it to you?

4. *The most important question you need to ask yourself is, are you really entitled to what it is that you want?* Do you think that most other reasonable people would agree with your idea that you are entitled to what you feel you should have? This will determine whether your anger is appropriate. It is unrealistic to expect others to always be able to meet your wants and needs, and it is certainly unrealistic to demand it. Even when you think that your needs should be met by someone else, they often are not. Life can be unfair. You cannot always expect life to be fair.

Often, you need actual input from other people to determine whether you are really objectively entitled to what you want from another person. That is why anger management skills are best taught in group sessions—you can benefit from the input of a variety of different people, and you can get a sampling of different views on the situation. This is also a reason why it is so important to have an empathic and reasonable, objective therapist help discuss your anger with you. Is it really appropriate for you to be angry about the situation about which you are angry? How easy is it to hear from others that you are not entitled to what you think you are entitled? Can you accept it? Why does your partner think or feel that you are not entitled to have what you think or feel you are entitled? What do they feel you are entitled? Would this be acceptable to you?

5. *If you find that you really are not entitled to what you want, why did you feel entitled to it?* Can you accept not having what you felt entitled? Can you accept it as being a preference, and not something you are entitled to and must have? How unhappy will you be if you do not get what you want, if your preferences are largely unfulfilled? Are you able to choose between being angry and being disappointed? Are you motivated to no longer feel angry? Very often the most appropriate response is being disappointed—not angry.

Can you accept being disappointed rather than being angry? Often anger acts as a defense against feeling depressed. Anger protects one's self-esteem, and therefore can have "antidepressant" functions, keeping the person from becoming depressed. Some people would rather be angry about their disappointment than depressed. This way their self-esteem remains largely intact.

6. *What other emotions or feelings do you have in response to your disappointment?* Does the disappointment make you feel sad, envious, jealous, resentful, frustrated, confused, hurt, disrespected, "put-down," anxious, suspicious, paranoid, "left out," unneeded, unrewarded, unrecognized, or disregarded? How damaged is your self-esteem? Do you feel the desire to regain some control over the relationship, to intimidate the person into behaving the way you want them to behave? Do you want to blame your partner? Do you feel the impulse to become angry with and intimidating to them again? How irresistible is this impulse? Can you imagine how you would feel if anger and blame were not emotions that you as a human could experience? Try to imagine how you would feel if anger were not in your emotional repertoire. Try to learn to express these feelings.

Direct expression of these feelings, and discussion of these feelings, is one of the aims of ROAR therapy. Very often the therapist needs to help the patient identify hidden emotions. The therapist might use facilitating statements such as, "If that happened to me I might feel sad or disappointed."

If the direct expression of the emotions is blocked, then there is the tendency to "act out" these feelings. Instead of telling your partner you are hurt and saddened by their insensitive remark, you slam the door. In the latter case, you are acting out your emotions rather than expressing and "dealing" with them. Anger frequently plays a role in "acting-out behaviors." Anger is usually the fuel of acting out.

7. *Are you able to tell the person with whom you are angry how you feel other than angry?* What other emotions can you communicate that you feel toward them? Can you tell the person how you feel using "I feel" statements (e.g., "I feel sad," or "I feel hurt") rather than becoming angry and blaming them? Can you become vulnerable rather than defend your pride? Can you swallow your pride?

How much do you blame your partner for your being angry? What percentage of your anger do you blame on your partner, and what percentage do you blame on others, or on yourself? Can you limit your expression of anger to just what you feel they are responsible for?

8. *Once you have shared your anger in a way that brings you closer to your partner—without threatening or excessively blaming him or her—what are the two of you going to do now?* What are the specific elements of the solution? What are each of you going to do differently? Can you engage in meaningful negotiation? How moved is each party by the pain of the other? How motivated is each person to really do things differently? Are there secret hidden agendas, such as one partner really wanting the relationship to fall apart so they can feel justified in leaving the relationship for someone else?

In actual ROAR therapy each step can be presented on a flip chart, and clients are reminded about each step by presenting a different page of the flip chart. There are eight flipcards, each with the following headings: Define why angry; Gap analysis; Entitlement analysis; Entitlement justification analysis; Preference and disappointment analysis; Feelings and self-esteem damage analysis; Communication and blame analysis; and Solution development and implementation. Each page of the flip chart contains the basic elements and tasks of that step of ROAR therapy.

ROAR therapy can be done with individuals or with couples, or in group or in family therapy. If one party of the problematic relationship does not want to be involved in therapy, this obviously hampers the effectiveness of the intervention, but individual ROAR therapy is possible and often quite useful. I often find it valuable to do the intervention first with each partner separately, and then bring them together to hear the other person's responses. I encourage active, effortful listening (with the partner trying to paraphrase the other's responses), and active, effortful negotiation (often with specific homework assignments that implement some of the specifically developed solutions).

Anger commonly accompanies Love Trauma Syndrome. Anger can become complicated and can involve property damage and physical aggression against others. When anger becomes tinged with paranoia and a desire for revenge, it can even result in murder. Although it is often important to get in touch with your anger, it is never appropriate to express your anger in such a way that you might harm another person or yourself. The expression of anger should be contained, and its appropriate expression might require the presence of a trained therapist who can monitor and help guide the expression of anger. Angry people should *never* have access to guns or to other weapons. If they do have such access, someone needs to intervene and remove the weapon.

I have some patients who describe listening to "angry music" while they are getting in touch with their angry feelings. They describe listening to songs that match their thoughts and feelings over and over until the anger is exhausted. This sort of music also enables you to better understand that you are not alone in having these feelings. You can get over them and go on. On a somewhat related note, I have had some people tell me that "Primal Scream Therapy" helped them recover from a love trauma. Their prolonged screaming is mixed with anger and terror, and eventually they claim to be able to "drain" themselves of these emotions and feel liberated.

Finally, it should be noted that some cognitive and rational behavior therapists who are "purists" rarely see anger as an appropriate response to any situation. Such therapists see anger as almost always representing an unreasonable expectation of others. Others can never be perfect. We might strive for perfection, but we can never achieve it.

Antidepressants in Love Trauma Syndrome

For some patients, self-help and talk therapies alone are not sufficient to break the severe depression and anxiety associated with their Love Trauma Syndrome. For patients with simple, acute, "uncomplicated," and less severe forms of Love Trauma Syndrome, most therapists would first advocate a trial of some psychotherapy alone (either individual, couples, group, or some combination). However, for those patients with severe and persistent Love Trauma Syndromes, especially when complicated by serious symptoms of hyperarousal and depression, medications such as antidepressants are often useful.

I am a great believer in the usefulness of psychotropic medications, especially antidepressant medications, in their ability to ameliorate the symptoms of severe and persistent (e.g., greater than 2 months in duration) Love Trauma Syndrome and its depressive complications. Sometimes other medications are also used as "antidepressant adjuvants" (i.e., in addition to the antidepressant medication). These adjuvant interventions (e.g., lithium, thyroid supplements, or even another antidepressant that operates on different brain neurotransmitter systems and has different clinical effects) can "boost" the overall antidepressant effect. Research on the most effective medications—and adjuvant strategies—for the treatment of Love Trauma Syndrome complicated by depression and anxiety should give us a better idea in the future of how to best treat specific patients.

It should be noted that medication treatment combined with psychotherapy can have a profound effect on the brain hyperarousal associated with Love Trauma Syndrome (see Figure 9.3). The reduction of brain hyperarousal is responsible for a number of the therapeutic benefits of treatment. The love trauma memories are taken off their "mental pedestal" for continuous contemplation, and can now be contemplated in a manner similar to other lifetime memories. After treatment, patients respond to love-trauma-related cues with much less physiological arousal. Psychotherapy helps patients understand how their brain's biological emergency responses to what are in reality innocuous cues are exaggerated and unnecessary. This allows patients to become less reactive to their hyperaroused periods.

Brain imaging studies have shown that "overactive" brain centers thought responsible for the experience of anxiety, depression, and dysphoric hyperarousal are made less active after weeks of successful treatment with an antidepressant (e.g., Drevets and Raichle, 1992; Kennedy, Javanmard, and Vaccarino, 1997). Antidepressants seem to be able to "turn down" overactive brain alarm centers; i.e., brain regions that alert us to the presence of danger. Note that antidepressants will not have an immediate therapeutic effect—it might take from weeks to months before a meaningful beneficial effect is realized. Sometimes the hyperarousal also needs to be addressed with anxiolytic medications such as lorazepam (Ativan), diazepam (Valium), alprazolam (Xanax), or clonazepam (Klonopin). Unfortunately, these anxiolytics provide only temporary

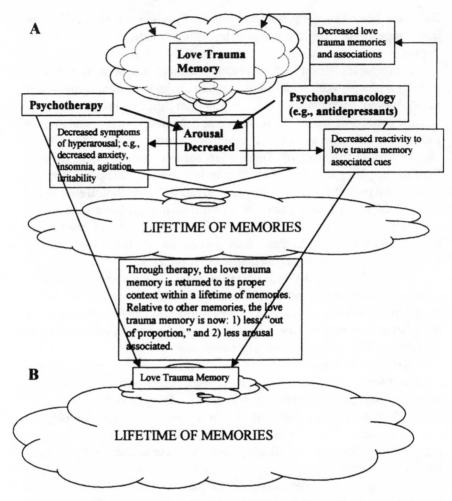

Figure 9.3   *Taking Love Trauma Memories off their "mental pedestal." Through psychotherapy and pharmacotherapy, there is transformation of A) separated love trauma memories (with a place in consciousness "out of proportion" to other lifetime memories), to B) love trauma memories that tower less over other memories. Hyperarousal is no longer associated with love trauma memories.*

relief, and it is the antidepressant that will lower the arousal more permanently. However, the anxiolytics can provide for a temporary "band-aid" while the antidepressants are taking their time to have a more enduring therapeutic effect. One serious problem with anxiolytic medications is that they are potentially addictive, and need to be used with great caution by people with Love Trauma Syndrome that is complicated by substance or alcohol abuse.

Some patients will begin to feel much better with their antidepressant medication, and will then stop taking their medication because they feel that they have recovered. They might also lower the dose of their antidepressant soon after beginning to experience a beneficial effect. Such people can then have a return of some hyperarousal symptoms within days to weeks of medication discontinuation or dose reduction. One common symptom of the return of hyperarousal is the reemergence of some sleep disturbance (e.g., insomnia, early morning awakening) or of irritability and anger. The antidepressant treatment should be reestablished to recover its full therapeutic effect.

Some Love Trauma Syndromes are associated with obsessions and ruminations about the love trauma event. Certain antidepressant medications (e.g., fluoxetine [Prozac], sertraline [Zoloft], paroxetine [Paxil]) are particularly good at helping decrease some of these unpleasant obsessions and mental fixations related to a love trauma event. Sometimes, higher doses of these medications need to be used to obtain the "antiobsessional" effects. However, conventional antidepressant doses of these medications are often effective in reducing the upsetting obsessions.

Hence, antidepressants can be used to address a number of different target symptoms of Love Trauma Syndrome, such as hyperarousal, depression, obsessional thoughts, and mental fixation on love trauma memories, thoughts, and feelings. They might even help some of the numbing and dissociative symptoms, and diminish social avoidance and avoidance of love-trauma-related cues. However, regardless of the target symptoms, it should be reemphasized that when using antidepressants the patient needs to remember that these medications do not work overnight. Antidepressant medications need time—on the order of several weeks—to take effect. Even then, the medications often need to be used for months more before the full effect is realized.

Additionally, these medications have side-effects—some of which are intolerable to the patient. If one antidepressant causes unpleasant side effects, other medications then need to be tried. If you and your doctor find that you are sensitive to side effects, remember that for most antidepressants it is useful to try a lower dose and slowly work your way up to a more effective dose. Some of the side effects of these medications will go away with time. You have to be patient (hence the term "patient"—you are called a patient because that is what you have to be during the process of healing from any illness).

Love-Trauma-Syndrome-Associated "Defeat Stress" and the Antidepressant Effect

Antidepressant medications are able to combat the effects of "defeat stress" in the brain. A love trauma is such a defeat stress, and animal research has shown that, when faced with an overwhelming stressor that causes defeat, animals on antidepressant medications continue physical activity and efforts to overcome the stress for longer periods than animals not receiving antidepressants. While being treated with an antidepressant, animals under stress are less likely to give up and appear helpless.

An example of how well antidepressants can help people with Love Trauma Syndrome is illustrated by a patient of mine whose husband had an affair with her sister. She discovered that the affair had been going on for years without her being aware of it. She felt betrayed by her husband and her sister, who eventually both ran off to another state to set up residence together. My patient became depressed, and for years felt inadequate and unattractive. When I first saw her, she was obsessed with visions of her husband and sister together sexually, and dreamed about them nightly. She had attempted suicide by overdose to get these thoughts out of her mind and to stop the love-trauma-related nightmares. Her standard and quality of living had fallen after her husband deserted her, and she was pessimistic that things would ever get better for her. She felt hopeless, helpless, ugly and of "low value."

After just a few weeks on the antidepressant Prozac, her upsetting nightmares and intrusive thoughts of her ex-husband and her sister disappeared, and her mood brightened. She no longer felt unattractive, and she began dressing quite stylishly. She no longer felt hopeless about her life. She was like a phoenix rising from the ashes—and rise from the ashes she did. She reengaged relationships with friends and relatives, improved her occupational performance as a school teacher, and increased her social activities. She rekindled her interests in writing poetry and playing the guitar, and even began performing at a local coffeehouse.

A number of my patients with Love Trauma Syndrome and depression have on their own taken the naturally occurring "phytotherapeutic" (i.e., herbal) antidepressant agent St. John's Wort (*Hypericum performatum* extract). This herbal remedy has been reported to be effective for the treatment of mild to moderate depression (Wheatley, 1997; Ernst, Rand, and Stevinson, 1998). For instance, one patient who came to me with what he called "relationship blues" (it was a chronic Love Trauma Syndrome mixed with depression) found St. John's Wort effective for improving his mood. It also reduced his overall "lovesick" feelings (i.e., a generalized malaise for which no medical cause could be found). Interestingly, one of the suspected activities of *Hypericum* is the inhibition of some "sickening substances" (i.e., depression, tiredness, anxiety, and other "ill feelings"—inducing substances) secreted during certain forms of stress. For instance, *Hypericum* has been reported to dramatically inhibit interleukin-6 production (Thiele et al., 1994). Interleukin-6 is one of many sickening substances secreted in response to a variety of physiological and emotional stressors. A whole new class of antidepressants is being developed by pharmaceutical companies that block another "sickening factor"—i.e., substance P (Kramer et al., 1998). Substance P is involved in the neural transmission and perception of pain. It is not known at this time if *Hypericum* blocks substance P. *Hypericum* has been reported to be useful in people with prominent somatic symptoms of depression, such as tiredness and fatigue (Hubner, Lande and Podzuweit, 1994).

Some recent studies found St. John's Wort to be as effective as conventional antidepressants, and without the side effects associated with the more conventional antidepressant medications. At this time psychiatrists are unable to predict which antidepressant will be best tolerated and most effective for a particular patient. *Hypericum* extracts have been reported to have effects on the brain similar to "synthetic" antidepressants, such as Prozac (fluoxetine), Zoloft (sertraline), or Celexa (citalopram). For instance, both synthetic antidepressants and *Hypericum* extract increase serotonin receptor binding in the brain.

Repetitive Transcranial Magnetic Stimulation (RTMS)

When Love Trauma Syndrome is complicated by severe depression and medications and psychotherapy prove ineffective, a new treatment called repetitive transcranial magnetic stimulation (rTMS) might be considered to help lessen symptoms of severe depression. In rTMS, a pulsing magnetic probe is placed over the scalp, and the pulsing magnetic field is able to pass through the scalp and skull and directly stimulate underlying brain cortical neurons. Early studies have found that rTMS can diminish symptoms of depression. Unfortunately, rTMS is not currently approved or routinely available for the treatment of depression, and it remains a research tool at this time (although a number of psychiatric research centers offer the treatment as a research intervention).

Unlike electroconvulsive shock (ECS) treatment for depression, rTMS does not require the use of anaesthesia or the induction of a seizure to be effective. Interestingly, the antidepressant effect of rTMS might involve neuronal brain mechanisms similar to ECS and antidepressant medications. Both ECS and antidepressants have been found to reverse psychological stress- and trauma-induced brain neuronal (i.e., nerve cell) "shrinkage." Recent studies have shown that ECS and antidepressants increase the production of certain brain cell growth factors, such as nerve growth factor (NGF) and brain-derived neurotrophic factor (BDNF; Duman and Vaidya, 1998; Duman et al., 1997, Morinobu et al., 1997). These brain growth factors increase the survival, growth, and synaptic strength (i.e., nerve cell connections or "connectivity") of brain neurons. Such changes are thought to underlie the therapeutic actions of antidepressant treatments such as antidepressant medications, ECS, and rTMS. While the stress-induced impoverished neuronal connections allow for a fixation on defeat-stress and trauma-related memories, thoughts, and feelings, antidepressant treatments permit the formation of new neuronal synaptic connections that are able to compete with the older stress- and trauma-forged connections. These new nerve connections can support different (i.e., non-trauma-related) memories, ways of thinking, feeling, and behaving (e.g., see Figure 9.3). Interestingly, many people have the mistaken notion that antidepressant medications can "damage" the brain. In fact, the opposite seems to be the case. The antidepressant medications, and even ECS, appear to be able to prevent and reverse stress- and trauma-induced neuronal injury. Antidepressant treatments are both "neuroprotective" and "neurorestorative." Whether rTMS is likewise a topic for future research.

Antipsychotic Medications and Love Trauma Syndrome

Some patients with severe Love Trauma Syndrome who are unable to resist their violent urges might need antipsychotic medication to quell their violent impulses. Some patients become dissociated and unresponsive to outside inputs. No one should underestimate the destructive potential of someone with a severe Love Trauma Syndrome and a history of prior violence. If alcohol or other drugs of abuse such as amphetamine or cocaine are also involved, the likelihood of violence increases further still. In these situations I feel that antipsychotic medications are often justified to help pacify the patient. Additionally, patients who are potentially violent might need inpatient psychiatric hospitalization to protect them and others from their violent urges.

As described in an earlier chapter, some people can become psychotic after a love trauma. When someone is psychotic they have problems differentiating reality from fantasy. They might hear voices or sounds that others do not hear. Sometimes they become paranoid, believing that there are people who want to hurt them, or take advantage of them, or see them do poorly and be unhappy. They might believe that others are following them, spying on them, stealing from them, or carefully monitoring their activities. Antipsychotic medications, such as olanzapine (Zyprexa), risperidone (Risperdal), and quetiapine (Seroquel) are used to treat psychosis.[2]

Not uncommonly, people who become psychotic in the context of a severe Love Trauma Syndrome develop delusions of jealousy. Delusions are false beliefs that are not grounded in reality. When someone has a delusion of jealousy, they become convinced that there are rivals for their romantic interests—when in fact there are none. They are constantly vigilant for romantic rivals, and often accuse their love interests of being unfaithful. One patient became convinced that his wife had "hundreds of affairs" while they were married—she in fact had none. She had been involved with just one other man (about whom my patient knew), and that was years before she was married, before she even knew my patient.

Patients with Love Trauma Syndrome complicated by delusions of jealousy sometimes need to be treated with antipsychotic medications. When appropriately treated, the patients (and those around them) become more comfortable. For instance, in the case of the patient described previously, after several months on an antipsychotic, he stopped talking about his wife's "affairs" completely, and accepted that she was "a good woman" and was probably being faithful to him. Such patients become less controlling and possessive as they are less concerned about potential rivals in their environment and about the fidelity of their mates.

Monitoring the Effectiveness of Therapy

Regardless of the treatments being used to help someone recover from a Love Trauma Syndrome, it is important that the effectiveness of the overall treatment be assessed on a regular basis. In chapter 2, I presented the Love Trauma Inventory (LTI), a questionnaire that patients can take to determine the severity of their condition. This yardstick can be used to measure how someone is doing over the course of therapy.

To follow a patient's progress during therapy for Love Trauma Syndrome, patients are given copies of the LTI and are encouraged to complete the test in the day or two before their next treatment session with me. I usually ask the patients to complete the questions while thinking about the way they felt since the last time I saw them (e.g., over the last week or two). I also encourage them to write in narrative statements about how they have felt over this time period (e.g., discuss particularly problematic reminders, or interventions they found helpful). It is often useful to plot their course on a graph, with their total scores indicated at each time point. In this way, the effectiveness of the different interventions that are being used can be assessed, and the most useful treatments for a patient can be selected. In this manner, treatment for Love Trauma Syndrome can be individualized for particular patients.

Finally, patients should not be discouraged if progress seems slow. Patients often want dramatic improvements in a short period of time. This is often not possible. Typically, the syndrome needs to be chipped away at slowly, bit by bit, until it becomes less and less of a problem for the patient.

Chapter Ten

Beware These Inconstant Lovers

I t is said that "an ounce of prevention is worth a pound of cure." For people who want to decrease their likelihood of becoming a victim of Love Trauma Syndrome, it might be useful to become aware of some "types" who can be unreliable partners.

There are certain people who initially appear to be attractive mates. They might be fun, wealthy, charming, witty, and capable of making you feel good (at least in the short run). Although they might be very appealing initially, some can serve you up a generous helping of love trauma. When you look at their history of relationships, problems emerge.

What follows is a brief list and description of some character types that should be avoided. If you do decide to become involved with such people and you are looking for a long-term, perhaps permanent relationship, make perfectly clear to these people what you want from the relationship. Describe to them the level of commitment that you expect. If you are not looking for a more permanent relationship, and you just want to have fun, then have your fun. However, many people who initially think that they are just going to "go along for the ride" end up becoming more involved than they thought, along with developing a case of Love Trauma Syndrome.

MANIC LOVERS

As implied in the previous paragraph, you need to be careful with whom you become romantically involved if you want to decrease your likelihood of being a victim of Love Trauma Syndrome. One person to be on the lookout for is the man or woman with manic or hypomanic tendencies. On the surface, such individuals appear to be very attractive partners, and are often quite charismatic. They exude enthusiasm and vitality. Manic and hypomanic people usually are focused on having fun, and they are usually successful at achieving this goal. They avidly seek out pleasurable experiences, and are unintimidated when they approach opportunities for pleasure. These people typically "feel good" all or much of the time, and are effective at making others around them also feel good. But such people are more likely to make you a victim of their poorly considered choices. They often choose what they feel will give them the most immediate pleasure, happiness, "fun," without concern for the longterm consequences of their actions.

The mechanisms in the brain that support feeling good also heighten appetitive interests and pursuits—that is, appetites for food, for sex, or for other rewarding activities. People with manic or hypomanic tendencies often have an increased interest in sex, and their libido can be quite high. In fact, they do have more sex. The sex they have is wilder and more uninhibited. If you are their partner, they might not want to have sex with only you. Their charisma makes them quite attractive to a variety of mates. People with satyriastic tendencies typically have some form of manic or hypomanic condition.

These people may become unfaithful to their partners, or they may stop going to work to pursue activities that they find more pleasurable (e.g., golf, going to the beach, having sex with whomever they want and can). Manics and hypomanics often ignore the painful consequences of their actions. They might ruin their marriages by impulsively becoming romantically involved with others. By the time they realize what has happened, irreversible damage has been done to their relationships.

An example of a person who inflicted a Love Trauma Syndrome on her husband is given by a woman who came to my office asking me to help her "deal" with her husband. She was a well-dressed, stiffly attractive 40-year-old who described her situation matter-of-factly and without emotion. She told me that she was one of the most successful real estate agents in the area and that recently she had taken on a boyfriend over 10 years her junior—much to the chagrin of her husband. Her husband, she explained, "had blown the whole thing out of proportion," and was in an "annoying, hysterical dither." She complained that he was keeping her up at night "with his endless whining." "It's a good thing I only need a few hours of sleep," she said. She wanted me to "set him straight." "Do you think you could calm him down for me, Dr. Rosse?" she asked. When I did speak with him, it was obvious he was in the throes of a full-blown Acute Love Trauma Syndrome.

She admitted that she did not like seeing her husband "so unhappy," but otherwise she denied distress. She smiled when she spoke of her boyfriend, and described enjoying the affair. "I feel like I'm twenty again," she told me. At one point she even told me about her boyfriend's copious amounts of ejaculate. "I've never seen anything like it," she told me in awe. "Maybe you need to check him out," she laughed. There was no hesitancy in the way she addressed me and she looked me straight in the eye, rarely averting her gaze. She even showed me a picture of her and her handsome lover taken outside a local restaurant. They both had wide smiles and very bright white teeth.

The Hypomanic/Manic Continuum

As described in an earlier chapter, people with hypomanic/manic tendencies can be uncommonly cheerful; be quite irritable when they do not get their way; have inflated self-esteem; have a decreased need for sleep; be overly talkative and productive at what they do; and, as described in the previous example, be excessively involved in pleasurable activities, including sex. Hypomania refers to a form of the condition less severe than mania.

However, there is a wide spectrum of hypomanic/manic-like symptoms that exists between being "normal" and having a full-blown mania. Sometimes somebody's hypomanic nature is quite subtle, and there does not appear to be anything "wrong" with the person.

For instance, there is a range of cheerfulness, from normative feelings of cheeriness to manic cheerfulness and euphoria. We all feel irritable from time to time, but if you turn up the volume on irritability you can approach manic levels of cantankerousness. Additionally, it is not unusual to feel self-confident, but when you consistently exaggerate your abilities and believe that you can do things that you really cannot, you are beginning to approach the manic end of the spectrum. Although many of us can get away with an occasional night of sleeping for only a few hours, not feeling tired after a couple of nights of little or no sleep is solidly in the manic end of the spectrum. Finally, although most impulses (e.g., to be unfaithful) are resistible, they become increasingly less resistible in the context of growing hypomania and mania.

At the more pathological end of the continuum, the hypomanic/manic character is possessed of an increasingly greater sense of vigor. From this increased sense of energy, coupled with a change in their assessment of the limits that the environment places on them, is born the bold risk-takers that these people can become. Hypomanic/manic people minimize the risks and the negative consequences of their actions. They do not appreciate that the choices and decisions that they make now have consequences that could affect them for their entire lives. On the other hand, people with more depressive predispositions have the opposite problems of their hypomanic/manic counterparts. Whereas hypomanic/manic people make decisions with little processing of the adverse consequences, depressives are obsessed with the possible dire outcomes of their decisions. Depressives can be paralyzed with their indecisiveness.

Hypomanic/manic people are not intimidated by the dangers of having affairs. Such activities can include not only sexual indiscretions, but also impulsive and poorly thought out business investments, multiple impulsive purchases, and spending sprees. Because of sexual indiscretions, I have seen marriages disintegrate because of the sexual activities of a partner during a manic episode.

For instance, a manic woman who was married was admitted to a psychiatric unit where I worked. She had met a man for the first time at the supermarket and later that day had sex with him. She was attracted to this man because "he was real cute" and had a tattoo of a flower on his arm. At the time of her admission to the psychiatric unit, she was clearly manic. Although her indiscretion was clearly secondary to her temporary manic state, her husband developed a severe Love Trauma Syndrome with which he dealt by ending the marriage in divorce.

Even much less severely afflicted hypomanic/manic characters can have problems resulting from inadequately processing the potential risks and consequences of their actions. This is why their relentless pursuit of fun can land them into trouble. The maxim, "for one moment's pleasure you can spend the rest of your life paying for it" is often wasted on these people. These people are willing to overstep the bounds of impropriety, even if it means that they are in danger of being caught.

This is why some of our leaders and others who achieve fame—be they politicians, sports figures, actors, brave soldiers and aviators, or corporate leaders—sometimes blunder. People who achieve such prominence tend to have hypomanic/manic qualities, and are drawn from a group of individuals who are more prone to have hypomanic traits. The hypomanic/manic-associated attributes (e.g., confidence, courage, fearlessness) that help them achieve success in their fields are often the same attributes that lead to their downfall and involvement in risky and questionable behaviors. The very boldness that gets them into their positions of leadership and fame gets them into trouble. Their strength is their Achilles heel.

The mild hypomania of the woman whom I described earlier in this chapter helped make her one of the most aggressive and successful real estate agents in her region. She met formal diagnostic criteria for syndromal hypomania. She actually described herself as feeling "high." "You know," she said to me, "the way you feel when you fall in love." She was irritable, and when I said something with which she did not agree she was quick to show her irritation. She seemed overly confident. She spoke constantly and it was hard to interrupt her, although she was quick to interrupt me. She was very productive at work, and in fact had a record year in sales. She slept less than about 5 hours each night, and reported "never" feeling tired. One of her complaints about her husband was that "he slept all the time." He was sleeping about 8 to 9 hours a night. "What does he want to do" she said to me, "sleep his life away?"

Her hypomania also facilitated her feeling ready to have an affair, and having the affair in a fairly open manner. She did not want to divorce her husband, and I believe her when she said she thought little about the problems that might arise from having an affair. However, her 15 years of marriage ended in divorce, and the family life of her 13-year-old son was disrupted, all to her dismay. Her position in her company was threatened when issues of sexual harassment were raised because she had an affair with a younger junior employee.

Because manic/hypomanic characters are less intimidated by risk, they are at greater risk of drug and alcohol addiction. As they are also impulsive, they can rush into action without fully thinking about the consequences of their actions. They cannot envision a time when they could not maintain voluntary control over what they do. "Other people might become addicted," they say to themselves, "but not me." They feel immune to addiction and rashly decide to sample addictive drugs. Many can become addicts.

Finally, the hypomanic/manic character is also quick to challenge the authority of others. Social conventions and rules are for other people to follow. Marriage and a commitment to others does not cramp their style when it comes to pursuing pleasurable sexual activities with inappropriate mates.

The hypomanic/manic characters described in the aforementioned paragraphs are fairly easy to identify, but the more typical characters encountered by most of us (and include many of us) are "form frustes," or lesser forms, of the manic and hypomanic patients described previously. These more typical characters show signs of being somewhere between "normal" and "manic."

If you want a rough gauge of how hypomanic/manic-like someone is, you can ask yourself the following questions about the person's *predominant* mood and behavior (answer "yes" or "no"):

1. Is the person always cheerful?
2. Are they quick to challenge the authority of others? Do they seem ready for a fight if necessary?
3. Do they seem confident and determined? Do they seek and confidently hold on to positions of dominance?
4. Is there an absence of self-doubt and of anxiety?
5. Do they appear energetic, sometimes tireless?
6. Do they dominate conversations? When they talk, do they express many ideas or jokes?
7. Are they very active socially, and do they have a wide range of acquaintances, friends, and allies?
8. Do they have very active sex lives with a partner (or partners)? Are they bold in their quest for partners (e.g., active and confident "pickup artists?")
9. In their academic and occupational pursuits, do they become very busy with ambitious projects?
10. Do they place a lot of importance on having fun, and go to great lengths to have it?

The greater the number of "yes" answers, the greater the likelihood that they have hypomanic/manic-like features. Note that a person with even mild hypomanic/manic traits who appears more toward the "normative" end of the spectrum of the characteristics described previously can get into trouble in their personal relationships. Even these individuals can suffer from a diminished perception of risk and minimization of potential onerous consequences. It is for this reason that they are more likely to get into trouble in general, but the classic problem for them is their tendency to get overly involved in pleasurable activities—that is, sex—without regard for adverse consequences. They might ruin their marriages by impulsively becoming romantically involved with others.

Hypomanic/manic people are more prone to becoming "victory sick" in the context of achieving some "victory" in their lives. When they are victory sick they are overly emboldened and have a dramatically diminished sense of risk. Their judgment becomes further impaired, and they end up engaging in risky and reckless behavior that gets them into trouble. One hypomanic/manic patient prone to becoming victory sick was a builder of office buildings. After completing a project, he would become elated and want to "party," and would develop satyristic tendencies. He was married with three children, and during these periods he had multiple affairs, often with prostitutes. His wife discovered that he was unfaithful, and their marriage ended in divorce.

Although these people might be fun to be around, if you're looking for love, and looking for someone who you want to be certain won't give you a generous helping of Love Trauma Syndrome, stay away from these sorts of individuals, especially if they display a lot of the features described previously. If you do get involved with such people, voice your concerns and make it very clear to them that you want them to honor their commitment to you. Express your expectations for the relationship and the limits of what you will tolerate. Consider precommitted relationship and premarriage counseling. Also consider periodic or ongoing counseling as a preventive measure. Even trivial problems in a relationship can drive a hypomanic/manic character into the arms of someone else.

Many hypomanic/manic characters can be tamed, although some only partially. They can learn how to be less impulsive and reckless. They can learn to discipline themselves and to contemplate possible negative outcomes of their behavior (especially after being burned for not doing so in the past). Some hypomanic/manic characters surround themselves with a partner, friends, and associates who send up warning flags urging them to consider the possible negative consequences of their actions. Some of these characters can learn to heed Horace's advice to "be bold and be sensible," i.e., balance their boldness with common sense.

THE PSYCHOPATH

Another type of person who is at first superficially attractive, charismatic, charming, and fun to be around is the psychopath (also called *antisocial personality*). If you get involved in a serious relationship with such a character, you are at high risk of suffering a love trauma. There are many other reasons to stay away from this sort of character, as psychopaths become involved in a wide range of illegal activities.

These people are masters of deception and disguise that is designed to disarm you so you can be more easily violated. Similar to hypomanic/manic characters, psychopaths like to party and have fun. They want to charm you and have sex with you. Some people like being around psychopaths because the lives of psychopaths can be full of excitement. However, the fun and adventure usually comes at tremendous cost to those who choose to associate with such people.

Psychopaths are not full "emotional beings." They lack the capacity for feeling guilt, shame, and anxiety about mistreating others. They practice the cognitive distortion of *minimization*, whereby they minimize in their minds the often horrible impact they have on their victims. They can minimize the unhappy consequences their behavior has on others to the point of frank denial. They do not become appropriately upset when they imagine doing bad things (e.g., cheating, robbing, murdering, having children whom they have no intention of helping to support, having multiple affairs). They lack the "empathic capacity" to feel what other people feel. Psychopaths are interested in satisfying their own needs with little attention being given to the needs of others. They are amoral individuals who boldly take from others without feeling guilt. The psychopath, or psychopathic or antisocial personality, is also sometimes referred to as a *sociopath*.

To acquire resources and rewards, psychopaths knowingly engage in behaviors that break established social rules and laws. The spectrum of antisocial behaviors includes stealing and the pursuit of other illegal activities. They also habitually fail to honor financial, social, and occupational obligations. They "con" others for personal profit or for pleasure. Although psychopaths typically are irresponsible parents and partners who inadequately provide for their children's welfare, they can also be seemingly dependable parents who provide for their family with illegally acquired resources. Many psychopaths operate within the guise of seemingly socially acceptable occupations and professions. It is thought that "white collar" psychopaths consume as much as 10% of the Gross National Product (GNP) of the United States.

What can be most chilling about psychopaths is their lack of remorse and their self-serving justifications for why they committed their crimes. They convince themselves that the victim somehow "deserved" their fate, or that their criminal act was some form of necessary "self-help" for a sociocultural condition not to their liking. These psychopaths do not see themselves as villains (in fact, they often see others as the villains).

Psychopaths come in "soft" and "hard" forms. The softer varieties of psychopathy are often the hardest to detect. The detection of softer psychopaths is further complicated by the fact that in our society some of the distinctions between soft psychopathy and acceptable social and business practices are blurred. The distinction is being worked out continually in our courts of civil law. For instance, what some might view as a "con job" might be viewed by others as good marketing and salesmanship. Although getting involved with a soft psychopath can provide you with short-term benefit, the longer-term consequences of associating with such individuals can be devastating to your social and financial standing.

The antisocial behaviors of psychopaths are becoming an increasing problem for our society. For instance, when I went to elementary school in the city, metal detectors were not present at the entrances to screen children for weapons. Now many elementary schools in cities have such metal detectors, and people are clamoring for more detectors to be installed. Increasing amounts of government resources are going toward efforts to contain the growing excess of antisocial behaviors in our society. Additionally, emboldening drugs of abuse (e.g., cocaine, alcohol, methamphetamine) have a multiplying effect on antisocial behavior, and increase the likelihood of the expression of psychopathic behaviors.

Another reason to stay away from psychopaths as romantic partners is that if you decide you want to leave the relationship, and the psychopath develops a Love Trauma Syndrome, they are more likely to resort to perverse means of acting out on their desire to punish you. Even if they are engaging in multiple affairs, they might be very possessive and demand fidelity on your part. Some more severely psychopathic individuals resist accepting failures in love by trying to threaten the rejecting partner into submission. The psychopath might even resort to the use of weapons such as knives or guns. This is a particularly dangerous way to express one's unhappiness about a love trauma, as some psychopaths end up using the weapons on others (i.e., the rejecting partner or accidental targets).

The Maximizing Cheat

Intermediate between "normals" and psychopaths are *maximizing cheats*. Although most of us cater to our selfish interests first, we are not all cheats. Cheats give others the sense that they are going to be treated fairly and be reciprocated, however, they have little intention of doing so. Cheats try to maximize what they can get out of relationships, while being aware that they are going to reciprocate as little as possible. Such people can be charming and suave, and can make you believe that you are going to be treated fairly. They are looking for "something for nothing" (or something for as close to nothing as they can get). When they maximize what they get, it's at someone else's expense.

One example of a cheat is given by a patient of mine who worked hard to have affairs with other women while he was married. He said he enjoyed the benefits of marriage (e.g., having children and a "place to hang his hat"). He also said that being married "is good for business—makes people think you're a good, family man." However, he also enjoyed his affairs. He said that his wife "trusted" him, and that she thought he was "a devoted and perfect husband." She did not know about his affairs, and he said if she discovered them "she would be devastated." To cover up his unfaithful activities, he told his wife that he was going on "business trips." In fact, the only business many of these trips involved was jumping into bed with other women. "I give them a good time," he said.

He was in touch with wanting to maximize what he could get out of life, and he articulated this as his philosophy of life. But he also said that cheating "came with the territory," claiming that others "just want to keep it all for themselves." "You have to cheat them before they cheat you" he said. "That's what's it all about." Although he thought it unlikely that his wife was having affairs, he said, "You never know."

He was also a cheat when it came to his business relationships. He even boasted to me about how certain business deals were clearly in his favor, and how the other parties did not realize how little they were getting out of the agreements. He once even brought in documents showing me how a particular deal was going to earn him hundreds of thousands of dollars. He said that the client was getting little in return. "I'm not going to refuse to take their money," he said."Do you feel guilty about this?" I asked the patient while marveling at the documents he was showing me. "Hell no," he said, sitting back in the chair laughing. "This is good business. Hell, this is great business" he exclaimed.

This patient, like many cheats, was not a formal psychopath. He did not violate formal laws in the way that more hardened psychopaths do. Instead, such cheats work hard to maximize what they can get out of life by cheating in ways that fall short of frank criminal behavior. However, if you build a personal or professional life with such a person, you might find yourself with little left after the betrayals have been discovered and the relationship has ended.

Cheats are also quite adept at developing self-serving justifications for their behavior. They convince themselves that their cheating is "justified." They sometimes blame the victim for their actions. A patient of mine who had an affair claimed that he did so because his wife had "a bad temper." In reality, his temper was far worse. He developed a list of justifications for leaving his wife of 20 years for a younger and more attractive partner. He was not willing to view himself as a "cheat" who violated his marriage vows to his wife. Instead, he viewed himself as someone who had been oppressed for so many years by "that witch" [his wife] and was now "breaking free" from his tormentor.

In fact, many cheats try to convert themselves from the status of a cheat to that of a "victim." I once had an adolescent patient who had sexually abused a 7-year-old child. This teenager was convinced that he was the victim of the 7-year-old. He repeatedly said that the child "came on to him," and did not attempt to repel his advances. After the teenager was caught, he blamed the 7-year-old for "leading me on." He became very distressed when I did not accept his victim status.

Cheats try to maximize what they can get for the least amount of effort. Such a position is illustrated by the fable of the Little Red Hen. In this story, the Little Red Hen has three animal friends. They watch her as she prepares to plant seeds to grow wheat. Before she puts the first seeds into the ground, the hen asks if any of her three friends would help her plant the seeds. They all decline. The wheat grows, and the Little Red Hen harvests the wheat, thrashes it, and takes it to the mill to be ground. However, before each step, the hen asks her friends to help her, but they always refuse. She takes the wheat to the mill herself, and prepares the processed wheat to be baked into a loaf of bread. Her companions stand idly by, not lifting a finger to help. Her friends do not even help her put the bread into the oven.

Finally, when the bread comes out of the oven, hot, and smelling delicious, the Little Red Hen sits at her kitchen table ready to eat the bread. She then turns to ask if any of her friends would help her eat the bread. Her three companions jump at the opportunity. But she blocks their access to the bread. She tells them that since they had done nothing to assist her in making the bread, they could not share in eating it. The moral of the story is that you should have to *earn* your access to resources.

However, the Little Red Hen's friends are examples of rather inept maximizing cheats. Better cheats employ strategies that enable them to exert minimal effort but still get their way. The hen's friends might have been able to enjoy eating the bread when it was finally baked. For instance, they might have said that ordinarily they would have loved to help her, but they had excuses for why they could not. For example, they might have said they were feeling ill and not up to helping her, or they were too busy with other chores. They might have begged her for some bread to eat, claiming to be on the verge of collapsing from starvation. Or they might have sworn that in the future they would be certain to be of more assistance, and that they had learned their lesson from the Little Red Hen. Such deceptions are only a few of the strategies used by maximizing cheats looking to get something for nothing.

Some maximizing cheats are quite adept at using deceptive attractiveness displays to capture their prey. They might claim access to resources, or a desire to share resources, when they really do not have access to the resources, or any willingness to share. When a person realizes that they have been so deceived, they feel betrayed. Even among primates, deceptive attractiveness displays have been observed by males pretending to have food that they are willing to exchange for sexual favors. In actuality, they do not have the promised food. The female primate does not become aware of the deception until after the sexual favor has been given.

A case example of how a person can become a victim of false attractiveness display woo is given by a patient of mine named Janice. When Janice first came into my office, her distress was made evident by her tears. Through these tears she told me the story of her relationship with her husband, Fred. She had met Fred at a university 6 years earlier where they were both graduate students. In his initial wooing of her, he told her that he was from a wealthy Southern family. He said that he was "lucky" he did not have to worry about making an income to get by. He was interested in just being a student.

After their relationship had become more intimate and sexual, she wondered why Fred did not take her home to meet his family. It was not until a year later that it became clear that his family was not wealthy—in fact, they were quite poor. He told her that he lied to her so that she "would not reject him," as he was so much in love with her. They had been living together for months, and overall the relationship seemed to be going well. She decided to stay in the relationship despite the evidence of his deception. They eventually were married, and she became the major wage earner in the family, even after the birth of their son Joey. Fred continued to try to complete graduate school.

What precipitated Janice coming into my office was that she was heartbroken after discovering that Fred was unfaithful. One day while she was straightening out papers on his desk, she found a letter that started with the words "Dear Judy." Wondering who Judy was, she continued to read the letter. In the letter Fred described Judy as the "love of his life." However, he went on to say that he could not go on with the relationship with her. This was because his wife "was mentally ill," and would not be able to tolerate the breakup of their marriage. He was breaking up with Judy "for the benefit of his family," and putting his "own needs second." He was hoping that Judy would "understand."

Since the birth of their child 3 years earlier, Janice had thought that Fred had been out late at night "working at the campus library" because "things had become too chaotic at home with little Joey in the apartment." "The apartment is so small, and there really was no quiet place to work. Joey had colic and it was hard to get him to sleep. Fred was always blaming Joey for his not being able to work in the apartment and needing to go to the library. But now I know he was out with Judy, and who knows who else."

Janice had chosen a bad mate, and had failed to respond to his first evidence of a major deception. She was brokenhearted.

THE NARCISSIST

Another type of character who might initially be quite appealing but would be a good candidate for leaving you with Love Trauma Syndrome is the narcissist. Simply put, narcissists are preoccupied with their own needs (with little concern for the needs of others). They feel "special" and important. People with narcissistic features boast about their achievements while deprecating the accomplishments of others. Nevertheless, narcissists can be quite adept at wooing mates, as they are often attractive and intelligent.

The term *narcissist* comes from the Greek legendary character Narcissus. Narcissus died because he was so preoccupied with his own beauty that he was unable to stop looking at his own reflection. In the Greek legend, Narcissus was so handsome that everyone wanted to be with him and love him. However, Narcissus snubbed all who approached him. He had no love or concern for others, only for himself. Finally, a rejected lover prayed to the gods for revenge, and the goddess Nemesis (the goddess of "righteous anger") answered the prayer. Nemesis caused Narcissus' demise by having him discover his own reflection in a clear pool of water as he was leaning over to get a drink. Seeing his reflection, he understood why others loved him, and he too thought he was beautiful. Narcissus fell in love with his own reflection, then wasted away and died of starvation staring longingly at his own image in the pond.

Like Narcissus, narcissists are forever focused on themselves. They are focused on their own greatness and pay little attention to others. They lack humility, although some can be quit proficient at displays of false modesty. Narcissists are usually arrogant, haughty, and obnoxious to others. Because of this, they can be difficult lovers, family members, friends, and colleagues.

Because narcissists feel that they are the best, they only want to associate with others who are also "the best." Therefore, they will only deal with "top" doctors, lawyers, teachers, and associate only with top institutions. They also want their mates to be the best. These are the people who are searching for the "perfect" mate. Good luck trying to live up to a narcissist's expectations.

If a narcissist does choose to associate with you, they usually can make you feel special, as narcissists make it clear that they only associate with others who are somehow special. They will elevate you to some special status to suit their needs to be surrounded by special, "beautiful," and important people. This elevation to special status can feel quite good to people who associate with narcissists. However, narcissists can be quick to snub those they regard as "unworthy" and no longer special and suited to the narcissist's needs. These snubs are often impolite and rude. Most narcissists do not want to be bothered with anyone who is not in some way special.

When the narcissist's selected special people or institutions disappoint them, they blame and self-servingly invent fault with the person or the institution. Narcissists are quick to "put down" anyone or anything that contradicts their grandiose sense of themselves. They seldom accept blame or interpretations of events that compromise their sense of greatness.

Narcissists feel entitled to special privileges, and often annoy others when they obtain services and resources (e.g., wealth) that they do not deserve. By virtue of their sense of special status and privilege, narcissists feel entitled to access resources without assuming reciprocal responsibilities (i.e., earning the resource access), and they take more than their "fair share." When their relationships are viewed objectively, narcissists are usually seen as taking advantage of others. They do not feel that they have to earn things or follow social protocols the way others do—narcissists feel they deserve things simply because they are special. They feel no guilt or shame about getting things they do not deserve. If they have an affair and break your heart, you can be assured that they will blame you.

Even slight challenges to the narcissist's authority and specialness are put down, often with unwarranted harshness. Sometimes narcissists will counter perceived slights and insults with physical violence. They become enraged at others who will not "reflect back" to them their greatness and importance. Narcissists will punish others for their sins of commission (i.e., perceived "put-downs" of the narcissist) and sins of omission (i.e., failing to praise the narcissist adequately). Narcissists need this sort of attention to maintain their sense of specialness.

Narcissistic Vulnerability to Love Trauma Syndrome

Interestingly, whereas persons with narcissistic personality features are more likely to inflict Love Trauma Syndromes on people who fall in love with them, many narcissists are more vulnerable themselves to developing a Love Trauma Syndrome when someone leaves them. Narcissists might feel entitled to do whatever they want in a relationship (e.g., have affairs), but are intolerant when their mates become similarly involved with others. Narcissists have a grandiose sense of themselves, and cannot conceive of anyone wanting to leave or abandon them. When someone they love does leave them, their positive and grandiose image of themselves is shattered, and they can develop a severe Love Trauma Syndrome.

Indeed, in those narcissists whose feeling of specialness rests on shaky ground, when they are abandoned, they can fall apart. Their myth of invulnerability is shattered, and they go on a rampage to retaliate against the person who destroyed their sense of specialness and importance. Narcissists can become angry, rageful, depressed, and anxious in the context of a breakup with someone they love. Not uncommonly, the narcissist has been involved in a long string of behaviors that have been offensive to the person whom they love (e.g., periodic verbal or even physical abuse). But when the person they love finally leaves them—or does something else that does not help prop up their self-esteem—they develop a Love Trauma Syndrome (that may even be complicated by violence).

The Alcoholic and Drug Addict

People who are addicted to alcohol or to other drugs of abuse such as cocaine or heroin are usually unable to attend to the reciprocating demands of a relationship. Because such addicts are slaves to their addiction, they are at high risk of neglecting the needs of their mate with whom they have become intimately involved. Their addiction comes first—they service the needs of others only after they have been able to satiate their needs for drugs and for alcohol.

Alcohol and addictive drugs such as cocaine and heroin appeal to and exploit our natural desire for euphoric experience, pleasure, and the deadening of emotional pain. To enable us to experience greater amounts of euphoric gratification, we have developed increasingly sophisticated ways to get pleasure-inducing substances to our brains. Crack cocaine is one such invention. "Crank" (smokeable methamphetamine) is another.

The word addiction comes from the Latin verb *addicere*, which means to bind a person to something. The addict is bound to their substance of abuse—and only secondarily to their mate and their family. There are three basic elements to addiction:

1. There is a *craving* for the substance to which they are addicted. Craving represents an intense desire that the addicted person experiences as a "need." Often, engaging the object of an addiction becomes as rewarding as eating or having sex. It might even replace the desire for sex. The craving also implies difficulty in resisting the urges to engage the object of the addiction and diminished control over these urges. Sometimes, the drive toward the object is automatic.

2. The addict increasingly uses the substances they crave over the course of their addiction. Alcoholics drink more alcohol, and crack addicts smoke larger amounts of cocaine. Addicts lose more and more control over the substance to which they are addicted.

3. An addiction has adverse effects on the addict's familial, social and occupational functioning, and on their health and wealth. Most people view the lifestyle of an addict as a vehicle on the road to ruin. Relationships are often destroyed during the course of an addiction.

People with an addiction represent a poor risk for a long-term relationship. If you fall in love with an addict, the relationship is at risk of ending in a Love Trauma Syndrome. The addict needs to be able to demonstrate that they can commit to remaining abstinent.

& Chapter Eleven

Making Peace

The Power of Love

T here are limits to the power of love, and you always run the risk of getting involved with people who might reject, betray, leave, or hurt you for one reason or another. Accepting this risk is part of the price we pay for intimacy, and some pain is also part of that price. Nevertheless, few things make life as worthwhile as the experience of love between two people. People need to have the capacity to repair relationships with loved ones whom they have offended. The ability to engage in reconciliation and to forgive is an innate and natural capacity.

Even with the potential of not winning in love, there are few endeavors more fulfilling and enjoyable. However, you need to choose your partners carefully, and watch out for cheats. In fact, people expend considerable effort by trying to figure out who would be a good partner for themselves. Some partners do more for you than others, and some are more reliable and steadfast. Failure to assess adequately the quality of your partners and how trustworthy or reliable they are can have disastrous effects on your success and happiness in life.

Can You Give Peace a Chance?

Alice was a middle-aged mother of three children who first came to me after her previously faithful husband of 14 years left her for his office assistant, a woman almost half her age. During the first few months of therapy we worked hard to help her find some relief from a severe Love

Trauma Syndrome. She had terrible insomnia, and sometimes was unable to get any sleep at all at night or during the day. All day and night she was plagued with intrusive thoughts and fantasies about her husband and his new love. She was sleep-deprived and often felt completely exhausted, but she still had to go to work and care for the three children, who became even more difficult to take care of after their father left them. After particularly difficult and stressful days she had fantasies of abandoning her children, hopping on an airplane, going to another state, and taking on a new identity. She had Medea Syndrome-like motivations for doing this, as she wanted to get back at her husband through their children. "He hurt me more than I ever knew I could be hurt," she said to me. "Let him and that bitch take care of his kids," she would say to me angrily. However, when she remembered (or was reminded) that these were her children also, she quickly dismissed her planned escape. "How could he do this to me?" she would often say through tears.

By 4 months after her husband's departure, she was beginning to do better. I knew she was doing better when I began to find her asleep in the waiting room prior to a session, rather than crying or pacing around the room. She was sleeping through the night, and she had begun to feel more rested and less stressed. Her intrusive thoughts and fantasies about her husband and his office assistant began to lessen. She settled into a new routine with the children, and began to think that she was going to survive without having to escape to a new life and start over. One week she came into my office stunned. Her husband had began to call her daily, asking for permission for him to return home "where he belonged." "I miss not coming home to kids and you," he said, crying. He told her he had broken off his affair with his office assistant, who was no longer working for him. He asked for her forgiveness, telling her she was "the love of his life." He said that leaving her was "the biggest mistake he had ever made." Now it was her husband who could not sleep at night, and who appeared to be tearful all of the time. He was missing a lot of days at work, and was worried about losing his job.

She had intensely conflicting emotions about what to do next. She was filled with Love-Trauma-Syndrome-related anger and desire for revenge, and was afraid that she would never be able to forgive him for the pain to which he subjected her. She wondered if she could ever trust him again. Her intrusive thoughts and fantasies about her husband and his office assistant in bed together began to plague her again. She wondered if she would ever want to resume a sexual relationship with him again. She

imagined that if she took him back she would want to "make him pay"—
"to punish the son-of-a-bitch, slowly." She did not feel ready to give peace
a chance.

However, she was quick to note that this was the first time that she
knew of that he had ever been unfaithful to her. Before leaving her some 4
months earlier, he had been an attentive husband and father, and had been
considerate of her needs and feelings. She found him handsome and desirable, and a part of her still loved him. She respected his intellect and his wit.

She also realized that they were having problems before he left. He
would complain from time to time that he felt "taken for granted," he
would express resentment that she focused more on the needs of the children than on him, and their sex life had become almost nonexistent. He
seemed moody and frankly depressed. She remembered waking up one
Sunday morning a few weeks before he left and finding him sitting at the
kitchen table staring out the window. "Then I realized he was crying," she
said. "It actually frightened me. I had never seen him cry before. I asked
him what the matter was, and he said nothing. And I was too freaked out
by it to say anything more. He got up and took a shower, and I was glad.
We probably should've gone into therapy or something then."

Is the Relationship Worth Saving?

The first step to repairing an injured alliance is to determine whether
the relationship is worth repairing. When a loved one has proven themselves time after time to be unworthy, attempts at repair are foolhardy.
There is an expression that says, "If I'm taken once, shame on you. If I'm
taken twice, shame on me." The only repair to be made with an unworthy
ally is to put them on notice that you are "on to them," and that you do not
intend to be taken advantage of anymore. There are times when casting
blame and being angry is appropriate; for example, in situations where
your partner has grossly violated the expectations, agreements, and responsibilities of the relationship. You need to keep your distance from people who are not trustworthy. Sometimes you need a period of time where
you hold on to your anger and keep your distance while you evaluate
what you should do next.

When a relationship falls apart, it is necessary to try to understand
what went wrong. Once it can be determined who is at fault, appropriate
apologies need to be made. Was the breakdown related to a misunder-
standing, or was there a clear violation of the alliance?

Sometimes, this is not so easy to determine. People sometimes will not agree that they have done something wrong for which an apology is owed. For instance, I once saw a couple who argued vigorously about the man's infidelity early in their relationship (before they were married). He thought that it was not a violation of their relationship for him to have dated others then; she thought it was. She learned about the affairs from one of his friends after they had been married for a few months. She thought he was a cheat, and he saw himself as unjustly accused. He thought he was entitled to date and have sex with others until their relationship became "more serious."

However, the two could not agree upon exactly when the relationship did become "serious." He argued that the relationship became serious when he stopped seeing other women. She thought that the relationship had become serious much earlier, when the two of them started to have sexual relations. He had initiated sexual relationships with other women after he had started having sex with his future wife. He did admit that he hid his affairs from her and that he had lied to her about what he was doing. However, they had never formally discussed whether it was acceptable for them to date and have sex with other people while they were seeing each other. He would not accept that he had done anything wrong, and she would not accept that she was being unreasonable about her expectations of fidelity early in their relationship.

Can the Relationship Be Saved?

He blamed her for the problems in their relationship (because she was "so unreasonable"), and she blamed him for their problems because he was "a cheat." I asked them to tell me how each of them would feel if blame and anger were not human emotions—they did not exist. Behind his blaming he did admit to some guilt for deceiving her, and behind her blame and anger was sadness and grief that "I had not won him over immediately, the way he had won me."

Although she took a hit to her self-esteem, he did as well. They were both able to see how the blame and anger were protective of their self-esteem, and that taking the hit to self-esteem results in a lot of dysphoric and sickening brain arousal. The case illustrates how even when partners want to save a relationship, it is very difficult to do so when one or both of them blame the other for the problems in the relationship. Relationships can be saved when blame and anger can be attenuated and the dysphoric feelings and hyperarousal behind the blame and anger can be explored and diminished. This might require the therapist to work with the couple on some days and also with each member individually—with the therapist having a commitment to the relationship and to each couple member.

"Swallowing Your Pride"

Part of the price of intimacy is needing to be able to swallow your pride. Unfortunately, swallowing your pride appears to have fallen out of fashion. People seem more interested in "standing up for their rights"— even when it involves stepping on the rights of others, or rupturing prized relationships. Of course, standing up for your rights protects your pride and your self-esteem, but at what expense to the relationship?

Swallowing your pride does result in the mental internalization of some defeat, and a cascade of brain events that results in some emotional and physical sickening. I knew when the man in the relationship described in the previous account accepted some of the responsibility for the problems—his head dropped and his voice weakened. He had taken the hit to his self-esteem. When she took the full hit to her self-esteem she sobbed uncontrollably, which also brought a tear to his eye. This is why people resist swallowing their pride—to do so can hurt. The advantage to doing so is that it allows you to preserve the relationship rather than defend your pride.

When you are able to swallow your pride, you begin to hear the other person's position without concern solely for defending your position and your pride. You can engage in active listening rather than being defensive. You give yourself permission to try to understand the other person's point of view, and this takes time and effort. When you try to convey your thoughts and feelings to your partner, your revealing how your think or feel should not have any hint of blaming the other person. If blaming statements (either explicit or implicit) are included in your communication, your partner will be put on the defensive, and little can be accomplished. Statements such as "You make me feel worthless" imply that it is the other person's fault for your feeling worthless. When trying to disclose your thoughts and feelings in a meaningful way to encourage open and honest communication, always use "I" statements instead of "you" statements. Instead of saying "You make me feel worthless," you should say "I feel worthless."

When both parties are able to swallow their pride and communicate their feelings, problems can be settled by compromise, and without fighting. In compromise, both parties share some defeat and subsequent sickening. The parties can adjust emotionally to their changed self-esteem, and peacemaking becomes possible. People need to be able to swallow their pride when appropriate.

The Paradox

One of the great dilemmas of being in relationships is that what might make you feel better (and maintain or increase your self-esteem) can create problems in your relationships. For instance, when you become more defensive and subtly distort reality to favor your position in a disagreement, it creates problems for people who are trying to get along with you. Remember that defenses are *automatic* self-serving distortions of reality that try to defend your self-esteem. Although the defensive position might enable you to feel better about yourself (and hence less depressed, anxious or otherwise sickened), it impairs your ability to solve the problems you have with others.

The problems that exist between people are linked to threats posed to their self-esteem. We instinctively move against anything that threatens our self-esteem by engaging our psychological defenses. Our brains try to resist any downward shifts in our self-esteem. Hence, the solutions we develop for interpersonal problems must consider the impact the solutions have on people's self-esteem and self-respect. If the solution seriously diminishes either of the parties' self-esteem, it will be rejected as unacceptable. Some people will go to extremes to resist the internalization of defeat. They want to block the sickening processes that promote feelings of lowered self-esteem.

When trying to improve relationships, both parties typically must share in feeling a little worse about themselves for the betterment of the relationship. The most workable solution to an interpersonal problem usually shares the pain as evenly as possible between the two parties. If one person experiences an unfair burden of the blame and pain for the relationship not working, attempts at working out a solution will be hampered. When fixing relationships, people might have to feel worse about themselves before they can feel better about themselves and the relationship. As the saying goes, "No pain, no gain."

Resisting the Blame Game

One test for determining how ready people are to work on a relationship is to ask each partner how much of the blame for the relationship problems they place on the other person, and how much they would accept. Ask them to assign percentages for the blame—a percentage to themselves, and a percentage their partners. If a person is willing to assign themselves some responsibility for the problems; for instance, they assign themselves 50% of the responsibility (while assigning the other 50% of the blame on their partner), you have someone with whom you will be able to work on improving the relationship. It means they are willing to accept some of the blame, they are not completely defensive about what is going on, and they do not experience a need to protect themselves at all costs— even if it means the dissolution of the relationship. However, if they are not willing to assign themselves any responsibility for the problems they are having in their relationship; that is, they assign themselves 0% responsibility for the problems, it is unlikely that you are going to be able to conduct a meaningful dialogue with the goal of improving the relationship.

Giving Someone a Second Chance

For some damaged relationships, the transgressions are not great, and repair is clearly worthwhile. Violators of explicit and implicit compacts in cooperative relationships can change. Even dramatic violators can correct prior transgressions. For instance, I had a patient who was addicted to crack cocaine for over 10 years. During his addiction he had taken advantage of his wife and her family time after time. When they allowed him to stay at their homes, he often stole money and possessions from them to support his habit. His wife and her family would no longer have anything to do with him.

When the patient recovered from his addiction, he made it a goal to repair his relationship with his wife, their children, and her family. He wrote carefully worded apologies to each of them. He began to work hard (taking on two jobs and working over 60 hours a week) so that he could send money to his wife and the family members from whom he had stolen. He began to send gifts to his wife, their children, their nephews, and their nieces on their birthdays and holidays. He sent cards to everyone at Christmas and Easter, and on their birthdays as well. He did this for over a year and a half before anyone in his family responded. It was his wife's sister who first replied to his gestures, and invited him to a Thanksgiving meal where his wife and children were also going to be. At that Thanksgiving table he thanked God for his family and for their forgiveness. He tangibly demonstrated that he had changed and eventually was accepted back into his family. His wife has a husband again, and his children have their father back.

The Formula for Repair

What this patient did illustrates the essential elements for repairing damaged relationships and bringing about reconciliation. These elements include:

1. a verbal or written sincere and formal *apology* for the wrongs you have committed;

2. appropriate and genuine contrite expressions accompanying the apology (e.g., appropriate penitent body postures, gestures and facial expressions—i.e., *physical expressions of contrition*), and possibly written expressions of contrition (e.g., in the form of cards) as well;

3. providing some compensation for past offenses and *gift giving* (and more extensive resource sharing);

4. expressions of your desire to be a better cooperative ally now and in the future (technically called *cooperative propositions*); and

5. *physical expressions of reconciliation* (e.g., handshaking, handholding, embracing, touching, kissing, signing of treaties).

As this case example illustrates, very often each of these elements needs to be repetitively implemented before the other party is willing to reengage in the relationship. Gift giving and resource sharing provide tangible evidence that people are willing to "reinvest" in each other. Of course, the ability to engage in gift giving and resource sharing is dependent on the wealth and resource holdings of the parties involved. Gift giving might also include providing services and support without the immediate expectation of reciprocity. The offended party might need considerable material and emotional compensation before the offender can be fully accepted back. In the context of reparations, they give without the expectation of necessarily receiving in return. They are paying for damages that they caused. They are making amends by giving up more than they will receive.

Only a few of the elements listed previously need to be engaged to initiate repair, and "partial" reconciliative efforts are often better than none. It is often the first step on the path to relationship repair. For instance, a partner might refuse to fully apologize, or offer what the other partner regards as only halfhearted apologies. Such partial apologies can appear "insincere" and be rejected.

However, there is a range of "genuineness" to apologies, and some people initially can only offer partial apologies. This is because the act of apologizing involves some acceptance of fault, which reduces their self-esteem. Again, this reduction of self-esteem induces some sickening phenomena and dysphoric hyperarousal in the person who is apologizing. More genuine and complete apologies are not offered in part to check sickening—at least partly.

As discussed in previous chapters and in this chapter (but worthy of repeating), the brain works hard to protect self-esteem. This is because in the ancient ancestral environment in which we evolved, drops in self-esteem would have diminished your confidence, which would have resulted in your feeling less able to access resources from the environment. This decreased access to resources ultimately would have translated into diminished survival potential for you and for your offspring. Hence, partial apologies might be all that someone can offer at a particular time. The reestablishment of an intimate relationship in the context of a Love Trauma Syndrome requires someone (or both partners) to accept some blame. Accepting some loss in self-esteem is part of the price we pay for intimacy (and it is usually worth the price). Luckily, partial apologies are often sufficient to end fighting and pave the way for later fuller expressions of reconciliation and apology.

Often reciprocal apologies need to be offered, and both parties share in the lowering of their self-esteem. Sometimes the needs of the individual to defend their self-esteem run counter to the needs of the couple attempting reconciliation. Usually both parties need to recognize their separate contributions to the problems in the relationship. It is actually quite rare that a relationship problems is caused solely by one of the parties. Both need to explore what their contribution to the problem is.

However, sometimes one of the partners assumes the "victim" role, and this "victimized" partner might have difficulty accepting their part in the problems and accept any blame or offer any apology. These victims might feel so low already that they often are unwilling to accept any further diminishment of their self-esteem. They are unable to apologize and lower themselves any more. They do not want to accept themselves as more damaged than they already are.

Sometimes the relationship healing and repair process takes time. For instance, the wife in one couple whom I was seeing was very angry with her husband for having an affair. He had a few complaints about her, including feeling "put down by her all the time," and feeling the need to find someone who was "not always on my case and making me feel like a child." She was unable to accept any blame—and she completely blamed her husband for their marital problems. However, a couple of months later, after church she admitted to her husband that she recognized that some of her behaviors had profound effects on their relationship. The priest had given a sermon that allowed her to appreciate her role in the problems she and her husband were having. She apologized to her husband for putting him down. The marriage was saved.

Likewise, it is often difficult for patients with Love Trauma Syndrome to forgive those who have wronged them. Such people are not ready to give up their anger and their resentment. Their anger shields their self-esteem—and they are not yet ready to give up this protection. These individuals find it difficult to *accept* the apology, and might appear to accept the apology only halfheartedly. The process of reconciliation is often a slow and painful ongoing process—not necessarily something that can be done in 5 minutes, or even over the course of day. Sometimes it takes years, and people have to be patient for the forgiveness process to proceed. Some people are unable to forgive completely, but some forgiveness is better than none. Repair of broken relationships takes time and effort.

People need to allow themselves to be vulnerable in relationships. Many people have grandiose and unrealistic expectations of the people whom they love and are crushed and/or angry when these expectations are not met. By allowing ourselves to be vulnerable, we can slowly become more intimate (not just sexually, but emotionally and spiritually) with those whom we love. Ideally, a romantic relationship involves more joy than pain, but some pain is inevitable in any relationship.

The Price of Admission

There is a "price of admission" to any relationship, and nobody is entitled to not pay. Besides paying an admission price, we also have to earn our keep. Some of us feel that what we get out of a relationship is not worth the price of admission or of keep. Our kin tend to give us the greatest support and access to resources for the least in expected return. (However, I have had many patients tell me that the expectations that family members had of them exceeded what the patients were willing to pay.)

The "price" of admission and of keep is both openly and covertly negotiated. Indeed, the expectations of the parties are at least tacitly agreed upon. We must accept that in any alliance, an "economic" relationship is forged. This economic relationship is based not only on monetary or material resource exchange, but also on the trade of other "goods" and "services," such as nurturance, emotional support, and companionship. This economic relationship can be renegotiated periodically, as is often done in couples therapy. When a couple's cooperative alliance breaks down, much couples work focuses on deciphering the currencies of the relationship and on articulating what each person feels is inequitable. The more asymmetry that someone feels or thinks exists in the "tit-for-tat" exchange of currency, the larger the couple's problem.

Each ally needs to do their "fair share" to maintain the alliance. Successful couples work requires being specific about the currencies of the relationship. For instance, do the members of the couple feel that they deserve more help with the chores around the house, with the children, or with financial matters? Do the members want more in the way of nurturance and demonstrations of emotional support, sexual favors, or more sensual, intellectual, or spiritual inputs? Does each partner support and boost the others' self-esteem, or are they "toxic" to feelings of self-worth? Much couples therapy centers on identifying these toxic elements and containing or neutralizing them.

THE BREAKDOWN OF COOPERATION

People have expectations of benefit from any relationship they are in. Some will try to exploit that benefit. When people extract their benefit, their partners carefully observe what is taken and develop a sense of what and how much is appropriate for them to take. We might feel entitled to access certain benefits (e.g., resources), but our partners might feel otherwise. Although we appear to have evolved as social animals capable of cooperation, we also appear to have the desire to try to maximize what we get out of relationships. When we try to maximize our share, we run the risk of exceeding what others regard as our fair share. However, not everyone tries to maximize their share. Some individuals take less than they give. This might be because some of us have lower opinions of ourselves and feel we must "pay a higher price" to earn our keep in the relationship. Such people often feel entitled to access less, whereas others believe that they should be able to access more than they are getting from the relationship.

Nevertheless, many of us try to maximize our share, and feel justified in doing so. People have an uncanny ability to rationalize their selfish interests. We feel entitled to a maximal share. At some point, our partners begin to see us as exceeding our fair share.

There is often a gap between what we view as being our fair share and what others regard as our fair share. Hence, what some will call taking their fair share, a partner might regard as "cheating." Sometimes, people who have habitually taken less feel cheated when they see others taking more. When our loved ones view us as exceeding our fair share, they begin to feel entitled to exceed their fair share as well.

One type of person especially prone to feel entitled to more than their fair share is the narcissist (or the person with narcissistic tendencies). By definition, narcissists feel entitled to special treatment. Because of their feelings of entitlement, narcissists tend to take more than what others regard as their fair share. Narcissists do not feel that they have to earn things or follow rules the way others do.

Another type of narcissistic person who feels entitled to special treatment are those who believe they are particularly good, moral, decent, or "nice." They often have features of obsessive–compulsive personality, and try to be as "perfect" in their behavior as possible (e.g., "perfectly nice"). They try to be perfect in their academic, social, familial, and occupational pursuits. Because they have put in such effort to be perfect, they feel entitled to some special recognition and attention. They expect some "payback" from others—although the others usually do not know that they have a bill! Because they try to be perfect (and they believe they have been successful at doing so), they expect others to try to behave perfectly toward them.

People having this type of obsessive–compulsive personality can be very demanding regarding getting what they feel entitled to in a relationship; that is, getting what they feel they "deserve," or "what they have earned." They have a rigid sense of what they have due to them, and their sense of what is fair might be tilted in their favor. If someone other than them takes more than their fair share, they become angry. They can become infuriated when they see others exceeding their fair share or "getting away with something." These individuals become righteously indignant and demand punishment and retribution. They do not want to feel cheated, do not tolerate seeing others cheated, and are zealous monitors for cheaters. At times they appear overzealous and "hypermoral."

Expressions of Appreciation

One of the ways feelings of entitlement poisons relationships is that it inhibits proper overt expressions of appreciation. Even in trusting relationships, people who help a partner expect—and deserve—clear expressions of recognition for their efforts. You must be wary of taking your partner for granted. Many relationship problems are related to partners being stingy with their expressions of appreciation. It's polite to thank someone who has helped you, and not doing so can rightfully upset the other person. Some people do not acknowledge the help they receive from others because they feel entitled to the assistance—no payback is required. They feel a gesture or statement of appreciation is unnecessary.

Overt expressions of appreciation represent acknowledgement that favors have been received—and your brain regards such acknowledgement as an indication that your favors stand a chance of being reciprocated. Your brain regards an ally to be a good ally when they do not take advantage of you. When you offer expressions of appreciation, you have recognized the price the other person has paid for supporting and maintaining the relationship. There is implicit acknowledgment that you are indebted to them. This expression of appreciation makes the other person feel better, and boosts their self-esteem. Their sense of RHP increases, as they have an ally who appreciates them and who will be available when needed.

When someone's assistance is not overtly appreciated, the helping partner is not reassured that their efforts have been noticed and that they stand a chance of being reciprocated. Your partner has the right to resent you when you have not expressed your appreciation openly. They will feel insecure about their prospects for having their efforts reciprocated at some time in the future, and they will wonder if they are being exploited in a relationship with you. They might begin to think that they are being cheated.

Detecting Cheaters

Some researchers have argued that the dramatic increase in human brain size and capacity over recent evolution is related to an increased need for brain processing power to help us navigate our sophisticated social system. Part of the increased processing power needed by our brains involves the detection of cheaters with whom we are in relationships.

Cheating involves deception. Investing in relationships with cheaters is costly for noncheaters. The longer the cheating is allowed to continue, the more one loses. The instinct is to break off relationships with cheaters and maintain relationship with people who cooperate. However, people who cooperate "unconditionally," that is, who cooperate and maintain relationships with cheaters and noncheaters alike, are often exploited by cheaters. We need to be able to recognize cheaters so that we can defect from those people who would exploit us. This defection "punishes" cheaters and helps to maintain noncheating cooperative behaviors in others.

This process of continuing to cooperate with noncheaters and defecting from cooperation with cheaters is sometimes referred to as the "win-stay, lose-shift" paradigm.[1] That is, if your cooperative efforts are rewarded with a truly cooperative partner, you "win." You "stay" in that relationship. If you discover that your partner is a cheat, you "lose." You leave the relationship—that is, you "shift"—and look for a more trustworthy partner.

The judicial system of our nation is dedicated to preventing and to detecting significant cheating, and to punishing the serious cheaters among us. Some sociology experts believe that one function of gossip is to hear from others in your group for whom to watch out. For instance, you want to know who might exploit you if you were to get into a relationship with them, and who might take more from you than they would give. Gossip provides you with advance intelligence on the integrity of the character of a potential love partner. It is one of the reasons that gossip regarding someone we love can have such an impact on us—especially when it reveals something about them that has been hidden from us. However, gossip can be distorted and tainted and can provide us with faulty information.

Another way of detecting potential cheaters before being duped is based on a careful examination of a potential mate's history of cooperation. What has been their level of cooperation in past relationships? Has the person acted responsibly, or have they neglected their responsibilities as spouses, parents, children, family members, friends, or co-workers? Have they honored their social obligations in the past? Has the person been caught cheating in relationships? Have they been deceptive? Do they have a history of cooperative relationships of long duration? Why did past cooperative alliances fall apart? Are they quick to offer flimsy rationalizations of their past failures as partners, or do they seem genuinely contrite and guilty about past derelictions? Have they tried to "undo" some of these past failures by compensating those whom they have wronged? Or do they simply offer excuses about why they do not have to do so? Remember, history has a way of repeating itself.

You can also get a sense of how cooperative a potential partner will be by observing firsthand the quality of their current cooperative relationships and interactions. Some people will try to show just how cooperative they can be (a form of attractiveness display). For instance, a patient of mine was trying to impress a woman of whom he was particularly fond. One day while the two of them were walking down a city street, they encountered an older woman laying on the sidewalk who was short of breath. He picked this older woman up and carried her three blocks to a nearby hospital emergency room. He said that his real motivation for doing this was to impress his girlfriend. (That day he also ended up on a hospital stretcher with severe lower back pain!)

If you engage in an relationship with someone with a dubious history of cooperation, or with someone who does not appear to engage in meaningful cooperative alliances in general—beware. You should enter into such a relationship only after you have examined their potential for repeating their poor performance as a partner. You need to assure yourself that their past or current deficits are not likely to emerge in the alliance with you.

Of course, no one is perfect, but some potential allies are more imperfect than others, and some should be avoided. You need to choose your loves carefully, especially for relationships that you want to be long lasting (e.g., a marriage). Sometimes, when you do not have enough data to make a clear-cut decision about somebody's worthiness, you simply have to trust your intuition. You can only hope your intuition has access to legitimate and sensible reasons for the decision you are making, and is not being blinded by your desperate desire to find someone to love. Be open to revising your assessments about your potential mate as you gain more access to information about their character.

Note that some partners are unable to reciprocate to your satisfaction because they are overcommitted to other cooperative ties and responsibilities. They might have to attend to time-consuming responsibilities to their children, work, or other important social obligations. Some people simply to do not have the skills to prioritize their commitments. However, some people use their being overcommitted as an excuse for giving less to you than they have received from you. It might be a guise for cheating.

Beware of Deceptive Attractiveness Displays

Some people use deceptive attractiveness displays to attract and maintain their relationships with partners. For instance, to gain your cooperation and allegiance, a person initially might feign attractiveness; for example, they might claim access to resources, or a desire to be a sharing partner—when they really have no such access or intention of doing so. When a person realizes that they have been so deceived, they feel betrayed.

As described in an earlier chapter, even among primates, deceptive attractiveness displays have been observed by males pretending to have food that they are willing to exchange for sexual favors. In actuality, they do not have the promised food. The female primate does not become aware of the deception until after the sexual favor has been given. Likewise, some people might pretend to want to repair a relationship, while having little to no intention of changing their behavior. Sometimes you need to decide to bail out of relationships that have little chance of succeeding. Some people have no intention of changing.

CAN'T GET NO SATISFACTION

Some people with narcissistic tendencies are not satisfied with the quality of their partners. No matter what their mate gives to them, it is never enough. It would only be good enough if it came from a better mate.

These people are always seeking better mates and friends. A relationship with a "better" ally makes them feel "better," and more important, increases their self-esteem. Certain people abandon allies whom they perceive as "imperfect" for "more perfect" ones. They typically "size up" their new potential partner before leaving their old one. They want to choose in favor of the best.

I have had patients spend years in such sizing-up efforts. They want to maximize what they can get out of the partners whom they chose. Often, they go on "fault finding" missions to rationalize why they are leaving their imperfect partner. I have seen patients use trumped-up charges to justify leaving perfectly good spouses and mates. The charges belie the underlying selfish and narcissistic motives for leaving the less appealing ally for someone more appealing.

Some people who continuously search for perfection in their partners lose opportunities for becoming involved with substantial mates. For instance, a man whom I once treated was a successful physician who wanted to be married. He said that he was on a quest for the "perfect" woman. He had been in a series of relationships, and when I saw him he was involved with a woman he characterized as "near-perfect." Her problems included what he regarded as defects in her grooming and complaints that her "hair was too thin" and not the right color. He said he wanted to be able to "sit at the kitchen table and look at a perfect woman." He told me that if he "settled for less" he would always "feel unsatisfied."

People who are always looking for someone better have little invest-ment in the current relationship. You will always be short-changed by such people, and they will be toxic to your self-esteem. Both parties need to focus their efforts on maintaining the current relationship, and not on searching for other relationships to bail out into in case the current rela-tionship fails. If someone is more interested in searching for another part-ner than in maintaining their current relationship, they are not interested in providing the commitment and sacrifice successful relationships demand. That commitment and sacrifice is the cross each of us has when we pay the price of intimacy with others—who are always somehow imperfect.

The Relationship Reborn

To renew a relationship, it is often important for both parties to give up their anger and blame and to replace it with disappointment that their partner was not able to live up to their expectations. Besides the basic ele-ments of reconciliation described previously, the rules, "economic" cur-rencies, and expectations under which the new relationship will operate should be made clearer.

Successful relationships have the capacity to renew themselves. The strength of the new relationship is usually dependent on the severity of the transgression that jeopardized the alliance in the first place. The new relationship will often remain tainted by heightened vigilance for future violations, although the taint can diminish over time as the partner contin-ues to demonstrate their worthiness.

The ability to forgive those who have violated your trust and to repair broken alliances helps you to maintain your relationship network. You should try to contain any damage done to an alliance with a worthy part-ner in an effort to maintain a mutually beneficial relationship. Worthy partners should be maintained—and there are few perfect partners.

Concluding Thoughts

T oday was a busy work day. I saw patients from 8:00 a.m. this morning to after 6:00 p.m. There was little time between patients, as I
was supervising and teaching three resident physicians who were
doing a psychiatry training rotation with me. One was an internist, another was a family practitioner, and the third was a psychiatrist. Together
we interviewed a variety of patients with different psychiatric conditions,
such as depression and PTSD.

"When you come down to it, Dr. Rosse," the internal medicine resident asked me about psychiatric patients in general, "aren't these just
weak people who need to be toughened up, who need a good talking to?"
This was not an insensitive man, but someone who was struggling to understand psychiatric problems.

My response came to me quickly. "Aren't people with diabetes, or hypertension, or heart disease also 'weak' people with vulnerabilities in either their pancreases, blood vessels, or hearts?" I said. "People with
psychiatric conditions have vulnerabilities in various brain regions—albeit
the specific brain areas involved are not well defined at this point in time."
He thought a moment, but he was still not satisfied. "But at least in medical conditions you can see what's wrong with them. In diabetes, you can
take their blood and measure their elevated blood sugar. In hypertension,
you can measure their blood pressure and see their blood pressure elevations. And with heart disease, you can take an electrocardiogram and see
their damaged hearts, or perform angiography and see their clogged arteries. In psychiatric conditions, like depression or PTSD, all's you have to

go on is what the patients' say. You have to take them on their word. There's no proof that they're ill. It's literally all in their heads."

I was too busy and too behind schedule to continue to reply to his challenges with lengthy discussions. I gave him my customary response to such questions that included the idea that psychiatry was still in its infancy and we had not yet progressed to the point where we had useful and accurate diagnostic tests for specific psychiatric disorders. I did mention that there were many, many studies clearly demonstrating that the brain and body functioning of people with severe psychiatric disturbances was clearly different than that of normal controls, but tests that were able to help us make specific psychiatric diagnoses were not yet available. To make accurate diagnoses, all we are able to do now is talk to patients, and see if they have a constellation of symptoms that meet criteria for the diagnosis of a specific psychiatric disorder. Additionally, you have to know the right questions to ask. We could also make psychological diagnoses by performing special psychological tests.

The one patient whom I would have seen today with a chronic Love Trauma Syndrome (over 20 years in duration) did not show up for his scheduled appointment. However I was not overly concerned because his treatment over the past year has gone very well and his symptoms are now minimal. He has been able to return to work and to other social activities and is fully functional again. He also started an exercise program for the first time in his life, and was trying to stop smoking. When I see him now one of his main preoccupations is making money "to make up for all that time I lost when I was moping around." His mood is now bright, and he no longer cries in my office.

When he first started coming to see me I could hardly get him out of my office after a session. After describing Love Trauma Syndrome to him during the first session we had, he repeatedly nodded his head in agreement. He told me that I was the first doctor who understood him. He felt relieved that there was a name for the condition he suffered from. He worked hard in therapy, and the antidepressant he took improved his mood, alleviated his insomnia, and decreased his anxiety and arousal. He went from thinking about his lost love almost every waking moment to almost never thinking about it.

However, driving home that evening, I became concerned that this book would not be able to convince certain people about the validity and importance of Love Trauma Syndrome. I knew that patients like the patient whom I described in the preceding paragraphs who had Love

Trauma Syndrome needed no convincing about the validity of the condition. However, people who had never experienced Love Trauma Syndrome, or who had never worked with a population of Love Trauma Syndrome victims, might not be able to appreciate the condition's significance. Because they could not see it in an abnormal laboratory value, or abnormal X-ray, they simply might not see it. Broken hearts are ubiquitous, but you can't detect them on an electrocardiogram. And not everyone who breaks up with someone whom they love develops a Love Trauma Syndrome. Most people develop only minor symptoms that are not of sufficient severity to consider them to have the full syndrome. A certain amount of distress is a normal response to a lost love. If you do not ask the proper questions, Love Trauma Syndrome will remain an invisible disease that will go undetected. It is often a hidden disease, as sufferers are often ashamed of their pain, and only talk about it to their closest confidants. Additionally, large scale studies establishing the condition's validity have not yet been performed.

As I was driving, I welcomed the slow rush hour traffic. It gave me more time to contemplate what I would put into the concluding chapter that my editor requested. I thought about how hard it was to get my trainees to appreciate the seriousness—and sometimes even the existence—of certain well-established psychiatric illnesses, such as PTSD. Convincing people of the importance of Love Trauma Syndrome was going to be a challenge.

On my way home, I stopped at my neighborhood coffee shop for my usual cafe latté with skim milk. This was the place where I loaded up on the caffeine that fueled much of the writing for this book. I sat down at a table and began to dissociate, staring off into space and hoping for some inspiration to come over me to help me write the concluding chapter. It was all that I had left of the book to write. I thought that the traditional final concluding statements I was so used to writing for academic articles—involving a brief technical summary of my findings and a dry outline of the implications of the findings, along with the obligatory "future research will be needed to further determine the validity of the current findings"—would not be a satisfying conclusion for most readers.

On the table in front of me was a copy of the day's newspaper, *The Washington Post*. As I began to flip through the paper and drink my coffee, a number of articles caught my eye. On the fifth page of the paper, one story described how a right-wing militia leader shot himself "after falling into despair over his pending divorce."

Another article on the same page told the story of the arrest of Ira Einhorn, a charismatic "New Age Guru" in the 1970s. The article described that he had been convicted for the murder of his girlfriend. Authorities say that Einhorn's girlfriend of many years had threatened to leave him, and that Einhorn beat her to death. He apparently broke her skull in 13 places, and stuffed her body in a trunk.

Just two pages later, there was a full page article titled "Murder–Suicide Reflects Rising Strain on Poor Hispanic Women—Isolated and Unable to Cope, Mother Shot Triplets and Herself." This article told the tragic story of a woman who murdered her three children and then herself after falling into a "deep despair over her abandonment" by her boyfriend, who "left her to marry another woman."

Then there was a whole section of the paper that day devoted to the testimony of Monica Lewinsky, the woman who was in love with President Clinton and had a now famous sexual affair with him over an 18-month period in 1995 and 1996. The section was five full pages, with a three-quarter inch bold headline, "You Let Me Down," a statement describing the way the love-struck Lewinsky felt about the object of her affection, who at that time was President Clinton, after he began to snub her. Much of the nation—if not the whole world—know the intimate details of the physical nature of their relationship. Monica Lewinsky described her love for President Clinton, and its associated joy while the relationship was going well, and her intense pain—and sometimes disappointment and anger—when he broke off the relationship. Lewinsky tried to discuss her heartache and suffering with her friend, Linda Tripp. What Monica did not realize was that her "friend" Linda tape recorded many of their personal conversations. Tripp later handed these tapes over to independent counsel Kenneth Starr, who was engaged in a sweeping investigation of any possible criminal activity in which the President might have been involved. Starr's report to Congress and to the country (and to the world for that matter) contained hundreds of pages of Monica's love letters to the President, and documentation of her testimony about their relationship. The transcripts of Ms. Lewinsky's statements included points at which she broke into tears. Monica's is the case of a Love Trauma Syndrome that would almost bring down a presidency. Had the heartbroken Monica Lewinsky not felt the need to discuss her suffering with a friend, Linda Tripp would have never recorded the phone conversations that lead to President Clinton's impeachment for purjury and obstruction of justice.

I finished off my Grande Cafe Latté, bought the paper, and having been fortified with the day's news and a lot of caffeine, went home to write my concluding chapter. My experience with the day's newspaper further validated for me the importance of the condition I had dubbed "The Love Trauma Syndrome." I realized that even for people who personally never had Love Trauma Syndrome, or who never worked with its sufferers, that the newspapers and television news were full of notorious examples of people acting destructively in response to a love trauma—examples of the worst (and thankfully rare) possible outcomes for people afflicted with the syndrome. The reader should note that the vast majority of people with Love Trauma Syndrome never do anything that makes it into the newspapers or television news. Other media, such as television dramas, cinema, the theater, and popular music, are also suffused with love trauma themes and various depictions of people with the malady. Even if people are lucky enough to escape their own personal experience with Love Trauma Syndrome, they would almost certainly have friends and family in whom they might be able to recognize the condition. This book would serve to help extend people's understanding of the affliction people previously called "brokenhearted."

In the final analysis, I hope this book has increased your awareness of Love Trauma Syndrome, convinced you of its importance, and has informed sufferers and clinicians of ways to recognize and overcome the condition. I am not advocating that Love Trauma Syndrome become a formal psychiatric diagnosis that could be found in the "Diagnostic and Statistical Manual (DSM) of Mental Disorders" (published by the American Psychiatric Association) used by mental health workers for assigning specific psychiatric diagnoses to patients. But I am advocating an increased awareness of the condition by laypersons, clinicians, and researchers. I have found that for certain patients there is therapeutic value to using the diagnostic label "Love Trauma Syndrome" with them—rather than more conventional and accepted designations such as "adjustment disorder" or "depressive disorder not otherwise specified." The Love Trauma Syndrome designation is something patients can identify with. I have seen patients' eyes open wide when I used the Love Trauma Syndrome diagnosis with them for the first time, their heads nodding in approval while they exclaim "Yes, that's it! That's what I have." I have never seen such cathartic responses in patients when I have told them that they are suffering from an "adjustment disorder" or "anxiety disorder not otherwise specified." Finally, I hope that this book stimulates future research, targeted at a better understanding of the syndrome, its treatment, and its relationship to other psychiatric disorders such as PTSD, depression, anxiety, obsessive-compulsive disorder, paranoia and delusional jealousy, dissociative disorders, adjustment disorder, and alcohol and substance use disorders.

May your hearts go forth to love, and if they break, may they heal and go forth to love again.

Endnotes

Foreword

1. Wang, Z., Hulihan, T. J., & Insel, T. (1997). Sexual and social experience is associated with different patterns of behavior and neural activation in male prairie voles. *Brain Research, 767,* 321–332.
2. Rosse, R. B., Fay-McCarthy, M., Collins, J. P., Risher-Flowers, D., Alim, T. N., & Deutsch, S. I. (1993). Transient compulsive foraging behavior associated with crack cocaine use. *Am J Psychiatry, 150*(1), 155–156.
3. Rosse, R. B., McCarthy, M. F., Collins, J. P., Alim, T. N., & Deutsch, S. I. (1994). The relationship between cocaine-induced paranoia and compulsive foraging: A preliminary report. *Addiction, 89,* 1097–1104.

Chapter 2

1. With "managed care" becoming the dominant force in most health care delivery systems, there is pressure to develop faster and "more efficient" ways to help patients overcome their emotional distress. Unfortunately, managed care administrators operate with a double agenda—they want to provide adequate mental health care while keeping costs down. Sometimes these two agendas conflict with each other. However people have long known that, usually, "You get what you pay for."

   Managed care administers are also distressed by the notion of "new" psychiatric disturbances such as Love Trauma Syndrome. They worry that these new conditions will escalate our already skyrocketing health care costs. Additionally, many argue that some of these new "lower grades" of psychopathology (e.g., various "minor" depressive syndromes and conditions such as Love

Trauma Syndrome) represent trivial conditions that are essentially "normal" reactions to the vicissitudes of life. Managed care administrators become concerned that mental health workers are creating a state of "dystopia" into which most of the population will fall—and that might drive health care costs higher. There is also the fear that mental health workers will overtreat people with lower grades of psychopathology—thereby exposing them to potentially harmful and unnecessary (not to mention costly) therapies.

However, most mental health practitioners treat emotional problems only if the condition causes the patient significant distress or interferes with the patient's social and occupational functioning. All psychopathology exists on a continuum with "normal" behavior, and mental health workers should be expert in determining what is a "normative" or a "pathologic" response to adverse events, and what problems deserve treatment, and which ones can be addressed with a "watchful waiting" attitude.

Unfortunately, I believe that people are often too quick to attribute their severe psychological distress to a "normal" reaction to adverse events. Because of this, only a fraction of the people who need mental health services ever receive such care. We know that it is easier to treat psychiatric problems when they are recognized early—often when the condition is in its more advanced prodromal stage, but has not yet emerged as a full, "clinically significant" syndrome. In the advanced prodromal stage, the person might be missing work occasionally because of their condition. However, by the time it has advanced into a "higher grade" more "clinically significant" condition, the person might no longer be able to function at work, and they might lose their job. If the condition has been allowed to progress into its more severe form, the person might require inpatient psychiatric hospitalization—the most costly of all psychiatric treatments. Treating lower grades of psychopathology helps keep patients out of the hospital. Now the cost of not treating the patient when their condition was in its lower grade form; that is, the cost to the patient, to their family, to their community, and to society, becomes much greater. "Psychoeconomic analysis" reveals how in the long run it is less costly to recognize and treat conditions of lesser severity. As will be more fully discussed in a later chapter, a condition such as Love Trauma Syndrome can become complicated by a myriad of serious psychiatric symptoms. It is cheaper and easier to treat it early in its course than after it has been compounded by other psychological problems.

Chapter 3

1. Most "fighting" involves exchanges of intimidation displays between competitors. Intimidation displays show how formidable an opponent you are, and are designed to "sicken" your adversaries and diminish their willingness to fight. The display tries to inculcate in your rival the idea that you cannot be defeated (or that you cannot be defeated easily). These displays try to make clear to the

adversary that if they choose to fight, it will be at tremendous cost to them. Such displays often include a certain amount of body language "ape talk," where the opponents might expand their chests or somehow try to make themselves look physically larger and more formidable than they really are in an attempt to intimidate. Opponents might try to loom over their adversaries to impart a sense of dominance. Intimidation displays also include attempts to focus attention on your strengths and your opponent's weaknesses. The overall aim of the display is to induce a sense of asymmetry between your power and your opponent's.

Intimidation displays engage "sizing up functions." Here the person sizes up their opponent's strength and compares it to their own. The person sizing up the situation assesses the likelihood of victory should the opponent be engaged in a fight. Throughout the animal kingdom, animals are known to go through a process of sizing up adversaries as part of their deciding to move against a foe. You size up your foe's intimidation display, and you assess their fighting ability. You also need to assess their access to allies, and to size up the number and strength of these allies. During the sizing-up process, you look for asymmetries in strength between you and your rival. Generally, the more asymmetry that can be found, the greater the likelihood that a challenge will follow. One party has sized up the situation as being in their favor. Sizing up allows you to predict the outcome of a fight, and allows one of the parties to cede defeat before having more damage inflicted upon them, or choose to fight if their brain calculates a high probability of their winning.

The person sizing up the situation is also determining whether they should engage in either "fight or flight" in response to the opponent's intimidation display. If a person sizes up their power as being less than their rival's, they can retreat and escape to avoid defeat.

2. Sloman, L., Price, J., Gilbert, P., & Gardner, R. (1994). Adaptive function of depression: Psychotherapeutic implications: *Am J Psychother, 48,* 401–416. This group also discusses how the loss of a love object (as can occur in a love trauma) triggers an ineffective anger and rage response, which later can progress into activation of the brain mechanisms responsible for generating ISS. They further describe how prolonged ISS becomes clinical depressive illness.

Chapter 4

1. In fact, any psychiatric condition (e.g., conditions such as schizophrenia, bipolar disorder, substance abuse disorders) can all be exacerbated by Love Trauma Syndrome.

2. People with rejection-sensitive dysphoria often have cravings for chocolate. Interestingly, there are certain catecholamines (e.g., phenylethylamine) in chocolate that appear to stabilize neural transmission in the social circuits in our brains in the context of social disruption (or the threat of such disturbance).

3. Distress displays help reintegrate a person into a social relationship or group. Such displays serve to attract—or reattract—mates and other allies. For instance, when the Gebusi tribespeople of New Guinea experience the uneasiness and fear of *abwida*, open displays of their distress are encouraged to "advertise" their vulnerability and promote their "return to good company." Such displays of *abwida* are prototypic distress displays.

   Distress displays can also serve to direct aggression away from the person in distress. In the context of a challenge, when one of the competitors emits a distress display, it is usually a signal that the displayer is ceding defeat. A distress display is a universal signal of defeat.

4. Names such as fluoxetine, sertraline, and paroxetine are "generic" names, whereas names such as Prozac, Zoloft, and Paxil are the respective trade names for these antidepressants. Trade names are given to medications by the pharmaceutical company that originally manufactured the medication. It would be a mistake to think that only the antidepressants listed here would work in patients with Love Trauma Syndrome complicated by depression. Any antidepressant could be useful. Promising new antidepressant medications not currently marketed in the United States include reboxetine, tianeptine, and substance p antagonists. Interestingly, effective antidepressants often have slightly different profiles in the way they effect different brain neurotransmitter systems (e.g., serotonin, norepinephrine, substance p) and neurotransmitter receptors (serotonin receptors, adrenergic receptors, sigma receptors, and substance p receptors). These different neuropharmacologic profiles are thought to be the reason that certain antidepressants are more effective for some people than others. The notion is that the brains of certain patients do better with certain antidepressants than others, and that the task of the psychiatrist is to find the antidepressant that works the best for a particular patient while having the fewest side effects. For instance, there is the sense among many knowledgeable psychiatrists that monoamine oxidase inhibitors (MAOi's) might be particularly beneficial in patients with prominent "atypical" features of depression (such as rejection sensitivity). However, newer antidepressants such as fluoxetine (Prozac) and sertraline (Zoloft) are usually employed first because they are easier to use and are associated with fewer side effects than MAOi's.

5. Promising new mood stabilizers currently under study include the anticonvulsant medications topiramate, tiagabine, oxcarbazepine, zonisamide, and vigabatrin.

6. The antianxiety agent buspirone (Buspar) is a nonaddictive antianxiety agent that can diminish symptoms of anxiety. However, unlike the other antianxiety agents described here, buspirone takes a number of weeks before the full benefit can be realized. Buspirone might be a useful agent in some patients with a Love Trauma Syndrome complicated by anxiety. Promising new antianxiety agents are under development, such as abecarnil.

Chapter 5

1. Interestingly, a person's hallucinating geometric designs or buzzing sounds is thought to sometimes signal their entrance into a more profound dissociative experience.
2. His premature ejaculation was also later cured, as medications such as sertraline can delay ejaculatory urges during sex. These medications can be used to treat premature ejaculation.
3. Your self-esteem is "calculated" in the emotional part of your brain (i.e., your limbic system). The calculations are made automatically and beneath your awareness. Your past victories and defeats in life figure prominently in these calculations. The more victory experiences you have had in your life—and the fewer defeats—the greater your self-esteem is likely to be. Simply put, victories raise self-esteem and defeats lower it. Victories heighten our sense of potency and embolden us to continue our more intrepid efforts. Defeats do the opposite. However, some people discount the importance of victories in their lives, and augment the significance of their defeats. These individuals will have low self-esteem despite the amount of success relative to failure they have experienced. Others magnify their successes and minimize their defeats. These people enjoy higher self-esteem than you would think they deserve. Low self-esteem increases one's vulnerability to Love Trauma Syndrome. Higher self-esteem is protective.

Chapter 7

1. Sometimes the demonization is only partial. With such partial demonization, the person does not become entirely evil. They might be seen as having parts of her or of him that are "bad" along with some "good" ones. If the person is able to mentally "compartmentalize" and keep separate in their brains the "bad" and the "good," then they might be able to remain conscious of only the bad characteristics—and lose touch with the good aspects of the person. With compartmentalizing we are able to keep focused on the bad at the exclusion of the good (and the converse can occur as well when someone is idealized). This ability to compartmentize and focus on only one aspect of a person's character at a time is sometimes referred to as "splitting."

Chapter 8

1. Guilbert, C. M., Custodian of the Standard Book of Common Prayer (1977). *The book of common prayer and administration of the sacramanents and other rites and ceremonies of the Church.* New York, NY, The Church Hymnal Corporation and The Seabury Press.

2. My grandfather died in 1985. Since then, when my mother is in crisis, she sometimes has dreams that my grandfather calls her up. "Sunny" [my mother's name], he says, "I'm calling long distance. Remember, *nothing important, nothing serious*. Gotta go now. Bye." Then he hangs up.

3. From Suzy Platt (Ed.; 1989, p. 276). *Respectfully Quoted—A Dictionary of Quotations Requested from the Congressional Research Service*. Washington, DC: Library of Congress. The Prayer is most often attributed to the late Christian theologian Reinhold Niebuhr (1892–1971; from *The A.A. Grapevine*, January, 1950, pp. 6–7). Some version of the prayer appears to have been in use by people within Alcoholics Anonymous (A.A.) since about 1940. The version most commonly used in A.A. meetings in my area is "God, grant me the serenity to accept the things I cannot change, the courage to change the things I can, and the wisdom to know the difference."

4. Even before the period of exhaustion sets in, Love Trauma Syndrome can result in considerable distractibility and difficulty in concentrating. People with Love Trauma Syndrome who have not reached the exhaustion stage still need to be good to themselves and to be careful with all physical activity to not accidently hurt themselves or others.

5. McWilliams, P. (1988). *You can't afford the luxury of a negative thought. A book for people with any life-threatening illness—Including life*. Los Angeles, CA: Prelude Press.

Chapter 9

1. Sometimes people who feel physically sick in the context of a Love Trauma Syndrome need to see a psychiatrist or other physician to rule out the presence of physical causes contributing to their distress. Any physical condition can be worsened by emotional stress—and the stress of Love Trauma Syndrome is significant. Psychiatrists and other physicians are trained to determine whether underlying physical conditions exist. I have had patients in the throes of a Love Trauma Syndrome tell me that they felt the most physically ill they had ever felt in their lives. Luckily, medical workup did not reveal serious medical conditions. Patients are then relieved that there are no serious underlying medical conditions with which to concern themselves, and they can focus on the psychological causes of their distress and unhappiness.

2. According to definitions provided in the Diagnostic Statistical Manual, Fourth Edition (DSM-IV, 1994), both Acute Stress Disorder (ASD) and Posttraumatic Stress Disorder (PTSD) occur after extremely traumatic, life-threatening events (e.g., car accidents with serious injuries, natural or manmade disasters where people were hurt severely, robbery at gunpoint, rape, torture, incarceration in a concentration camp, terrorist attack). Both ASD and PTSD are characterized by symptoms of "reexperiencing" the trauma (e.g., in the form of intrusive

thoughts, memories, flashbacks, and nightmares), increased arousal (e.g., in form of exaggerated startle, anxiety, fear, distractibility, insomnia, hypervigilance, and irritability and outbursts of anger), and avoidance of any cues or reminders of the traumatic event. In both ASD and PTSD, the symptoms are severe enough to cause significant personal distress and interfere with social, academic, or occupational functioning. ASD begins within the first month of the trauma and lasts at least 2 days but a maximum of 4 weeks. The onset of PTSD can be within three months after the trauma, but to earn the diagnosis of PTSD, the symptoms need to have been a problem for at least 4 weeks. If the symptoms of ASD last for more than a month, the diagnosis is changed to PTSD. ASD and PTSD are further differentiated by ASD having more prominent dissociative symptoms. To earn a diagnosis of ASD according to DSM-IV, a person has to have experienced at least 3 of the dissociative symptoms listed: 1. a sense of "numbing," detachment, or reduced or absent emotional responsiveness, 2. reduced awareness of their environment (e.g., "feeling dazed"), 3. derealization (a sense that the world seems strange, weird, unreal, or that the previously familiar now seems unfamiliar), 4. depersonalization (a sense that you feel detached from your emotions, thoughts, and feelings), and 5. dissociative amnesia (e.g., memory loss for aspects of the trauma). However, PTSD is also commonly associated with dissociative symptoms, including emotional numbing, feelings of detachment, reduced emotionality (e.g., diminished ability to experience "loving" feelings), and amnesia for aspects of the trauma.

In ASD, PTSD, and Love Trauma Syndrome, the stressors are psychologically overwhelming. But in ASD and PTSD, the stressors are overwhelming and life-threatening. These life-threatening stresses would be traumatic to most people. In Love Trauma Syndrome, the precipitating stressor is not life-threatening, and not as uniformly traumatic to people as the precipitating stressors in ASD and PTSD. Compared to ASD and PTSD, in Love Trauma Syndrome the threshold has been lowered for the required severity of stressor when making a diagnosis.

Chapter 11

1. Malinski, M. (1993). Cooperation wins and stays. *Nature, 364,* 12–13.

Bibliography

Abrams, K. M., & Robinson, G. E. (1998). Stalking. Part I: An overview of the problem. *Can J Psychiatry, 43,* 473–476.

Akiskal, H. S. (1986). The clinical significance of the "soft" bipolar spectrum. *Psychiatric Annals, 16,* 667–671.

Akiskal, H. S. (1996). The prevalent clinical spectrum of bipolar disorders: Beyond DSM-IV. *J Clin Psychopharmacology, 16,* 4S–14S.

Alcock, J. (1989). *Animal behavior: An evolutionary approach* (4th ed.). Sunderland, MA: Sinauer Associates, Inc.

Allman, W. F. (1994). The stone age present: How evolution has shaped modern life: From sex, violence, and language to emotions, morals, and communities. New York: Simon and Schuster.

American Psychiatric Association. (1994). *Diagnostic and statistical manual of mental disorders* (4th ed.). Washington, DC.

Ardrey, R. (1976). *The hunting hypothesis: A personal conclusion concerning the evolutionary nature of man.* New York: Atheneum.

Aune, K. S., Comstock, J. (1997). Effect of relationship length on the experience, expression, and perceived appropriateness of jealousy. *J Soc Psychol, 137,* 23–31.

Axelrod, R. (1984). The evolution of cooperation. New York: Basic Books.

Axelrod, R., Hamilton, W. D. (1981). The evolution of cooperation. *Science, 211,* 1390–1396.

Baker, R. (1996). *Sperm wars: The science of sex.* New York: Basic Books.

Barkow, J. H., Cosmides, L., Tooby, J. (1992). The Adapted Mind: Evolutionary Psychology and the Generation of Culture. New York: Oxford Univ. Press.

Bliss, E. L. (1984). A symptom profile of patients with multiple personalities, including MMPI results. *J Nerv Ment Dis, 172,* 197–202.

Bliss, E. L., Larson, E. M. (1985). Sexual criminality and hypnotizability. *J Nerv Ment Dis*, 173, 522–526.

Blore, D. C. (1997). Use of EMDR to treat morbid jealousy: A case study. *Br J Nurs*, 6, 984–988.

Burns, D. D. (1980). *Feeling good: The new mood therapy*. New York: Avon.

Burns, D. D., Nolen-Hoeksema, S. (1992). Therapeutic empathy and recovery from depression in cognitive-behavioral therapy: A structural equation model. *J Consult Clin Psychol*, 60, 441–449.

Buss, D. M. (1995). The evolution of desire: Strategies of human mating. New York: Basic Books.

Byrne, A., Yatham, L. N. (1989). Pimozide in pathological jealousy. *Br J Psychiatry*, 155, 249–251.

Cano, A., O'Leary, K. D. (1997). Romantic jealousy and affairs: Research and implications for couple therapy. *J Sex Marital Ther*, 23, 249–275.

Carter, L, & Minirth F. (1997). *The choosing to forgive workbook. A 12 part comprehensive plan to overcome your struggle to forgive and find lasting healing*. Nashville, TN: Thomas Nelson Publishers.

Clark, M., & Carpenter, T. (1997). *Without a doubt*. New York: Viking Press.

Cleckley, H. (1976). *The mask of sanity*. Saint Louis, MO: C.V. Mosby Company.

Conner, T. J., Kelly, J. P., & Leonard, B. E. (1997). Forced swim test-induced neurochemical, endocrine, and immune changes in the rat. *Pharmacol Biochem Behav*, 58, 961–967.

Cook, P. W. (1997). *Abused men: The hidden side of domestic violence*. Westport, CT: Praeger Publishers.

Cooper, D. A. (1997). *God is a verb*. New York: Riverhead Books.

Cott, J. M., Fugh-Berman, A. (1998). Is St. John's wort (Hypericum performatum) an effective antidepressant? *J Nerv Ment Dis*, 186, 500–501.

Daly, M., Wilson, M. (1988). Homicide. New York: Hawthorne.

Darwin, C. (1874). *The descent of man* (2nd ed.). London: Murray.

Dawkins, R. (1976). *The selfish gene*. New York: Oxford University Press.

De Waal, F. (1982). *Chimpanzee politics. Power and sex among apes*. New York: Harper Colophon Books.

De Waal, F. (1989). *Peacemaking among primates*. Cambridge, MA: Harvard University Press.

Drevets, W. C., Raichle, M. E. (1992). Neuroanatomical circuits in depression: Implications for treatment mechanisms. *Psychopharmacol Bull*, 28, 261–274.

Duman, R. S., Heninger, G. R., Nestler, E. J. (1997). A molecular and cellular theory of depression. *Arch Gen Psychiatry*, 54, 597–606.

Duman, R. S., Vaidya, V. A. (1998). Molecular and cellular actions of chronic electroconvulsive seizures. *J ECT*, 14, 181–193.

Ellis, A., & Harper, R. A. (1975). *Guide to rational living*. Los Angeles: Wilshire Book Co.

Emery, G., & Campbell, J. (1986). *Rapid relief from emotional distress*. New York: Rawson Associates.

Ernst, E., Rand, J. I., Stevinson, C. (1998). Complementary therapies for depression: An overview. *Arch Gen Psychiatry, 55*, 1026–1032.

Fava, M., Rosenbaum, J. F., Pava, J. A., McCarthy, M. K., Steingard, R.J., & Bouffides, E. (1993). Anger attacks in unipolar depression, Part 1: Clinical correlates and response to fluoxetine treatment. *Am J Psychiatry, 150*, 1158–1163.

Felson, R. B. (1997). Anger, aggression, and violence in love triangles. *Violence Vict, 12*, 345–362.

Fieve, R. R. (1975). *Moodswing: The third revolution in psychiatry*. New York: William Morrow and Company, Inc.

Finch, R. (1998). *The power of prayer*. Boca Raton, FL: Globe Communications Corp.

Foundation for inner peace: A course in miracles. Combined Volume. (2nd ed.). New York: (1996). Viking Press.

Freinkel, A., Koopman, C., Spiegel, D. (1994). Dissociative symptoms in media eyewitnesses of an execution. *Am J Psychiatry, 151*, 1335–1339.

Friedman, M. J. (1988). Toward rational pharmacotherapy for posttraumatic stress disorder: An interim report. *Am J Psychiatry, 145*, 281–285.

Fuhrman, M. (1997). *Murder in Brentwood*. New York: Zebra Books, Kensington Publishing Corporation.

Gacono, C. B., Meloy, J. R., Heaven, T. R. (1990). A Rorschach investigation of narcissism and hysteria in antisocial personality. *J Pers Assess, 55*, 270–279.

Gardner, R. (1995). Sociobiology and its applications to psychiatry. In H. I. Kaplan & B. J. Saddock (Eds.), *The comprehensive textbook of psychiatry VI* (vol. 1, pp. 365–375). Baltimore: Williams and Wilkens.

George, M. S., Wassermann, E. M., Williams, W., Callahan, A., Ketter, T. A., Basser, P., Hallett, M., Post, R. M. (1995). Daily repetitive transcranial magnetic stimulation improves mood in depression. *Neuroreport, 6*, 1854–1856.

George, M. S., Wassermann, E. M., Kimbrell, T. A., Little, J. T., Williams, W., Danielson, A. L., Greenberg, B. D., Hallett, M., Post, R. M. (1997). Mood improvement following daily left prefrontal repetitive transcranial magnetic stimulation in patients with depression: A placebo-controlled crossover trial. *Am J Psychiatry, 154*, 1752–1756.

Gilbert, P. (1997). The evolution of social attractiveness and its role in shame, humiliation, guilt and therapy. *Br J Med Psychol, 70*, 113–147.

Gilbert, P., & Allan, S. (1998). The role of defeat and entrapment (arrested flight) in depression: An exploration of an evolutionary view. *Psychological Med, 28*, 585–598.

Glaser, R., Kiecolt-Glaser, J. K., Malarkey, W. B., Sheridan, J. F. (1998). The influence of psychological stress on the immune response to vaccines. *Ann NY Acad Sci, 840*, 649–655.

Goldenberg, D. L. (1996). Fibromyalgia, chronic fatigue syndrome, and myofascial pain. *Curr Opin Rheumatol, 8*, 113–123.

Good, K. (1991). *Into the heart. One man's pursuit of love and knowledge among the Yanomama*. New York: Simon and Shuster.

Goodall, J. (1990). *Through a window. My thirty years with the chimpanzees of Gombe*. Boston: Houghton Mifflin Company.

Gould, R. A., Ball, S., Kaspi, S. P., Otto, M. W., Pollack, M. H., Shekhar, A., & Fava, M. (1996). Prevalence and correlates of anger attacks: A two site study. *J Affect Disord, 39*, 31–38.

Graves, R. (1992). *The Greek Myths: Combined Edition*. London: Penguin Books.

Hamilton, E. (1942). *Mythology*. Boston: Little, Brown and Company.

Ho, A. P., Gillin, J. C., Buchsbaum, M. S., Wu, J. C., Abel, L., Bunney, W. E., Jr. (1996). Brain glucose metabolism during non-rapid eye movement sleep in major depression. A positron emission tomography study. *Arch Gen Psychiatry, 53*, 645–652.

Holt, P. L. (1981). Stressful life events preceding road traffic accidents. *Injury, 13*, 111–115.

Horney, K. (1994 reissue). *Self-Analysis*. New York: W. W. Norton and Company.

Hornig, M., Mozley, P. D., & Amsterdam, J. D. (1997). HMPAO SPECT brain imaging in treatment-resistant depression. *Prog Neuropsychopharmacol Biol Psychiatry, 21*, 1097–1114.

Horowitz, M. J. (1986). Stress-response syndromes: A review of posttraumatic and adjustment disorders. *Hosp Community Psychiatry, 37*, 241–249.

Hryvniak, M. R., & Rosse, R. B. (1989). Concurrent psychiatric illness in inpatients with post-traumatic stress disorder. *Military Medicine, 154*(8), 399–401.

Hubner, W. D., Lande, S., & Podzuweit, H. (1994). Hypericum treatment of mild depressions with somatic symptoms. *J Geriatr Psychiatry Neurol, 7* (Suppl 1), S12–14.

Hunt, M. G. (1998). The only way out is through: Emotional processing and recovery after a depressing life event. *Behav Res Ther, 36*, 361–384.

Insel, T. R. (1997). A neurobiological basis of social attachment. *Am J Psychiatry, 154*, 726–735.

Irwin, H. J. (1998). Attitudinal predictors of dissociation: Hostility and powerlessness. *J Psychol, 132*, 389–400.

Irwin, M., Costlow, C., Williams, H., Artin, K. H., Chan, C. Y., Stinson, D. L., Levin, M. J., Hayward, A. R., Oxman, M. N. (1998). Cellular immunity to varicellazoster virus in patients with major depression. *J Infect Dis, 178*(1), S104–108.

John, I. H., Stoddart, D. M., & Mallick, J. (1995). Towards a sociobiological model of depression. A marsupial model (*Petaurus breviceps*). *Br J Psychiatry, 166*, 475–479.

Jung, C. G., Von Franz, M. L., Henderson, J. L., Jacobi, J., Jaffe, A. (1964). *Man and His Symbols*. New York: Doubleday and Company, Inc.

Kennedy, S. H., Javanmard, M., & Vaccarino, F. J. (1997). A review of functional neuroimaging in mood disorders: Positron emission tomography and depression. *Can J Psychiatry, 42*, 467–475.

Kienlen, K. K., Birmingham, D. L., Solberg, K. B., O'Regan, J. T., Meloy, J. R. (1997). A comparative study of psychotic and nonpsychotic stalking. *J Am Acad Psychiatry Law*, 25, 317–334.

Kitayama, I., Yaga, T., Kayahara, T., Nakano, K., Murase, S., Otani, M., & Nomura, J. (1997). Long-term stress degenerates, but imipramine regenerates, noradrenergic axons in the rat cerebral cortex. *Biol Psychiatry*, 42, 687–696.

Klerman, G. L., Weissman, M. M., Rounsaville, B. J., & Chevron, E. S. (1984). *Interpersonal psychotherapy of depression*. New York: Basic Books, Inc.

Knauft, B. M. (1987). Reconsidering violence in simple human societies. *Current Anthropology*, 28, 457–500.

Kramer, P. D. (1993). *Listening to Prozac. A psychiatrist explores antidepressant drugs and the remaking of the self*. New York: Viking.

Kudryavtseva, N. N., Bakshtanovskaya, I. V., & Koryakina, L. A. (1991). Social model of depression in mice of C57BL/6J strain. *Pharmacol Biochem Behav*, 38, 315–320.

Kupfer, D. J., Frank, E. (1997). Role of psychosocial factors in the onset of major depression. *Ann NY Acad Sci*, 807, 429–439.

Kura, T., & Kura, K. (1998). War of attrition with individual differences on RHP. *J Theor Biol*, 193, 335–344.

Lacomte, D., & Fornes, P. (1998). Homicide followed by suicide: Paris and its suburbs, 1991–1996. *J Forensic Sci*, 43, 760–764.

Lane, R. D. (1990). Successful fluoxetine treatment of pathologic jealousy. *J Clin Psychiatry*, 51, 345–346.

Lange, T., Vannatter, P., & Moldea, D. E. (1997). *Evidence dismissed: The inside story of the police investigation of O.J. Simpson*. New York: Pocket Books.

Lazarus, A. A., & Lazarus, C. N. (1997). *The 60-second shrink. 101 strategies for staying sane in a crazy world*. San Luis Obispo, CA: Impact Publishers.

Leong, G. B., Silva, J. A., Garza-Trevino, E. S., Oliva, D. Jr., Ferrari, M. M., Komanduri, R. V., Caldwell, J. C. (1994). The dangerousness of persons with the Othello syndrome. *J Forensic Sci*, 39, 1445–1454.

Lynch, J. J. (1985). *The language of the heart. The body's response to human dialogue*. New York: Basic Book Publishers, Inc.

Maggio, R. (1987). *The nonsexist word finder. A dictionary of gender-free usage*. Phoenix, AZ: Oryx Press.

Malinski, M. (1993). Cooperation wins and stays. *Nature*, 364, 12–13.

Marshall, R. D., Schneier, F. R., Fallon, B. A., Knight, C. B., Abbate, L. A., Goetz, D., Campeas, R., & Liebowitz, M. R. (1998). An open trial of paroxetine in patients with noncombat-related, chronic posttraumatic stress disorder. *J Clin Psychopharmacol*, 18, 10–18.

Marzuk, P. M., Tardiff, K., Hirsch, C. S. (1992). The epidemiology of murder-suicide. *JAMA*, 267, 179–183.

Masterson, J. F. (1981). *The narcissistic and borderline disorders. An integrated developmental approach*. New York: Brunner Mazel.

Mathes, E. W., Adams, H. E., Davies, R. M. (1985). Jealousy: loss of relationship rewards, loss of self-esteem, depression, anxiety, and anger. *J Pers Soc Psychol*,
48, 1552–1561.

Mathes, E. W., Verstraete, C. (1993). Jealous aggression: who is the target, the
beloved or the rival. *Psychol Rep*, *72*, 1071–1074.

Matsuda, S., Peng, H., Yoshimura, H., Wen, T. C., Fukuda, T., & Sakanaka, M.
(1996). Persistent c-fos expression in the brains of mice with chronic social
stress. *Neurosci Res*, *26*, 157–170.

McIntosh, E. G., Matthews, C. O. (1992). Use of direct coping resources in dealing
with jealousy. *Psychol Rep*, *70*, 1037–1038.

McNamara, P., Durso, R. (1991). Reversible pathologic jealousy (Othello syndrome) associated with amantadine. *J Geriatr Psychiatry Neurol*, *4*, 157–159.

McNeely, R. L., & Robinson-Simpson, G. (1987). The truth about domestic violence: A falsely framed issue. *Social Work*, *32*, 485–490.

McWilliams, P. (1988). *You can't afford the luxury of a negative thought. A book for people with any life-threatening illness—including life*. Los Angeles: Prelude Press.

Milroy, C. M. (1995). The epidemiology of homicide–suicide (dyadic death). *Forensic Sci Int*, *71*, 117–122.

Modestin, J., Ebner, G., Junghan, M., Erni, T. (1996). Dissociative experiences and
dissociative disorders in acute psychiatric inpatients. *Compr Psychiatry*, *37*,
355–361.

Morinobu, S., Strausbaugh, H., Terwilliger, R., Duman, R. S. (1997). Regulation of
c-Fos and NGF1-A by antidepressant treatments. *Synapse*, *25*, 313–320.

Mullen, P. E. (1991). Jealousy: the pathology of passion. *Br J Psychiatry*, *158*, 593–601.

Mullen, P. E., Martin, J. (1994). Jealousy: a community study. *Br J. Psychiatry*, *164*,
35–43.

Murphy, C. M., Meyer, S. L., O'Leary, K. D. (1994). Dependency characteristics of
partner assaultive men. *J Abnorm Psychol*, *103*, 729–735.

Nagy, L. M., Morgan, C. A., Southwick, S. M., & Charney, D. S. (1993). Open
prospective trial of fluoxetine for posttraumatic stress disorder. *J Clin Psychopharmacol*, *13*, 107–113.

Nesse, R. M., Berridge, K. C. (1997). Psychoactive drug use in evolutionary perspective. *Science*, *278*, 63–66.

Nesse, R. M., & Williams, G. C. (1994). *Why we get sick. The new science of Darwinian
medicine*. New York: Times Books, Random House.

Nowak, M., & Sigmund, K. (1993). A strategy of win-stay, lose-shift that outper-
forms tit-for-tat in the Prisoner's Dilemma game. *Nature*, *364*, 56–58.

O'Leary, K. D., Barling, J., Arias, I., Rosenbaum, A., Malone, J., & Tyree, A. (1989).
Prevalence and stability of physical aggression between spouses: A longitudi-
nal analysis. *Journal of Consulting and Clinical Psychology*, *57*, 263–268.

Omer, H., Da Verona, M. (1991). Doctor Iago's treatment of Othello. *Am J Psychother*, *45*, 99–112.

Orion, D. R. (1997). *I know you really love me: A psychiatrist's journal of erotomania, stalking, and obsessive love.* New York: MacMillan General.

Palermo, G. B., Smith, M. B., Jenzten, J. M., Henry, T. E., Konicek, P. J., Peterson, G. F., Singh, R. P., & Witeck, M. J. (1997). Murder–suicide of the jealous paranoia type: A multicenter statistical pilot study. *Am J Forensic Med Pathol, 18,* 373–383.

Parker, G., Barrett, E. (1997). Morbid jealousy as a variant of obsessive-compulsive disorder. *Aust N Z J Psychiatry, 31,* 133–138.

Parrott, W. G., Smith, R. H. (1993). Distinguishing the experiences of envy and jealousy. *J Pers Soc Psychol, 64,* 906–920.

Pearson, P. (1997). *When she was bad: Violent women and the myth of innocence.* New York: Viking Press.

Pincus, T., Fraser, L., & Pearce, S. (1998). Do chronic pain patients "Stroop" on pain stimuli? *Br J Clin Psychol, 37,* 49–58.

Pipher, M. (1994). *Reviving Ophelia: Saving the selves of adolescent girls.* New York: Ballantine Books.

Powell, C., & Forde, G. (1997). *The self-hypnosis kit.* New York: Penguin, USA.

Price, J. S. (1967). Hypothesis: The dominance hierarchy and the evolution of mental illness. *Lancet, 2,* 243.

Price, J. S., Sloman, L., Gardner, R., Jr., Gilbert, P., & Pohde, P. (1994). The social competition hypothesis of depression. *Br J Psychiatry, 164,* 309–315.

Ratey, J. J., Johnson, C. (1997). *Shadow Syndromes.* New York: Pantheon Books.

Rauch, S. L., Shin, L. M., Whalen, P. J., Pitman, R. K. (1998). Neuroimaging and the neuroanatomy of Posttraumatic Stress Disorder. *CNS Spectrums, 3*(7) (Suppl. 2), 30–41.

Real, T. (1997). *I don't want to talk about it. Overcoming the secret legacy of male depression.* New York: Fireside.

Retfalvi, P., Rosse, R. B., & Deutsch, S. I. (1997). Fibromyalgia: A neuropsychiatric perspective. *Journal of Musculoskeletal Medicine, 14,* 52–61.

Reynolds, M., & Brewin, C. R. (1998). Intrusive cognitions, coping strategies and emotional responses in depression, posttraumatic stress disorder and a non-clinical population. *Behav Res Ther, 36,* 135–147.

Rosse, R. B., Collins, J. P., McCarthy, M. F., Alim, T. N., Wyatt, R. J., & Deutsch, S. I. (1994). Phenomenologic comparison of the idiopathic psychosis of schizophrenia and drug-induced cocaine and phencyclidine psychoses: A retrospective study. *Clinical Neuropharmacology, 17*(4), 359–369.

Rosse, R. B., Deutsch, L. H., & Deutsch, S. I. (1995). Medical assessment and laboratory testing in psychiatry. In H. I. Kaplan & B. J. Sadock (Eds.), *Comprehensive textbook of psychiatry* (6th ed., pp. 601–619). Baltimore: Williams and Wilkins.

Rosse, R. B., Martin, M., Morihisa, J. M. (1989). Treatment of atypical psychosis. In T. B. Karasu & A. Frances (Eds.), *Treatment of psychiatric disorders* (pp. 1697–1712). Washington, DC: APA Press.

Rosse, R. B., Fay-McCarthy, M., Collins, J. P., Risher-Flowers, D., Alim, T. N., & Deutsch, S. I. (1993). Transient compulsive foraging behavior associated with crack cocaine use. *Am J Psychiatry, 150*(1),155–156.

Rosse, R. B., Giese, A. A., Deutsch, S. I., & Morihisa, J. M. (1989). *Laboratory and diagnostic testing in psychiatry.* Washington, DC: American Psychiatric Press, Inc.

Sapolsky, R. M. (1994). *Why zebras don't get ulcers. A guide to stress, stress-related diseases, and coping.* New York: W.H. Freeman and Company.

Scheier, M. F., Matthews, K. A., Owens, J. F., Magovern, G. J., Sr., Lefebvre, R. C., Abbott, R. A., Carver, C. S. (1989). Dispositional optimism and recovery from coronary artery bypass surgery: The beneficial effects on physical and psychological well-being. *J Pers Soc Psychol, 57,* 1024–1040.

Schmidt, K., Hill, L., Guthrie, G. (1977). Running amok. *Int J Soc Psychiatry, 23,* 264–274.

Segerstrom, S. C., Taylor, S. E., Kemeny, M. E., Fahey, J. L. (1998). Optimism is associated with mood, coping, and immune change in response to stress. *J Pers Soc Psychol, 74,* 1646–1655.

Seligman, M. (1998). *Learned optimism.* New York: Pocket Books.

Selye, H. (1976). *The stress of life* (rev. ed.). New York: McGraw-Hill Book Company.

Shalev A. Y., Freedman, S., Peri, T., Brandes, D., Sahar, T., Orr, S. P., & Pitman, R. K. (1998). Prospective study of posttraumatic stress disorder and depression following trauma. *Am J Psychiatry, 155,* 630–637.

Shalev A. Y., Sahar, T., Freedman, S., Peri, T., Glick, N., Brandes, D., Orr, S. P., & Pitman, R. K. (1998). A prospective study of heart rate response following trauma and the subsequent development of posttraumatic stress disorder. *Arch Gen Psychiatry, 55,* 553–539.

Shapiro, F., & Forrest, M. S. (1997). *EMDR: The breakthrough therapy for overcoming anxiety, stress, and trauma.* New York: Basic Books.

Sharpsteen, D. J., Kirkpatrick, L. A. (1997). Romantic jealousy and adult romantic attachment. *J Pers Soc Psychol, 72,* 627–640.

Sheline, Y. I., Gado, M. H., & Price, J. L. (1998). Amygdala core nuclei volumes are decreased in recurrent major depression. *Neuroreport, 9,* 2023–2028.

Sherman, J. J. (1998). Effects of psychotherapeutic treatments for PTSD: A meta-analysis of controlled clinical trials. *J Trauma Stress, 11,* 413–435.

Sherrill, J. T., Anderson, B., Frank, E., Reynolds, C. F., III, Tu, X. M., Patterson, D., Ritenour, A., Kupfer, D. J. (1997). Is life stress more likely to provoke depressive episodes in women than in men? *Depress Anxiety, 6,* 95–105.

Sloman, L., Price, J., Gilbert, P., & Gardner, R. (1994). Adaptive function of depression: Psychotherapeutic implications: *Am J Psychother, 48,* 401–416.

Southwick, S. M., Bremner, D., Krystal, J. H., & Charney, D. S. (1994). Psychobiologic research in posttraumatic stress disorder. *Psychiatr Clin North Am, 17,* 251–264.

Spiegel, D., Sephton, S. E., Terr, A. I., Stites, D. P. (1998). Effects of psychosocial treatment in prolonging cancer survival may be mediated by neuroimmune pathways. *Ann NY Acad Sci, 840,* 674–683.

Spring, J. A., & Spring, M. (1996). *After the affair: Healing the pain and rebuilding trust when a partner has been unfaithful.* New York: Harper Collins.

Stefanski, V. (1998). Social stress in loser rats: Opposite immunological effects in submissive and subdominant males. *Physiol Behav, 63,* 605–613.

Stein, D. J., Hollander, E., Josephson, S. C. (1994). Serotonin reuptake blockers for the treatment of obsessional jealousy. *J Clin Psychiatry, 55,* 30–33.

Steiner, J. (1996). Revenge and resentment in the "Oedipus situation." *Int J Psychoanal, 77,* 433–443.

Stevens, A., Price, J. (1996). *Evolutionary psychiatry: A new beginning.* New York: Routledge.

Stroebel, C. F. (1982). *QR: The quieting reflex.* New York: Berkeley Books.

Subotnik, R. (1993). *Surviving infidelity: Making decisions, recovering from the pain.* Holbrook: Adams Publishing.

Taylor, P. J., Kopelman, M. D. (1984). Amnesia for criminal offences. *Psychol Med, 14,* 581–588.

Thiele, B., Brink, I., Ploch, M. (1994). Modulation of cytokine expression by hypericum extract. *J Geriatr Psychiatry Neurol, 7*(1) (Suppl. 1), S60–62.

Toobin, J. (1996). *The run of his life. The people v. O.J. Simpson.* New York: Touchstone. Simon and Schuster.

Townsend, J. M. (1995). Sex without emotional involvement: an evolutionary interpretation of sex differences. *Arch Sex Behav, 24,* 173–206.

van der Kolk, B. A. (1994). The body keeps the score: Memory and the evolving psychobiology of posttraumatic stress. *Harv Rev Psychiatry, 1,* 253–265.

van der Kolk, B. A. (1997). The psychobiology of posttraumatic stress disorder. *J Clin Psychiatry, 58* (suppl. 9), 16–24.

van der Kolk, B. A., Dreyfuss, D., Michaels, M., Shera, D., Berkowitz, R., Fisler, R., & Saxe, G. (1994). Fluoxetine in posttraumatic stress disorder. *J Clin Psychiatry, 55,* 517–522.

van der Kolk, B. A., & Fisler, R. (1995). Dissociation and the fragmentary nature of traumatic memories: Overview and exploratory study. *J Trauma Stress, 8,* 505–525.

van der Kolk, B. A., Herron, N., & Hostetler, A. (1994). The history of trauma in psychiatry. *Psychiatr Clin North Am, 17,* 583–600.

van der Kolk, B. A., Pelcovitz, D., Roth, S., Mandel, F. S., McFarlane, A., & Herman, J. L. (1996). Dissociation, somatization, and affect dysregulation: The complexity of adaptation of trauma. *Am J Psychiatry, 153*(suppl. 7), 83–93.

Violoa, J., Ditzler, T., Batzer, W., Harazin, J., Adams, D., Lettich, L., & Berigan, T. (1997). Pharmacological management of posttraumatic stress disorder: Clinical summary of a five-year retrospective study, 1990–1995. *Mil Med, 162,* 616–619.

Wang, Z., Hulihan, T. J., & Insel, T. R. (1997). Sexual and social experience is associated with different patterns of behavior and neural activation in male prairie voles. *Brain Res, 767*, 321–323.

Wenegrat, B. (1990). *Sociobiological psychiatry: A new conceptual framework.* Lexington, MA: Lexington Press.

Wheatley, D. (1997). LI 160, an extract of St. John's wort, versus amitriptyline in mildly to moderately depressed outpatients—a controlled 6-week clinical trial. *Pharmacopsychiatry, 30* (Suppl. 2), 77–80.

Wilson, E. O. (1975). *Sociobiology: The new synthesis.* Cambridge: Harvard University Press.

Wilson, E. O. (1978). *On Human Nature.* London: Harvard University Press.

Wing, Y. K., Lee, S., Chiu, H. F., Ho, C. K., Chen, C. N. (1994). A patient with coexisting narcolepsy and morbid jealousy showing favourable response to fluoxetine. *Postgrad Med J, 70*, 34–36.

Wright, R. (1994). *The moral animal. Why we are the way we are. The new science of evolutionary psychology.* New York: Vintage Books, Random House.

Young, L. J., Wang, Z., & Insel, T. R. (1998). Neuroendocrine bases of monogamy. *Trends Neurosci, 21*, 71–75.

Zajonc, R. B. (1985). Emotion and facial efference: A theory reclaimed. *Science, 228*, 15–21.

Zeanah, C. H. (1993). *Handbook of infant mental health.* New York: Guilford Press.

Index

Page numbers in *italics* refer to figures. Page numbers followed by '*t*' refer to tables. Page numbers followed by '*n*' refer to end notes.